WE ASKED, "WHY NOT?"

THE FIRSTHAND STORY OF THE 1968 GEORGIA CHALLENGE DELEGATION WHEN POLITICS IN THE SOUTH WAS CHANGED FOREVER

PARKER HUDSON

CONTENTS

FOREWORD

BY TAYLOR BRANCH

Until recently, I had no idea Parker Hudson preserved this adventure from our youth. We went our separate ways for fifty-six years and barely took the trouble to find each other and reminisce. So it's fair to ask why any reader today should care about the intense daily whirlwind described in these pages.

Depending on your age, you may be curious about 1968. Parker captures at gut level the watershed year when our country seemed to be coming apart over the war in Viet Nam. Major cities exploded concurrently over Martin Luther King's assassination on April 4. A month later, by freakish chance, Robert Kennedy grilled me for hours about why more students did not support him for president. I was awed.

Within thirty days, as Parker and I were graduating from college, Senator Kennedy was assassinated, too. We went home to Atlanta discovering in common a feverish compulsion to do something. Anything. It made us pursue any sage or pipedream reformer we could find while holding down summer jobs. After eight weeks of the petty trials and chaos recounted here, we wound up as credentialed delegates inside Chicago's tumultuous Democratic National Convention. Television screens showed battered demonstrators downtown answer a police riot with their chant: "The whole world is watching!"

Parker delivers an old-fashioned coming-of-age story inside a preposterous miracle. We were twenty-one, naïve, and mostly lost but never done. He could have adjusted the narrative to lend us more dignity, but no, we behave as though the world depends on finding six discussion leaders or a hundred dollars by tomorrow.

His minute-by-minute detail promises something more in spite of all expectation. I had forgotten ninety percent of the gambits and half the people he recalls, but I can vouch for his authentic balance. Parker mixes extraordinary competence with a judge's temperament. He gives our fellow nobodies every chance to prove themselves. He treats the future legend John Lewis objectively in stride as someone who may help.

Passages that introduce Julian Bond are especially poignant for me. I ironed his shirts at the hotel in Chicago. Julian spoke for our challenge delegation on national television, and he felt exalted to us, though just 27. He and I became close friends for decades until his death in 2015.

This book also stirs a private memory by including our few encounters with Fannie Lou Hamer. Parker is more than generous to mention my separate task when we kept splitting up on the run, but he did not go with me for the hour or so I spent alone with Mrs. Hamer. Just offstage at the convention, in sight of the speaker's podium and TV lights, I was charged to make sure nobody snatched her away before a complex maneuver yielded to Mississippi for her wildcat speech to nominate Edward Kennedy to be president. In the excruciating tension, I asked if there was an outline or text somewhere. She shook her head and replied, "The Lord will tell me what to say."

Remote consultations scuttled this last-gasp surprise. The sharecropper with a prophetic voice did not get to propose another Kennedy to extricate us from Viet Nam.

Even so, the bloody conflict abroad merged with civil rights at home to motivate every leaflet and wild scheme in Parker's account. The nation was mired in undeclared war fought mostly by conscripts. Monthly draft quotas, set by the president alone, confronted our generation with a summons to kill and be killed in Asia, or dodge and evade, or even resist in prison. Millions anguished with loved ones over duty and conscience.

To reconsider the war required changing the president. In Georgia, that meant appealing to the Democratic Party because we were still a one-party region built on white supremacy. This historical fact is widely repressed in retrospect, but the southern GOP hardly existed. It did not bother to run candidates for many offices, having been scorned for a hundred years as the Yankee outfit created to perpetuate Lincoln's war. We grew up hearing elders say local Republicans were scarce as hen's teeth or polar bears. Of necessity, the South's pioneer GOP leaders were converted Democrats like Newt Gingrich and the fervent segregationist Strom Thurmond.

Democrats were wrenching their heritage in the opposite direction. We challenged the national party to reject white rule personified in Georgia by Governor Lester Maddox, who had acquired fame and very likely his mandate by defying the 1964 civil rights law with a pistol. Readers can glimpse our struggle all the way up from the integrated meetings in rural Georgia to floor fights at the Democratic National Convention. Parker recreates yesteryear vividly in Chicago with the pay phones, typewriters, and four-dollar hotel rooms. In seating us, Thomas Jefferson's original Democratic Party committed formally at last to equal votes and cross-racial representation.

Our cause spurred genuine two-party competition in the future, often for the first time. Ironically, this result penalized coalition Democrats at least temporarily across the South and beyond. GOP candidates sprouted from nowhere into the presumptive majority choice for white voters, dominating a rebranded Solid South. Race uprooted partisan allegiances, inspired patriotism, and muffled democratic values all at once. No other political force in American history packs remotely comparable voltage.

Parker simplifies these difficult issues. He admits with clarity and candor that our ragtag challengers—thrown together at an open convention—did not truly represent contemporary Georgia Democrats. Segregationists and Viet Nam war hawks doubtless would have crushed us in a primary or official caucus, but state law recognized no voter participation of any kind. Governor Maddox appointed every delegate with zero input from the public. Georgia, like many states then, allowed a party boss to select delegates to nominate a U.S. president who could wage war by executive power. The process excluded voters of every political stripe.

This was our bedrock complaint. We wanted the famous checks and balances to be grounded in fair elections. Cynics have ridiculed "We the People" and buried the American experiment ever since James Fenimore Cooper, who said democracy is just a playground for demagogues. Some people say so again today.

We tried hard to be good citizens in the emergency of our time. Maybe there are lessons here. Thanks to Parker for reuniting us in quite a yarn if nothing else, which I hope you enjoy.

Baltimore
June 2024

INTRODUCTION

2024

When the events recounted here first began early in the summer of 1968, I was twenty years old. Taylor Branch was five months older and wiser.

We wanted to change a few things, like being drafted to fight the Vietnam War, but there were no obvious ways to engage with the Democrat-controlled government of Georgia, run from the top by a segregationist governor, Lester Maddox.

This is the story of how we looked into what might be possible to do, anyway, and wound up eight weeks later as Georgia Challenge Delegates to the Democratic Convention in Chicago, organizing the delegation's logistics and writing Julian Bond's press releases, among a lot of other things.

It's actually a pretty crazy story, which I hope entertains, educates, and encourages you.

How does this manuscript even exist today? It literally has been in a file on a shelf in our attic for over fifty years. I started re-reading it six months ago and decided, at age seventy-six, that I ought to share it.

In October of 1968 I was studying at London School of Economics as a Marshall Scholar, when the Vietnam War protests shut down the school for three weeks. I used that time to sit in my room in Commonwealth Hall and to write out a day-by-day history of all that we had done just a few months earlier.

So that's what you will read—the unvarnished thoughts of the twenty-one-year-old me. Other than some typos and minor word choices, I've not "updated" the contents to conform with any current conventions or attitudes. It is pure 1968.

The manuscript has only been out of our attic twice. Years ago Julian Bond asked me to send a copy to the University of Virginia Library, to a special section of his "papers," which I did. A Guide to the Papers of Julian Bond, 1897-2006 Bond, Julian, Papers 13347 (virginia.edu)[1]. And then in 2017, Donnie Summerlin, an historian at the University of Georgia, used a copy for his work, "The Best of Georgia in Chicago[2]." In that much broader, well-written historical document, he refers to these pages as "the most comprehensive first-hand account of the events of the Georgia delegate challenge in 1968."

This is no high-level analysis of political trends or realigning forces from a national perspective. This is one young man's experience across one summer of intense activity with a good friend, including occasional summaries and observations which I hope keep it interesting.

Short biographies for most of the key individuals with whom we interacted are provided at the end of the book.

And we've created what I hope will be a "living" Gallery of Photos and Documents at our website, www.parkerhudson.com/1968gallery, where you will find photos that I took at the convention, press clippings, our mimeographed press releases, and more.

As you read down this page you'll travel back fifty-six years to the mindset and attitudes of a much younger writer.

And remember that from here on a present tense verb is 1968-present tense.

One final thought before starting. When you read about these events and how we succeeded or failed at a certain important task, please keep in mind that none of the following existed: cellphones, the internet, personal computers, word processors, fax machines, overnight delivery, inexpensive copy machines, cheap long-distance calls, digital cameras, four-function

---

1. https://ead.lib.virginia.edu/vivaxtf/view?docId=uva-sc/viu00259.xml#adminlink
2. https://bit.ly/3ykFJz7

calculators, search engines, personal printers, or videos. If you needed to tell someone something, you either had to meet with them face-to-face, send a human messenger, write them a letter, or call their home or business phone and hope that they were there and answered. There were no other options.

How any of us accomplished anything in those days seems a bit of a mystery. But, somehow, we did.

Enjoy.

1968

Before this summer, despite a definite general interest, I had little real understanding of all that is involved in either a local political organization or a national party convention. I began to write this book in the belief that there are other people like me who might find the day-to-day account of a non-politician's first brush with national politics, culminating in the Georgia Challenge at the Democratic National Convention in Chicago entertaining and illuminating. I have written in the first person to emphasize the limitations involved. This is no masterful treatise on political science.

It represents only the experiences and impressions of one young person during one summer of political involvement. There is little or no lengthy character development, simply because, unfortunately, I knew most of the people concerned only as members of organizations. With both people and events, I can offer only little analysis; mine are mostly impressions. But it was the events themselves and the impressions of the moment which, for me, made the summer so interesting.

This book divides rather logically into two parts, the first of which relates the growth of the McCarthy campaign in Georgia. Ours was a campaign of amateurs; none of us was a wise veteran with previous political experience. The problems, the infightings, the mistakes, the financial crises, and the small victories which we encountered as we tried to make McCarthy's name known throughout Georgia may prove of interest both to other non-politicians and also to anyone else who seriously starts out to move the nation from his own hometown.

The second half of the book recounts the experiences of those of us on the Georgia Delegation of Loyal National Democrats—the Georgia

Challenge Delegation—from the delegation's birth in Macon to our Credentials Committee hearing to our final seating at the Democratic National Convention and the nomination of our leader, Julian Bond, for Vice President of the United States. Ours was, I think, a unique victory in the history of convention politics.

This chronicle of the strategies and the political realities involved in our struggle may provide, beyond entertainment, the first general documentation of the, until now, largely oral tradition surrounding the details of a challenge delegation. It is my sincerest hope that every state Democratic Party will initiate real internal reforms and encourage broad participation in all state party affairs, thereby making such challenges never again necessary. Only in this way can the Democratic Party, or any party, nurture strong support and really represent the political desires of its supporters.

But should this needed change not occur, then perhaps the details recounted herein, plus the significant reforms incorporated in the party rules by the 1968 Democratic Convention, will prove of use to anyone in later years who seeks to change a situation in his state similar to the one we found in Georgia in 1968.

I came away from that summer convinced that, with the possible exception of national campaign strategy, politics is largely the art of applied common sense. I hope, above all else, that the experiences recounted in this book might encourage others to use political involvement as a powerful force for starting to approach the problems which beset our country today.

THE SPRING AND JUNE:
FRUSTRATION AND SILENCE

Taylor Branch and I graduated from the University of North Carolina and returned home to Atlanta early in June. Taylor was to be married within a week, and I immediately began a long-awaited summer job downtown in the Credit Department at the Citizens & Southern National Bank.

During the previous winter and spring at Chapel Hill, we had witnessed a significant change in campus attitudes towards America's war in Vietnam. Only a year before our student government had been unable to appropriate the funds necessary for a simple referendum on the war, because views were so divided. But by the spring of 1968, there had been a tremendous growth of anti-war sentiment; and it was by then almost impossible to find anyone who would actively argue the Administration's side on the war.

As both the war and student conversation about the war escalated throughout the winter, my simple intellectual hostility toward the war turned into morose personal despair. One could no longer have a meal with friends without someone at the table inevitably asking "What are you going to do next year?" referring to the Draft and its constant presence in all our lives.

Most of us also followed the war's ups and downs daily, and I can remember watching CBS one night during the Tet Offensive when an

American flag was run up the Hue flagpole by mistake just after the town had been retaken by the South. We next saw in living color the machine gun death of four terrified young Vietcong, followed immediately by a commercial about the gastric pains of a somewhat overweight American who had just eaten too much.

I could not believe that our country could afford to spend $35 billion a year, with our cities in tumult, nor 20,000 men dead, myself and friends possibly soon to join them, on a war which seemed unwinnable and whose prime motive seemed to be merely the retention of a particular military government in South Vietnam.

For a period of about a week right after the Tet Offensive I was not fit to be with because of my depression over the war and its costs to our people and to the people of Vietnam. But I eventually got it out of myself by writing a six-page letter to my Congressmen. From Senator Russell's office I got an exact copy of the same reply I had received to an earlier letter, three months before. Obviously such letter writing was having little impact on the powers that be, but it made me feel better to tell them what I thought.

————

As the spring blossomed, time grew short for those of us about to graduate. Constantly one was pounded with the Reserves, the Peace Corps, teaching, jail, etc., etc. Everyone had to make his own final decision. Most of my friends' draft boards were still giving deferments for teaching or for the Peace Corps, so many hedged against all possible events and sent applications everywhere. Some genuinely wanted never to serve in the armed forces. But most, I think, like myself, had no real bones about some sort of national service. It was just that the Vietnam war seemed the wrong issue over which to give one's life, especially when one not only thought that we could never win, but also felt that perhaps we were morally and historically wrong for being there in the first place.

Such was the feeling among many of us, students of the same general age group who only a few years before had been flocking to the Peace Corps from a genuine desire to help change the world. Now it looked like maybe it was more important to "change America first." At any rate, our Atlanta Draft Board was giving no such deferments, so Taylor and I were sweating, though Taylor would probably get a permanent deferment due to an earlier near-fatal motorcycle accident.

But with the spring came the primaries. I remember the New Hampshire primary was on March 12th, because it was the day a group of us drove over to Raleigh to take our Naval OCS physicals, having somehow managed to speed up the by-then three month long waiting list for application interviews. As we drove back from what was to be my first of three such exams, the early returns from New Hampshire were just coming in, and that night we watched in amazement as Gene McCarthy polled as many votes as the Democratic President of the nation, an unbelievable victory for the challenger. The McCarthy "children's campaign" was just out of its embryo; but it had worked, winning the admiration, the thanks, and the curiosity of those of us not lucky enough to have helped.

Shortly the first McCarthy for President headquarters in North Carolina opened in Chapel Hill. Many of us went by, purchased stickers and buttons, and left our names for future work. Perhaps a "McCarthy for President" sticker on one's bumper was a political and respectable way for many of us to say publicly about the war what we felt inside.

McCarthy's campaign picked up, and soon so did Robert Kennedy's. Though most of us in Chapel Hill felt we were too far from the primaries themselves to participate, or were too small a minority to have any impact in North Carolina, nevertheless we followed the campaigns constantly; and, in a way, McCarthy's cause and Kennedy's cause became very much our own causes. I suppose I started to feel like both my own future and the future of our country depended, in some part, on the effect which those two intense campaigns could have on our nation's voters.

This feeling about the importance of the McCarthy and the Kennedy campaigns was, of course, magnified by President Johnson's withdrawal from the race on March 31st. It then seemed, suddenly, almost unbelievably, that there was a real chance for peace in Vietnam and for change at home. Those first weeks of April most of us were quite relieved, believing that we had finally pulled back from the brink and were quickly on the way to peace and recovery. But by May the brink was still there and the only troops pulled back were the ones needed to guard the White House from rioters.

With the primaries and the spring came Dave Mixner, the newly appointed head of the McCarthy campaign in the South. For the moment "the South" was limited to North Carolina, as the McCarthy organization was still very much feeling its way everywhere, and especially so in the South. Dave and I met on a warm day at the north end of our campus during a somewhat over-rated outdoor anti-Vietnam teach-in, and I immediately liked him. He has a soft-spoken, friendly manner which belies his dedication and political acumen. I was later to find out that his parents were migratory farm workers and that he had first been beaten by the police when he was twelve years old for helping to organize strikes among the migratory laborers.

By 1968 Dave was a devoted Democrat of twenty-two who had dropped out of his job to help the McCarthy campaign. One of his assets was that he could recite from memory all of the procedural rules for every Democratic convention in every state in the union. When I told him that I was from Atlanta and that I might want to get involved during the summer, he set up a luncheon date for the two of us and Taylor.

Over the daily special at a Chapel Hill restaurant we discussed the campaign in general, the upcoming primaries, and the McCarthy strategy for the South. At that point the emphasis in all non-primary states was to be on influencing delegates already chosen, and Dave talked about establishing a McCarthy Southern Information Center in Atlanta in early June, even tentatively offering us the managerial positions therein. I was stunned by this sudden offer to help administrate a national "political" organization, something which I knew nothing about.

As both Taylor and I already had jobs lined up for the summer, and as we were both feeling rather inadequate besides, we turned down Dave's offer but promised to keep in touch. Dave stayed on in North Carolina for about a week, trying to get some sort of organization established, first mainly in the academic centers. He was typical of many, many young men and women in their mid-twenties whom I met later. He had heard Gene McCarthy, believed him to be the best candidate, quit his job, and literally had not had one day of rest since joining the campaign. He soon left Chapel Hill and moved back to Washington for new instructions and a new location assignment.

I was personally too much involved with trying to graduate and in my roommate's campaign for President of the Student Body to think seriously about contributing significantly to the North Carolina McCarthy organization. Student government elections at Carolina are run on a large scale, with those involved spending months in preparation; and many of us were helping my roommate, Jed Dietz, on what developed into a very close three-way race. Martin Luther King, Jr. was killed in Memphis a few days before the elections were to take place, and a few of us were downtown in Jed's campaign headquarters the night of Dr. King's murder, worried very much about what everybody in the country was worried about, from the security of our town to the viability of our nation.

I think we were the only people downtown that night, and there were reports that black people in Carrboro, Chapel Hill's black appendage, were in the streets and were soon going to march into town. I was really worried, both for them and for us; and I was relieved when it started to rain heavily, until I thought what a comment it was on our society when one's security depended on the weather. Later that week several of us watched on television as thousands of people in Atlanta joined hands and sang "We Shall Overcome," a eulogy to a dream which seemed to die twice that spring.

Over our spring vacation I joined friends in Miami. Taylor had gone to Atlanta to make arrangements for his wedding. He returned with news of a small meeting and the birth of Georgians for McCarthy, led by a Dr. Arthur Evans, an Emory University professor. In Chapel Hill, Dave Mixner was back and organizing buses to go to Indiana for work during the last weekend before that state's primary. Taylor had a Friday night band job but flew off early the next morning. He did canvas work for McCarthy in the first Kennedy-McCarthy confrontation, and he spent two hours in the Indianapolis airport after it was over, talking with Bobby Kennedy over breakfast.

The airport was apparently almost deserted when Bobby Kennedy arrived and spotted Taylor and a female co-worker, complete in McCarthy badges, waiting for their planes. Bobby offered them breakfast because he said he wanted to find out why it was that so many young people were for McCarthy: what followed was a long dialogue about the campaigns, the war, the draft, and youth. Taylor came away immensely impressed, after promising Bobby Kennedy that, if he ever got the chance, he would write a book about the draft and its effects on American youth.

Taylor returned to Chapel Hill. Only the California primary remained, and we all made the most of these last weeks at school, though not particularly for political involvement. I began to think in terms of what I was going to do when drafted, as I had been lucky enough to win a Marshall Scholarship for two years of postgraduate Economics study at The London School of Economics, and I wanted to go very badly.

By the first of June I had decided that were I drafted, I would drop out of my job and spend as much time as possible before reporting by helping with either the Kennedy or the McCarthy campaign, as that sort of involvement seemed to me the most critically important work one could do, if one sincerely believed that both the war and our cities needed changing rapidly.

I returned to Atlanta after graduation on June 4th, suffering from a severe back pain which had a habit of striking without warning once or twice every year, nearly incapacitating me for almost a week. I planned to start work the next day, and when my alarm radio went off early that Wednesday morning there was a special report from the California hospital where Robert Kennedy lay mortally wounded.

For me Robert Kennedy had personified the dynamic sort of liberalism for which most of us were longing by that next September. Sometimes his personal zeal, his strong will, or simply his name caused people to detract from his sincerity and his judgment: I can remember thinking that way at times in March when he first announced. But after a summer of political involvement and two weeks at the Democratic National Convention, I am convinced that it was just his sort of will, determination and charisma which are perhaps the most important qualities for a leader hoping to nurture broad support while constantly pushing for change.

Bobby Kennedy seemed to have those qualities about him: he was the true political man, in the best sense of the word, and his loss left a gap which other leaders, though possessing many of the same qualities, just did not seem quite able to fill.

But in early June I felt only that a great man had been murdered: I could not then myself foresee all that his death might mean. Taylor was married that second Saturday in June, the day of Robert Kennedy's funeral. Many of us walked straight from the broadcast of Edward Kennedy's moving eulogy for his slain brother into the chapel where Taylor was to marry Cathy Porter, a girl he had been dating for years. Several good friends from UNC were down for the event, and soon we were all standing on the church steps throwing marshmallows as Taylor and Cathy sped off for the airport and their honeymoon.

———

June, 1968, was exactly like the previous two Junes for me, at least in daily routine. I was a summer trainee at an Atlanta bank; "summer trainee" only because I expected to be either drafted or in England by October. My 1955 Chevrolet and I would thread our way downtown early every morning and fight the traffic and the heat on the way home every afternoon. My job was credit investigation and analysis, a very good way to learn about people and businesses in a short while. The people I worked with were top rate, the job was educational; and since I enjoyed living at my parents' home in Atlanta, I was rather happy with my immediate surroundings. On the weekends a group of us continued our two-year tradition of lazy tube trips down the Chattahoochee River near our home, and there was always some sort of nightly diversion.

But below the surface this was a very different June. No one in Atlanta seemed to know that a war was going on, that hundreds of Americans and Vietnamese were dying weekly, that the loss to our nation in men and creative potential was irreplaceable: or at least no one ever seemed to talk about it. Taylor and I came right from a campus where the war was on everyone's lips, where news reports were followed daily, where young men were having to make very real and very difficult decisions about their lives and our war, where the war and its effects upon our nation literally permeated every life and every day. We came from that sort of aware, worried and concerned daily academic experience and were swallowed by the incredible silence and total unconcern of middle-class America.

I had been a "hawk," I suppose, during my first year at Carolina; but by being forced in discussions to defend my beliefs and to analyze their foundations, I had come to a synthesis of beliefs which, at least in those more simple days of that 1968 spring, seemed more balanced and correct. The depressing thing about Atlanta in June was not that everyone was hawkish or that everyone had the "wrong" ideas. The really depressing thing was that, relative to our immediate past experience, no one seemed to be thinking or talking about the war at all.

All through the spring, during my first course on Chinese history, I kept thinking how little we average Americans know about China, and yet how much we accept our government's policies without even questioning them. That same feeling now came back to me about Atlanta and the Vietnam war in June. Usually when a luncheon discussion turned to the war people shook their heads politely, said something about how bad it all was, disclaimed any real knowledge of what was happening, and ordered dessert. And probably that same day another few hundred men were killed and another hundred million dollars were spent.

Or, if people did talk about the war at all, it was usually in State Department stereotypes. Not that Taylor, myself, or any of our friends by any means had even some of the answers; we just genuinely wanted to talk to people about the war and, to challenge views with which we disagreed. The depressing thing for us was that there seemed to be few views and even less talk. The silence was nearly complete.

Taylor and Cathy were living for the summer in a small one room apartment in the Boys Dorm at Westminster, our old prep school. Taylor was teaching there for the summer before doing graduate work in political science at Princeton, and he helped look after the school's boarding students. One night in late June, Jim Creech, George Wiley, two other recent UNC graduates working for the summer at a settlement house in Atlanta, and myself were at Taylor and Cathy's for an after-dinner talk.

In between Cathy's trips to the refrigerator and Taylor's trips to quiet the residents, we occupied the chairs and the floor of the apartment and discussed our impressions of the war and its impact on the people of Atlanta. All of us had been struck by the seeming silence of the city. As the night went on we began considering some sort of action to get people to think: at one point we were even contemplating hanging large signs from expressway overpasses during the rush hours, or else erecting a miniature graveyard of little crosses on an expressway interchange. Such thoughts, of course, were on the order of daydreams, but such was our frustration and our concern.

On a later occasion we expressed this feeling to some "over 30" friends of ours, the Pendergrasts, who shared our views on the war. They soon set up an evening meeting for us with Albert Bows, the president of the Atlanta Chamber of Commerce, to talk over our feelings about the war and the seeming local apathy. Mr. Bows turned out to be the ideal businessman and exactly the kind of man I had pictured as an "Atlanta leader." One good thing about Atlanta is that it is still small enough so that the men who control the real commercial power of the city can all sit around one large meeting table. An even better thing is that not only is this sort of meeting possible, but it is done quite regularly, and the men involved feel a real sense of responsibility to help make Atlanta work.

From the first primitive days of desegregation to the present struggle over jobs for the "hard core unemployed," and over city planning, these leaders have helped prevent the kind of plague which hit so many other Southern cities. They have provided the leadership which the whole city could follow and be proud of. They know that they have only begun, and they continue to search for new methods while providing the kind of atmosphere in which change can more naturally occur. There is even a group called "the good guys," a club of young Atlanta businessmen who anonymously devote their time to significant community projects.

The specifics of all this Taylor and I found out at our meeting with Mr. Bows, who is both proud of his work and concerned to do more. He admitted that he did not concern himself with the Vietnam war very much. But perhaps he was right in pointing out that there were more than enough problems for Atlanta businessmen to solve without tackling the war. Besides, he remarked, surely such energies could be used much more productively locally than in questioning the federal government's handling of the war.

I think on the whole that we had to agree with him about the best use of rather scarce time and activity. But in the end Mr. Bows did offer to set up a luncheon meeting for us with one of the "good guys' and to secure us, possibly, a date to address the Junior Chamber of Commerce about our concerns

While we agreed with Mr. Bows about what Atlanta businessmen could best be doing, I think that our main concern was that all Atlantans should be thinking and talking about a war which was affecting them directly one way or another. Eventually it occurred to me that perhaps people tend to think and to talk about issues over which they have some control; that is, why should one concern himself with the Vietnam war when he has no way to affect it?

In other states, if one felt so moved, there was, at least, the state Democratic Party through which, theoretically, one could hope to register a vote for change. The specific machinery for involvement varied from state to state, being most effective, of course, in states where there were presidential primaries. Georgia, however, was at the other end of the spectrum: and there was no provision at all for any local involvement in the state party.

Georgia had voted Democratic in every national election from 1864 to 1960. There was not even a Republican Party in Georgia until the early 1960's, and the Democratic Party is so entrenched in the state government that it is at times difficult to tell where the party stops and the government begins. I use the term "party" very loosely when referring to Georgia, for only in Fulton County, part of Atlanta, is there any semblance at all of party machinery.

Nowhere in the entire state of Georgia are there party caucuses, precinct meetings, or county conventions: they have never been needed. The necessary day-to-day maintenance is done by people appointed from the top in Atlanta. It has "always been like this in Georgia"; the Democratic Party has been in power for so long and has been challenged so little that it has never felt the need to establish local machinery for local involvement. The party is, in fact, run only by a small group of men at the top of the state government.

The most overt example of this hierarchical set-up is the party rule whereby the gubernatorial candidate of the party (read Governor of the state) and the party chairman personally appoint all of the Georgia delegates to the Democratic National Convention. For one thinking about involvement in the national party as a way to change either local conditions or a national policy, the Georgia Democratic Party is doubly frustrating: not only is there all of the entrenched establishment which exists in every other state; but in Georgia, and throughout the South, there is not even any prescribed method to go about changing that establishment or the party ideology it represents.

Possibly this is one reason why men like Al Bows do not concern themselves with national issues, because they have no way to be of any effect. Until there is some sort of change in the way both of our parties in Georgia are run, I must agree with him that such men's time is better spent where they can have some influence, and that is limited mainly to local issues.

It was not until July, after glimpses of the involvement of other young people in their own state party organizations, that I really sorted out the problem in Georgia. During June, like anyone else brought up in Georgia, it never even dawned on me to use party involvement as a means for change; such was just totally out of the realm of my past experience. Instead, I haphazardly looked here and there for something meaningful to do, not even recognizing the real problem.

For a while I thought I would try to work with a young couple organizing a softball league in a large part of Atlanta's black neighborhood. After going to a few games I was impressed by my own incapacity to add anything significant to what was already being done and also with the community spirit and friendliness which is totally lost in white society: perhaps this community spirit is one of the qualities which black culture has to contribute to America if ever given a chance. At any rate, both Taylor and I spent June in this state of suspended animation, vaguely looking for something to do but not quite sure what or how.

Georgians For McCarthy had, since that spring, been growing slowly and trying to settle an internal dispute over leadership. The group in Atlanta was still centered in the Emory University academic community. State organization, except in Athens at the University of Georgia, was virtually nil. One protagonist in the organization's leadership dispute was Joe Gross, the founder, who had been the only Georgian at the Convention of Concerned Democrats the previous fall. Mr. Gross, I was later told, envisioned himself rather as the leader of liberal Georgia, and he apparently continually reminded everyone of that fact, obviously leading to personal leadership problems.

The other protagonist in the dispute was Dr. Arthur Evans, the Emory University professor who had formerly been a student of Gene McCarthy. Dr. Evans is the epitome of the university professor: terribly nice, genuinely dedicated, somewhat forgetful, and seldom pushy, with an amazing capacity to work; seemingly a man more suited to lead an organization of equals. The dispute was apparently settled in June in favor of Dr. Evans: "apparently" because I was not involved in the organization at the time and also because Joe Gross still controlled the checking account containing the organization's limited funds. Though Taylor and I missed this original trouble, it was to come up again continually during the summer.

We had both phoned Dr. Evans early in June and expressed our willingness to help the group in any way we could. Our first answer came the last week in June when I received a phone call at work from a woman who said that Dr. Evans had given her my name as someone who might be interested in going to Chicago that weekend for a "general meeting," to be called the Coalition For An Open Convention.

All sorts of "important people" were supposed to be there, and the purposes of the two-day meeting were, first, to find some common ground on which McCarthy and former Kennedy followers could agree and, second, to work for the convention in August.

No other details were available, but she wanted to know if I, and my friend Taylor Branch, would be interested in going; we would, of course, have to pay our own way. Taylor and I talked it over and though we were not sure exactly what the meeting would be about, we were quite interested and decided to join the group.

That Friday night I attended my first Georgians For McCarthy meeting, held in Dr. Evans' home. There were about thirty people there, of all ages and both sexes. Most somehow seemed involved either with academics or the professions. I arrived a little late and knew no one, but I stood in the back and listened with interest. Dr. Evans introduced Charles Negaro, who had just arrived from Washington; I thought at the time his name was Charles, but Dr. Evans used three different names throughout the evening and I wasn't quite sure.

Charles turned out to be another middle-twenty McCarthy field worker, like Dave Mixner. He had quit his lawyer job after hearing McCarthy in New Hampshire and, though he had had no political experience before the McCarthy campaign, was assigned as field man for Georgia, Alabama, Mississippi, and I don't know where else: a job easily requiring an army, not just one man. In fact Charlie was to stay with us in Atlanta throughout the summer, an assignment which most of us were to feel was a blessing; but a few were to resent him and what he was trying to do as, incredibly, a "meddler from Washington."

At this, my first meeting, the topics discussed were the recent opening of the first McCarthy Storefront in Atlanta, a fund-raising mailing to be sent out, and a possible visit by Senator McCarthy. The rent for the storefront and the deposit on the only telephone had come largely from Dr. Evans' own pocket; the phone was, it turned out, a pay phone because the deposit for a pay phone was much less than for a regular phone. Just exactly who was going to man this office or for what purpose it was to be used had not really been sorted out, but it had been decided by the group that such a storefront was one logical starting point for any wider organization.

The mailing was a bit of a problem because of the money needed for postage and the fact that any money collected by the mailing would be paid into the account still controlled by Joe Gross. The possible visit by McCarthy was Charlie Negaro's subject, and as he spoke it dawned on me what a real undertaking such a visit would be. Decisions would have to be made about where, if at all, the senator would address a large crowd, where he would go, what he would do, etc. The local organization would also have to do the crowd building, the busing, the interest building and all the other behind-the-scenes activities necessary for a successful visit. That night the talk centered on which park would be best for an outdoor speech, but nothing was decided because the possibility of a visit was still uncertain and because such an undertaking would obviously require some guidelines from the national office.

My impressions of this first meeting and its business were mixed. The group was academic, homogeneous, and obviously new to participation politics. I felt comfortable in their presence; but even though the thought did not explicitly occur to me, I was nevertheless vaguely aware that a statewide presidential campaign would require more than genuinely well-meaning academics from one community in one city. At that time, though, I had no way of knowing whether this group—more or less—constituted the entire McCarthy organization, or whether there were similar groups meeting all over the state.

This meeting remains unique in my memory, because it was the last general meeting we ever held. Looking back, I realize that the organization was then undergoing a crucial alteration from an essentially self-concerned, mail-oriented discussion group into an outer-directed nucleus groping toward necessary political activism. We never again repeated the numbers of that night's meeting simply because there were not enough people able to make the time commitment implied by the transformation.

I'm not sure whether our subsequent smaller leadership is attributable to our own particular situation or is instead a general phenomenon. But it took us too long to realize the implications of this transformation, with the result that large numbers of potentially capable community leaders were left semi-involved on the periphery of the full time state organization, with no clearly defined role of either participation or of community responsibility.

When the meeting was over and the hat had been passed for contributions toward the storefront rent – and a new telephone – I introduced myself to Charlie and to Dr. Evans. Charlie was, at that point, planning a quick trip to Alabama; but he gave me his number at the Dinkler Plaza Hotel, where he was staying, and asked that I call him during the next week concerning a Southern Regional McCarthy Information Center. I left shortly because I had to get up early the next morning. But I got little sleep that night; I suppose I was a little excited about the weekend meeting in Chicago. I awoke at about 5 o'clock and drove over to pick up Taylor, who was in a usual state of last-minute material organization for the trip. That morning we flew off to Chicago; and though many people both then and later were to deride the Coalition For An Open Convention and its purpose, one of its immediate effects on Taylor and me was that neither of us was to get more than about six hours sleep any night for the next two months.

2

THE COALITION AND OUR FIRST INVOLVEMENT

The Coalition For An Open Convention (COC) was, at least in part, the brainchild of Al Lowenstein; and it was in his name that the "call" had gone out. I had first met Al a little over a year before when he had come to UNC to debate a State Department official on the Vietnam War. One of Al's greatest distinctions is that, at various times, he is damned by both the right and the left; I think this derision is because he is a genuinely activist liberal who believes that certain parts of our society should be changed, but basically from within the system.

Al, too, graduated from the University of North Carolina, right after World War II; he then co-founded the National Student Association at a time when communist youth organizations were growing rapidly in world strength and needed strong opposition. Since his service in the Korean War he has spent the last fifteen years in various roles, ranging from lawyer to teacher to civil rights worker to Hubert Humphrey's foreign policy advisor to what I can only call a "free-lance liberal." Al has dedicated his life, as simplistic as this sounds, to trying to right the wrongs of the world, never losing a basic liberal faith in people's ability to choose the right course, if only they are given all the relevant information.

This belief in the democratic process, coupled with a driving conviction that the Johnson escalation of the Vietnam War was morally, historically, and economically the wrong course of action for America, led Al to buck the liberal Democratic establishment he had been at least tacitly a part of and to start a crusade to get people to re-evaluate their stand on the war.

It was in the spring of 1967 that Al tore apart a State Department official in a UNC debate (it is perhaps significant that, at the time, the hawks complained that the State Department representative was somehow "chosen" by the doves, because he was so inept: later this same man was part of our national negotiating team in Paris). During that spring and summer Al was involved with groups all over the country trying to formulate some sort of coordinated anti-war program, while our cities burned.

In the fall of 1967, Al and others were instrumental in persuading Gene McCarthy to challenge President Johnson. They saw clearly, and often won thereby the disdain and distrust of the militant left, that the real way to bring about change in the society, be it over the war or black oppression, was not to throw bricks or to threaten violence, but instead to channel the energies and the frustrations of people opposed to the status quo into the system, into some form of acceptable action. Violence might get attention, but real change could only come when people were genuinely persuaded, when the system was made to work.

It was this understanding on the part of men like Gene McCarthy and Al Lowenstein – that what was needed was a political alternative, to be weighed, debated and fought for like any other political alternative – which saved America a great deal of possible violence; and which gave large numbers of American youth a chance not only to operate within the system, but also, in many instances, to succeed brilliantly. And, looked at from the perspective of November,1967, they had in fact changed perceptions quite a bit by August, 1968.

But the struggle along the way, by early July,1968, had been difficult. In a way Al had been too successful, for the spring produced not one, but two anti-war candidates. Al personally probably would have preferred it if Robert Kennedy had been the one to enter the race during the winter. But Kennedy did not enter until, to those on the outside at least, it seemed that Gene McCarthy had first proved the possibility of success. Whatever the reasons for Kennedy's late entry, by June 5th the Kennedy and McCarthy camps, while united on issues, had rather bitterly fought against each other in the later primaries, and real antagonism raged between them.

With Robert Kennedy's death, many of his supporters switched to

McCarthy; others, perhaps most, felt that all was lost and refused to remain involved. By late June there was a potential crisis developing. Not only were critical man hours of work being lost by former Kennedy supporters who remained aloof; but also, perhaps more to the immediate point, Kennedy delegates to the Democratic National Convention were being wooed by the forces of Hubert Humphrey, and there was a strong possibility that they might capitulate during July, leaving little hope at all for anyone else.

The purposes of the Coalition For An Open Convention were rather complex, and feelings about it were mixed. To people already partisan for McCarthy, the COC was either a blessing or a curse, depending on whether one felt it provided a holding action for those about to announce for Humphrey or whether one felt it only delayed longer the inevitable choice which had to be made in favor of McCarthy, thereby prolonging inexcusable inaction.

But for the majority of the over 1,000 participants, I think the COC served three purposes: First, it provided, at just the right time, an issues-oriented broad base for keeping landslide support from going to Humphrey: the importance of this base was crucially clear in the case of black delegates, who individually did not particularly want to alienate Humphrey but who were afraid that, by giving him their support too early the 1968 Convention would become another 1964 steam-roller in which the establishment power was so strong that no change, nor even any open debate, would be possible.

Second, the COC provided anew a somewhat papered-over, yet basically united, front of active liberals who would confront the party establishment with demands for both internal and external change. By late August the machinery set up by the COC did not really prove very effective itself, but at that point in early July, when the reports of Humphrey's strength were growing daily, the Coalition's combined boost upon the individual state delegations were crucial in encouraging a state by state "last push" before August.

And third, the COC provided a very useful forum for swapping the ideas and tactics which had already proved successful in campaigns at different ends of the country. I offer this analysis only from the benefit of hindsight gained by the end of the convention and from events later in the summer; that some leaders were then able to see the need for the COC from foresight must say something about the political expertise of a rising generation.

Taylor and I arrived at the Sherman House, a rather plain Chicago convention hotel, early Saturday morning, accompanying Dr. Evans and two students from Georgia – as far as we knew, the total of Georgia's representation. We checked in and then set about trying to discover what our two-day meeting was to be about. Taylor and I registered at the official booth in the large, somewhat cluttered lobby, rather luckily, it happened, as "adults" (as opposed to "students," those being the two broad classifications).

In the lobby we met friends from North Carolina, then went upstairs to meet Bob Powell, a friend and former President of the Student Body at UNC, who, it turned out, was typical of the above-mentioned former Kennedy supporters who were still undecided about McCarthy. After a rather discouraging talk with him about unity, we went downstairs again for the first official function: a preliminary news conference held by the callers of the coalition.

Al Lowenstein and the others sat at a long table on a small platform in a conference room made into a press room by the inclusion of several strong movie lamps and rows of chairs assembled near the head table. The press representatives continuously taped, filmed, and recorded every word; and their questions, though probably mechanical to most of them, seemed exceptionally perceptive to me. Al and his colleagues handled these questions with good sense and honesty: they answered that they were not sure about what was going to happen over the next two days, since it was the purpose of the meeting to decide about courses of action. They only hoped that, at least, issues would be brought up and decided upon which all of the participants could unite behind as fundamental to a liberal Democratic Convention in August.

Taylor and I sat on the side of the conference room while the questioning went on. This was one of my first experiences in saturation national press coverage, and it was interesting to watch the furrowed brows of the writers while trying to record an answer and the nervous fingers of the cameramen while attempting to quickly change a roll of film. With the news conference over, everyone adjourned to the larger "convention hall" for the official opening of the meeting.

On the way out, by chance, Taylor and I struck up a conversation with a rather large man we had spied standing at the back of the room during the interview. Except for his face, which made him seem a bit too soft spoken, he easily could have played the stereotype role of a small-town Southern sheriff, complete with silver-gray hair and a cigar stub stuck in the corner of his mouth. But George Walsh turned out to be anything but a stereotype: he was a lawyer from Decatur (a suburb of Atlanta) who had heard about the Coalition For an Open Convention and had independently decided to come, hoping to share his ideas with other lawyers present, as he was furiously working on a court injunction trying to bar Lester Maddox's hand-picked delegation from representing Georgia at the Democratic National Convention. We were glad to meet a fellow Georgian, and I think it encouraged us a great deal to realize that there was already at least one man trying to do something about our "system" in Georgia.

The COC lasted all day Saturday and all-day Sunday, with no time allotted for lunch on either day. The program was evenly balanced between speeches and working meetings on various subjects: delegate influence, vital issues to be included in the Democratic Party platform, general strategy for the next seven weeks, etc. In all, it was a very free-wheeling potpourri of people and subjects, and one would find small groups of people meeting all over the hotel discussing everything from the urban crisis to a fourth party. Anyone could plan a caucus at any time when a room was available; there were caucuses for "Kennedy Supporters," "Fourth Party Supporters," and "Challenge Delegations."

While these meetings were going on, besides participating in many of them, the students (probably about 1/5 of the total attendance) were holding their own meetings and caucuses. Taylor and I went to a few student meetings for a while, but the general level of debate was on the wording of a statement to the effect that if the national party conventions did not loosen up their undemocratic procedures, then the students would consider whatever government was elected in November as being illegal and would not feel bound to abide by its laws (i.e., especially, the draft).

We realized that the most vital and relevant discussions, if one was most concerned with actually changing things in the short run, were not being done in meetings like these, but instead in the small workshops, especially the one quickly begun by lawyers like Mr. Walsh and the one on challenge delegations. For in these workshops one could meet people with experience and ideas which might really prove useful for work at home in Georgia.

Late that Saturday afternoon in the hotel lobby Taylor pointed out Rev. Ed King, the young white man who, with Fannie Lou Hamer, had been one of the leaders of the 1964 Mississippi Freedom Democratic Party challenge delegation. About an hour later we spotted him again; and, since our curiosity had been aroused by all that was going on, we asked him if he had a few minutes to tell us about his 1964 experience, as we were "sort of interested in running a challenge from Georgia"(!). Where these words came from I do not know. Probably they were aroused simply by seeing Rev. King, and perhaps we never would have thought of a challenge delegation had we not met him.

I, of course, knew of the 1964 Mississippi challenge, but only vaguely; and not once had the thought of a Georgia challenge struck me until that Saturday, simply because I had been thinking in terms of general "political organization," not a challenge to the system itself. As with most ideas, the challenge delegation first came up casually and then grew in importance over the weekend and later weeks—as our understanding of both the Georgia and the national political situations also grew. Perhaps to Rev. King we seemed quite committed to a challenge; but at the time we were simply sampling his experiences, as we were genuinely trying to sample all the new experiences around us.

Rev. King spent an hour with us, explaining the specific details of how one goes about a challenge, a subject on which we were totally ignorant. In Mississippi they had worked for four years prior to the 1964 convention building a completely new party as both an internal and an external challenge to the regular Democratic Party of the governor; that is, they not only had planned to challenge at the national convention, but they also had run local candidates throughout the state.

They spent months precisely documenting examples of discrimination on the part of the regular party and its lack of local involvement, this evidence to be included in all the all-important challenge brief to be submitted to the convention Credentials Committee. After all of this work, and armed with their documented evidence, the delegation leaders arrived at the 1964 Democratic Convention hoping to unseat the "regulars" and to be recognized as the only democratic Democratic Party of Mississippi. What followed was, in Ed King's words, a fiasco.

Lyndon Johnson's forces had maintained such complete control over the convention and had so little wanted any issue to "rock the boat" that they were not about to decide the Mississippi case on its merits. Instead, as a "compromise," Ed King and Fannie Lou Hamer were offered two "seats at large" – with the Alaska delegation – while the rest of their delegation stayed out and the regulars stayed in.

It was Hubert Humphrey himself, said Rev. King, who came to them with tears in his eyes, acting as LBJ's hatchet man, begging that they accept the compromise if they wanted him (HHH) to get the Vice-presidential nomination. In the end they had no choice; and it was this debacle, according to Rev. King, which helped turn Stokely Carmichael and other SNCC radicals away from the "system." They had worked long and hard for the Mississippi Freedom Democratic Party (MFDP), assuming that the system would work fairly, only to run into what they easily considered political back-stabbing from short-sighted politicians.

The only two beneficial results of the 1964 challenge were, first, that with relatively little work in 1968, the MFDP was almost assured of being seated. Second, Governor Hughes of New Jersey had specified in the Call to the 1968 Convention that all state delegations should be chosen by some broadly democratic process and should include significant representation from all minorities within the state: a potential and forceful argument for challenging any official delegation which did not fulfill the1968 Call's requirements. As to when challenge briefs had to be in for 1968, Rev. King thought it was about August first.

Later that afternoon we attended a meeting of ten lawyers, including Mr. Walsh from Georgia. They were discussing both formal legal action and also the preparation of challenge briefs for the Credentials Committee of the Democratic National Convention. Mr. Walsh was most interested in the former, and he mentioned a post-1964 Texas case in which a federal court had ruled that "one man one vote" must extend at least to the district level in political parties. One lawyer had been involved with the 1964 MFDP challenge, and another was preparing a challenge in New York, based upon the arbitrary pro-Humphrey action of the executive committee of the state Democratic Party in selecting half of its delegates.

After supper in a splendid Greek restaurant with some Chicago friends, we returned to the Sherman House for more meetings. By this point Taylor and I were beginning to feel involved, and we set up a caucus for the

Southern states to talk about common problems and strategies. Late that night about twenty of us assembled in a rather ornate meeting room with a red carpet and chandeliers, typical of those tucked here and there in the hotels of a convention city.

There, besides our Georgia delegation, we met Mr. John Cashin, leader of the National Democratic Party of Alabama, centered in Huntsville. His party was trying to formulate a challenge from a state where, according to Mr. Cashin, the electors were already pledged to George Wallace. There, too, were representatives from Texas, where the "unit rule" - the right of a simple majority to elect all the delegates to the next higher level in the state's convention structure – was enforced at the local level, meaning that by the time the delegates to the state convention had been chosen, all opposition was neatly eliminated.

There, too, was Hans Reinisch, a New York businessman who had come along to see what we were doing and who vaguely hinted that there might be some seed money available from New York to get Southern challenges off the ground. We talked for about an hour, but since each state was in many ways a unique case, there was not too much that we could do for each other except to swap information about the technicalities of challenging and to promise to keep in contact during the summer.

On Sunday the convention continued, hoping for a near-supper ending for those who wanted to attend a fund-raising rally for Gene McCarthy, featuring Peter, Paul and Mary, other stars, and the senator himself; the rally happened to be going on that same weekend, though it was unconnected with the COC. The Sunday meetings were more like large workshops, and Taylor and I became more and more involved.

When thrust into such a fluid, dynamic meeting, one cannot help but feel part of the energy all around. It began to strike me how completely dedicated all the delegates seemed to be to changing both national policies and state procedures, how much they felt it was their fight, as if believing that if they did not tackle these problems, then nobody would. But these people, hoping to win influence in August, were fighting against systems infinitely more democratic than anything in Georgia, if only because their state had a "system," a state organization, something to fight through or against. Democrats from Oregon just could not believe how the Democratic Party of Georgia was (or was not) managed.

Taylor and I both slowly came to realize for the first time at the COC, by talking with people from other states, how undemocratic Georgia really is and how much there is need for change. But it also began to dawn on us what a unique opportunity we might have for changing things that year, based mainly on the Hughes' Call To The Convention and on the blatant flaunting(flouting) of this Call by our governor, who was only doing what all past Georgia governors had done, but who that year happened to be Lester Maddox, the man known throughout the nation for his famous photograph in which he is brandishing a pistol to keep black people out of his restaurant. (VERY run-on!)

The more we learned politically about other states, the more we knew what we were missing as Georgians; the more we personally felt that we could help to do something about it, and the more we felt that such an opportunity might not present itself again for years.

But how? There we weren't sure of anything. I remember one woman from New York telling us that, since <u>anything</u> we might do would be, strictly speaking, extra-legal as far as the Democratic Party was concerned, the important thing was just to do something, almost anything, to do it well, and to come to Chicago in August with a challenge: the important issue not being how we chose our delegates, but how the "official" delegation chose theirs.

Of course the more support that could be generated along the way, and the more representative our delegation could be, the better, if we wanted not only to challenge the old way but also to look toward building in the future. But the important thing, on that last day of June, was to do *something*.

At the final COC session, Al, acting as chairman, took motions from the various committees. One of the most hotly debated motions asserted that we would never support Hubert Humphrey unless he changed his stand on the war. Many felt that this affirmation was necessary if the "liberal wing" of the party was not again to be ignored at convention time, confidently being expected to return as always to the fold in October and to help the cause once it was Democrats vs. Nixon. The motion passed, and a few people walked out. The student caucus also brought up its resolution about not feeling obliged to respect the laws of the land if the election system were not made more democratic.

On this and several other "radical" motions, the caucus system proved, by chance, a great blessing: a resolution passed in a caucus could be aired and could receive its due press time, but the body as a whole was never asked to vote on it – a quite convenient system. As a final resolution we established a continuing committee to carry on the work of the COC, hoping to establish a headquarters in Chicago which would act as a coordination body for the nationwide attempt to keep the nomination out of the hands of any one candidate until the issues had been settled.

As the COC came to a close, Taylor and I pitched in and added our small part: we hurriedly compiled brief summaries from ten different states as to how democratically delegates were elected around the country. We had these summaries typed up and run off; then we stapled a bunch together and gave away as many as we could as people were leaving. We hoped that such information would prove useful in the hands of McCarthy and Kennedy delegates to the Democratic National Convention from primary states, who might want to let their fellow delegates know about the selection processes in states not quite so lucky.

As we were leaving to get tickets for the McCarthy rally, we met Ed King again in the lobby; he was having to change travel plans because the COC meetings had lasted so late. He told me that he could not go home to Mississippi that night, since he still considered it too dangerous to arrive in his hometown after midnight.

Though the McCarthy Speak Out auditorium was almost full, Taylor, myself and two friends got in easily and had good seats for what was a splendid show. After an hour of entertainment by several stars, including Peter, Paul and Mary, the house lights came up and the master of ceremonies began the task of raising funds for the national campaign.

This was my first personal encounter with large-crowd fund raising. It seemed a bit pushed at first, though after people started giving, it all seemed quite natural for the M.C. to ask, "Now who is going to donate a day's air travel to the campaign?" "Who is going to donate a week's expenses for 10 area coordinators?" etc. After about half an hour they had raised nearly a hundred thousand dollars in pledges, though I'm not sure how much was actually collected; and, from the point of view of a national campaign, this amount might have been disappointing.

Following Richard Goodwin's introduction, Senator McCarthy entered to a thunderous applause by a packed house. His speech was to me both inspiring and low key: the former possibly because it was the first time I had ever seen him, and I wanted him to be; the second because he just was.

He spoke in general terms about the war, the campaign, and the final push towards the convention in August, ending with a still confident hope for victory.

After another ovation at the end of the rally, our Chicago friends loaded us, our luggage and our bottle of bourbon into their sportscar, and we headed for a little tavern they knew about. Little wasn't the word: tiny was more like it. After a while Taylor and I wound up talking together outside in the adjoining alley, leaning on a car, occasionally going inside for mixers. It had been an eventful two days, and we were full of a vague sense of wanting to do something. We talked and planned in that alleyway for about an hour, as a gentle rain started to fall.

After a while we just decided (!) to go ahead and run a challenge delegation from Georgia. Even if we could not do much for Gene McCarthy, and even though we knew that we would probably lose, we hoped that our try might make some difference for 1972. It was a "what have we got to lose?" kind of a decision, with the prospect of changing things so possible that it excited us, and with no understanding at all about what was to be involved.

As we talked and sipped we evolved a tentative plan for a newspaper poll. From somewhere we would get the needed money (from our New York businessman friend?), then we would run a rough kind of an election. In early August polling places would be set up in Atlanta shopping areas as well as in the centers of other cities throughout the state. In two subsequent Sunday papers we would publish full page challenges to readers to "vote" for their Democratic presidential candidate on "ballots" provided (including a space for write-ins), these ballots to be mailed into a central polling location. The ad would also specify an Atlanta phone number which people could call collect in order to vote; and during this "voting week" our polling places throughout the state would be open.

Each ballot would require the voter's name, to prevent duplication. When all votes were counted, a delegation would somehow be chosen – we did not give these details much thought – pledged to vote the percentages as recorded on these ballots on the first round (as is usual) at the Democratic National Convention. Armed with these ballots and representing "the people of Georgia," this delegation would then challenge the delegation hand-picked by Lester Maddox.

Though such a system sounds bizarre, it offered us the possibility of generating the maximum interest and protest against the current system with a minimum of staff and state-wide organization. Whether such a delegation ever got to Chicago or not, we hoped we could at least dramatically point out to the people of Georgia the inadequacy of the present system and at the same time start people thinking about the need for change.

We even thought of a name for our new-found organization: first it was "Georgia Democrats for Democracy," but then we changed it to the somewhat double-meaning title of "Georgians for a Democratic Convention." We sketched in our minds how the "voting pages" in the newspapers would look. Taylor and I then took the final decisive plunge of long-term commitment: we decided that the next day he would take out a post office box in our new name and that I would open a checking account with no money. At that point we swore that, if there was anything that we could do during the next seven weeks that could get Gene McCarthy just one vote from Georgia, we would come back to that same tavern after the convention and really celebrate together.

We were feeling rather proud of ourselves and excited about the future as we later boarded the airport bus; and the night had not been without merit: at 9 p.m. we had been listening to Gene McCarthy; by midnight we had laid the "plans" for the Georgia challenge; at 2:30 we were at the airport and already high; by 6 a.m. we were in Atlanta, and at 8:30 I was at my desk and on the job. If it seems impossible that two twenty-one year-olds should have been half-seriously planning a state challenge for the Democratic National Convention, please remember that we had never done such a thing before, and so a challenge seemed to us equally as possible or as impossible as anything else.

That Monday night, July 1st, after opening our GDC checking account while at work, I was at home watching a local 6 o'clock news broadcast before supper. Near the end they presented an interview with a gentleman identified as Mr. Al Kehrer, the chairman of a group called The Georgia Democratic Party Forum. During the interview Mr. Kehrer announced the Forum's intention to go ahead with its planned challenge to the Lester Maddox delegation at the Democratic National Convention!

Here was an organization and a plan which Taylor and I had heard absolutely nothing about, and we obviously needed to find out what the Forum was and what its challenge plans were.

After calling Taylor, I phoned Mr. Kehrer. At that time I did not want to divulge any of our own "plans," so I just asked questions and told him that I was interested. He said that the Forum was planning to hold a convention in Macon (about ninety miles south of Atlanta) later that month and that he hoped that "all national political figures will be represented on our delegation." He further stated that plans were already underway to write a challenge brief, based mainly on Lester Maddox's disloyalty to the national Democratic Party, his support for George Wallace, and, therefore, his disqualification as the man who should choose Georgia's delegates. Mr. Kehrer put me on the Forum's mailing list and promised to send me an application form.

One other thing had struck me about that same TV newscast: immediately following Mr. Kehrer's interview, a filmed interview with our governor, Lester Maddox, was presented, in which Governor Maddox was asked what he thought about the Forum's challenge. In characteristic form, Governor Maddox replied that such a challenge was the work of radical elements and that, if the reporter examined their beliefs, he would probably find that "they didn't differ too much from the policies of the communist leaders in Moscow."

How ridiculous, how ironic a statement for him, of all people, to make. Governor Maddox was ascribing the bugaboo of "communist sympathizers" to a group of people he probably knew nothing about while, ironically, he sat at the pinnacle of a totalitarian centralized party which would probably easily rival anything Mr. Brezhnev or Mr. Kosygin could think up. The Georgia Democratic Party, in July, 1968, was a classic example of a party run by "democratic centralism," meaning that all communication was basically one way: from the top.

The Democratic Party of Georgia was being run with no local meetings, no caucuses, no state convention, and no election of officials. How much more could a young Russian be excluded from influencing his national ruling party than I was excluded from influencing the national Democratic party? And yet I was being asked to go "defend democracy" in Vietnam at the time when I was coming to question how much democracy I really had under our present system. One thing must be said in Governor Maddox's favor, though: I don't think he had the malicious intent that we usually ascribe to the Kremlin rulers; I'm sure it just quite honestly never occurred to him the kind of system he was perpetuating.

After my phone call to Mr. Kehrer, Taylor and I obviously had to talk, so I drove over to his apartment. As usual, Taylor had too much to do, between reading, correcting papers, and trying to keep civil order in the Boys Hall. Cathy was working on a lecture for the Bible class which she was teaching for the summer. I reported my phone call to Mr. Kehrer and, after a long talk, we decided that Taylor should now call him trying to find out exactly what sort of "Humphrey-McCarthy-McGovern" split Mr. Kehrer foresaw for the delegation, and also trying to set up a meeting for the three of us.

Taylor called, and Mr. Kehrer said that he foresaw a delegation 'representing all Democratic presidential candidates." Taylor then divulged his link with my call, told Mr. Kehrer that we had just been to the Coalition for an open Convention, that we had been thinking about a challenge, and that it would probably be good to have a meeting to share our experiences and our plans. Mr. Kehrer was more than agreeable, and we planned to meet late the following afternoon in his office, near the bank where I worked in downtown Atlanta.

We then called Dr. Evans; he told us that there would be a "working meeting" of Georgians For McCarthy the next night at his home, if we would like to attend. He also told us that Mary Beth McCarthy was coming to Atlanta to represent her uncle during the city's Fourth of July festivities, especially at the Young Democratic Club-Young Republican Club Charity Ball the night of July third. Dr. Evans wanted to know if I would like to be her escort. I wasn't sure of my plans but said that it would probably be alright. He and Taylor then talked about the possibility of a reception for Miss McCarthy on Thursday night, the Fourth. Taylor said he would try to get it organized. Cathy's parents were going away for the holiday, and he would try to get permission to use their home for that night.

While Cathy called her mother, Taylor and I talked about the need to invite some people to the reception who had financial resources and who might be willing to donate to our campaign and our challenge delegation causes. We hoped that even if Atlanta businessmen might not feel inclined to give directly to the McCarthy campaign, they might be more easily induced to give to a Georgia challenge delegation designed to shake up "the way things had always been."

On the assumption that businessmen are best approached by another businessman, I then called Hans Reinisch in New York and told him that we had "something going" in Georgia. I asked if he had yet received any promises of money for us (somewhat premature), and then I broached the subject of Mary Beth McCarthy's visit and our still unplanned reception. He said that he would love to "fly south" and that he would be in Atlanta on Wednesday to help us. I left Taylor and Cathy while they collectively tried to put together an invitation list for the "right people" for Cathy to call the next day.

I began that Tuesday at the Army Induction Center. The week before I had taken my draft physical; in fact, I had been forced to gamble and to volunteer for it. The directors of the Marshall Scholarship wanted to know by August whether I would be able to go to England, but my draft board would not get around to processing me until September, unless I requested an earlier examination.

At my first examination that June, in the midst of all that is a military physical examination, I had produced a copy of a letter from my doctor regarding my recurrent serious back trouble. I had sent the original of the letter to my draft board, but it was not included with my records at the examination center. Luckily, I wound up with an agreeable doctor, and though he could not decide my fate on just the strength of my doctor's letter, he set a date for me to see the Army's special orthopedic surgeon. Tuesday being that date, I appeared bright and early to be x-rayed. By late that afternoon I had a one year "physically unfit" rating, and I was very happy.

I then drove over to meet Taylor at Mr. Kehrer's office, which occupied two modern rooms in one of the new Atlanta office towers. On the door was "AFL-CIO Human Rights Office." It was about 5 pm and raining heavily outside when I entered. Mr. Kehrer's secretary showed me into his office. After greeting me, Mr. Kehrer spoke with his secretary, who was apparently leaving for a vacation and was trying to get her work caught up. Mr. Kehrer is tall, with a somewhat flat, not unpleasant face and graying hair that makes him look "fiftyish."

I picked up some of the Forum literature which was lying on a table and looked quickly through it while he talked with his secretary. I immediately discovered that the Georgian Democratic Party Forum was the name taken by the loose coalition of Georgia liberals who had been involved in the Ellis Arnall write-in campaign against Lester Maddox in 1966, and who were about the only "liberal force" left with any sort of organization. Now they were embarked upon the challenge to Lester Maddox's delegation.

Taylor arrived shortly, as did Rev. John Morris, whom Mr. Kehrer had invited. Rev. Morris is immediately striking as a friendly, concerned person, with somewhat curly brown hair and an almost Buster Brown, near-boyish face. He came in smoking a cigar and carrying the latest copy of *The Atlanta Journal*: Lester Maddox had finally published the names of those on his delegation to the Democratic National Convention. He and Mr. Kehrer spent a minute looking over the list, pointing out people whom they knew off hand to have either John Birch Society or Ku Klux Klan affiliations. Rev. Morris was at our meeting and was showing such interest in the Maddox delegates, it turned out, because he was in charge of gathering information and writing the Forum's challenge brief.

We quickly started talking, with Taylor and I roughly sketching our experience at the COC the weekend before and relating our plans for a newspaper poll in an attempt to get as many Georgians as possible involved in the delegate selection process. When Mr. Kehrer pointed out the enormous cost involved in such newspaper ads (which I really had not known before), we replied that we hoped to get some funds from New York. But we emphasized that ours were only dreams really, and that we were interested in the Forum's plans.

Mr. Kehrer related that at a Forum meeting in June, with representatives from almost all of Georgia's ten congressional districts, about a hundred Forum members had voted to go ahead with the challenge, only after repeated failures to persuade the state Democratic officials to reform the delegate selection process. They had appointed a steering committee to plan the necessary details, with Mr. Kehrer as chairman (both of the committee and the Forum). This committee, which included Rev. Morris, was going to meet that weekend in Macon to plan a full-scale convention for later that month, probably at the Dempsey Hotel, Macon's largest.

Although all the details were still to be worked out, Mr. Kehrer foresaw an "open convention," where any Georgia Democrat who would sign a loyalty pledge to the national party would be free to vote. Since Georgia had ten districts and 43 votes at the national convention, Mr. Kehrer thought that the Macon convention would be divided up by districts for the purpose of electing four delegates and four alternatives each, with the remainder of the delegates and any vacancies left by district attendance to be filled in from the reconvened entire convention.

When we got around to the subject of national presidential candidates, Mr. Kehrer said that he was a Humphrey supporter but that he did not want to sacrifice possible gains for Georgia by playing partisan politics; that is, he foresaw a mixed delegation, but he spoke in the terms of 60%-40% Humphrey-McCarthy, obviously feeling that a basically pro-Humphrey delegation would get the best hearing from the Humphrey-dominated Credentials Committee.

Rev. Morris said that one day he wore a Humphrey button, the next day a McCarthy button, but that his wife was strongly pro-McCarthy. Taylor and I let our sentiments be known, but we also agreed with Mr. Kehrer about the delegate split, and 40% of the vote was certainly about 40% more than McCarthy was going to get from the just-named Maddox delegation.

The more we spoke the more I started to think in terms of integrating our two plans, if possible. That is, if the money could be found, I hoped that we could first run the newspaper poll and then elect the challenge delegation in Macon at the Forum convention, pledging the delegation to vote the poll percentages on the first ballot. This seemed the ideal system to me, from the point of view of presenting a strong cause to the Credentials Committee; but when I mentioned it to Mr. Kehrer, he seemed skeptical, though he said that he would bring it up at the planning committee's meeting.

One thing that we did convince them of was the desirability of moving the Macon convention back into August, for two reasons. One was due to the time needed to get the convention organized. But more importantly, Taylor and I felt, it would be best to wait until after the Republican Convention, when interest would naturally be turning to the Democrats. If held too soon, "our" convention might get lost and forgotten in the mostly Republican press. But, if timed correctly before the Democratic National Convention, it could arouse maximum national interest and might thereby ride with the increasing momentum into the Democratic National Convention. Both Mr. Kehrer and Rev. Morris did seem amiable to this proposal, and when we left we all promised to keep in touch.

Walking back to our cars, Taylor and I discussed the situation. It seemed to us that just exactly what we lacked the Forum already had: an at least partially functioning state organization. The Forum's convention idea was both more and less grandiose than our own plan: more so in the state organization required; but much less so in the amount of money actually needed. And as Mr. Kehrer had pointed out, the Forum's budget was limited to a few hundred dollars. On the other hand, if Hans could come through with the necessary funds, the state-wide newspaper poll seemed intuitively a more democratic system, presenting a stronger case to be representative of the people of Georgia at the Democratic National Convention. We drove home for quick suppers, and then Taylor picked me up to go over to Dr. Evans' home for our first working meeting with Georgians For McCarthy.

At this July 2nd meeting, in addition to Dr. Evans and Charlie Negaro, we found Nick Beluso, Ken Martin, Richard Ramseur and Les Leopold, none of whom were yet members of Georgians For McCarthy. Mr. Beluso and his friend Ken Martin were quiet during most of the meeting. They were men of about forty who had previously been involved in local Atlanta politics, who were interested in McCarthy, and who wanted to see what sort of a McCarthy organization was forming. Richard Ramseur, also an older man, who was rather thin and had an incredible "Georgia" accent, was in the same position.

Les Leopold was a college student who had "dropped out for McCarthy"; along with others he had been responsible for "crowd building" in southern California. Charlie had asked the national organization for help, and Les had arrived to lend a hand. Also at the meeting was Joe Gross, the founder of Georgians For McCarthy, who was then in charge of "state organization," while Dr. Evans was nominally co-chairman in charge of the more delicate Atlanta operations. A late arrival was Marilyn Grayboff, the almost too enthusiastic and stubborn "press officer" of Georgians For McCarthy.

After introductions all around, we pulled our chairs together in the Evans' living room and got down to business in a manner that was to become standard throughout the summer: the most pressing issue was taken up first. In this case it was Mary Beth McCarthy's visit. She was due to arrive the next day and I agreed to escort her to the YDC-YRC Fourth of July Ball. Taylor had secured his new parents-in-law's home for a reception, and Cathy had been phoning all day issuing invitations to the few couples not already otherwise occupied.

Marilyn Grayboff was holding a smaller supper reception at her house on the night of the charity ball; she had also arranged for Mary Beth and me to be the guests on "Atlanta Now," an hour-long live TV talk show on the Fourth of July, following our official opening of the Atlanta McCarthy storefront. I announced that Han Reinisch was supposed to arrive the afternoon of the Fourth, hopefully to help at Mary Beth's reception that night. The situation seemed well in hand on our first subject.

Next came the possibility of a visit from Senator McCarthy himself; Charlie had passed the word up that the Fulton County Democratic Club was having a fund-raising dinner on July 18th, and there was a slight chance that the senator might be able to attend. Any details for such a visit would have to await national approval, but throughout this discussion and those on finances and organization in general, the tip of a summer long iceberg appeared for the first time – the tension between Charlie and Les, on the one hand, representing the national McCarthy organization, and we "Georgians," on the other hand, our side usually being taken most vigorously by Joe Gross.

Mr. Gross, who already had a few hundred dollars in an account which he controlled and who was preparing our third order of business – a statewide fund-raising mailing, giving his home as the return address – basically believed that Georgians For McCarthy was just that and should be run by Georgians. In my view, the ensuing hour's discussion was both embarrassing and out of place at the time, as we were really accomplishing so little anyway. But Mr. Gross seemed to believe that, before doing anything, we had first to spend time deciding just who we were, whom we represented, and where the clear boundaries of responsibility and authority lay. It was also obvious from his tone that he considered his own views critical to any sound decision, implying that he had been in Georgia for twenty years and knew best what was needed (and, therefore, that "outsiders" did not).

Charlie Negaro took all this, as he was to take all later barbs, fairly well. He was our only link with the national campaign; he and Les were expecting to devote 18 hours a day to the campaign, an impossible task for the rest of us with our regular jobs. Nothing that Charlie had yet said or done would lead any of us to believe that he was going to be "making decisions behind our backs";he was just too much a concerned idealist to do so; besides, I'm sure he felt that he was in Atlanta to help us, not for his own health or aggrandizement.

These were, at least, my impressions of him as he sat smoking his pipe and running his hand across his curly hair while listening to Mr. Gross. I felt that the last thing Charlie was about to come up with was hostility; but Mr. Gross, who I suppose was most concerned with the responsibility for decision making, pressed Charlie about our local autonomy. Charlie, whose only fault, I think, was to say things bluntly in a sometimes unpolitical way, responded that, yes, if he thought we were going to try to do something which he felt to be detrimental to the national campaign, he would do all that he could to veto it.

I felt that this was not an unreasonable position, and what we were going to do that would be so detrimental, anyway, I do not know. But I'm afraid that Mr. Gross was then convinced, somehow, that we had all been stripped of our decision-making powers and that we were henceforth the pawns of a young inexperienced lawyer from "somewhere" else.

I was becoming a little embarrassed by this shadow boxing. At that crucial time it seemed to me that we should be trying to build some sort of teamwork, based on respect and trust, for a hard push ahead, not wasting time and creating ill feeling over issues which were largely irrelevant.

Nick Beluso changed the subject by expressing the possibility that we could use his office in the west end of town as a second storefront, since he was in the tax business and only used his office six months out of the year. He also said that he had been down to the new McCarthy storefront, that it was an impossible place to work in, and that what was was needed was an "executive office" somewhere in a hotel where we could do our critical planning and phone calling. Here, finally, were some constructive ideas. Mr. Beluso would not then say whether he was willing to involve himself in our organization, but he said that he would think it over.

Richard Ramseur offered that he had been involved with state-wide fund raising before and might know some people to contact. He was also in the printing business and offered to do all of our printing at cost. Mr. Gross said that the new state-wide mailing was going ahead slowly, being restricted by funds for the stamps and enough time for him to seal and mail the letters. Just before the meeting broke up, Mrs. Grayboff invited us to come to her house early the next evening, before the other guests and Mary Beth McCarthy arrived, to continue our planning with more of the original members of Georgians For McCarthy.

We broke up late that evening, and on the way home Taylor and I discussed the day's events. On one hand, we were greatly encouraged by the previously unknown work of the Georgia Forum. Our plans of two nights before might have to be altered, but more importantly there was a functioning state organization with good ideas already at work. We were also encouraged by our late-night meeting. Four new men with divergent talents and contacts had arrived, plus ourselves.

If we kept up that kind of growth, we might just possibly be able to tackle the enormous job of a real state campaign. On the other hand, Taylor and I were veterans of several student campaigns and organizations in which one usually assumed everyone's good intention, divided up the tasks, and got on with the necessary work as efficiently as possible, without doubting a person's ability to get something done unless he proved himself unreliable.

Coming from such an "all equals" background, and confronted with the inconceivable details of a state campaign, we were convinced that, while Mr. Gross had some valid theoretical points, hours spent in his kind of debate were going to get us nowhere. Charlie seemed to us to be basically like ourselves, a well-meaning non-politician who was trying to change things through political means. Like him, we were interested in results, and we hoped that he would not feel unwanted and leave for somewhere else.

Early the next evening the same group reconvened in Marilyn Grayboff's basement, except that Mr. Gross and Mr. Ramseur were not present, and both the Besdines attended. Several decisions made at this meeting were to prove important for the summer's work. Mrs. Grayboff, our conscientious hostess, tried to contribute to the meeting while constantly running upstairs to make sure that her daughters were properly preparing everything. As we sat in the usual circle of chairs, Mr. Beluso led off by saying that he had given more thought to the idea of a state headquarters and that he was prepared to underwrite a three-room suite in the Dinkler Plaza Hotel (where Charlie was staying) in downtown Atlanta. He specifically used the word underwrite. He hoped that Georgians For McCarthy could pay the headquarters' $100 a week rent from the income such a suite could bring in; but should it not, he said that he was willing to gamble the difference. He also said that he knew a sign printer and was prepared to have two huge "McCarthy for President Headquarters" signs placed outside the hotel.

All this was contingent, he added, upon him having some personal control over what happened, because, after all, he said, we all expected to "get something out of this thing"; and Mr. Beluso, who had been to an earlier Democratic Convention for Stevenson, hoped to go again. Perhaps I was just too young, but never had it occurred to me that one worked for McCarthy to "get something out of it"—except possibly an end of the Vietnam War. Though I instinctively grimaced at his words, on the inside, I said nothing. For as with so many expressions, suggestions, and activities of those days, I rarely felt capable of criticism. Everything being new, one expression seemed just as politically valid as the next. Perhaps, in Mr. Gross' terms, I should have openly questioned; instead, Mr. Beluso's remark simply stayed with me as one part of my impressions of him. And besides, he had just offered us a state headquarters.

Mrs. Bresdine gave a quick financial report on our one hundred dollar bank account and a brief history of the whole checking account situation. Mr. Gross still maintained one checking account, titled "Georgians For McCarthy." Another account, "Georgians For McCarthy of Atlanta," was controlled by Dr. Evans and herself and was originally designed to handle the receipts and expenses of the Atlanta storefront. This financial division had been accepted as part of the leadership settlement earlier in the summer, but it was obviously impractical for a growing organization.

Then we talked about the overall problem of organization. Someone said that he believed the group had grown a great deal in just the past two weeks, and it would have to if it were to be successful, and that it was naturally time to expand the leadership if decisions were to be decentralized. Charlie proposed that the co-chairmen be doubled from Dr. Evans and Mr. Gross; and he nominated Mr. Beluso and Taylor to fill the new positions, if they were willing to serve. Dr. Evans was more than agreeable to such an expansion, but Mr. Gross was not present.

To my relief, Mr. Beluso said that he would be delighted with the post, if he was wanted. Taylor, of course, said yes. Mrs. Besdine further proposed that the financial chaos be ended by uniting both checking accounts under this new leadership, with a majority vote of the co-chairmen necessary to spend over $10 at one time.

I think we all voted to accept these proposals, and that was all there was to it. We then defined four areas of general responsibility for the co-chairmen: Dr. Evans, the Atlanta storefront and operations; Mr. Gross, state organization; Mr. Beluso, the new state headquarters; Taylor, the coordination between the McCarthy campaign and whatever challenge attempt was finally organized. In addition, Mr. Ramseur would be in charge of fund raising: Mrs. Besdine would still be treasurer; Mr. Martin would help Mr. Beluso, while also looking into the legal possibility of us forming a corporation, with himself to be the unpaid fiscal agent; I was to work specifically on the challenge delegation with the Forum.

None of these delineations of responsibility were ever strictly followed later, since we all usually wound-up pitching in together on whatever had to be done; but they seemed logical at the time. We went upstairs to greet our guests, and I felt as if we were finally getting something organized and moving.

Meetings like the one just described were typical of all those during the next seven weeks. Charlie's proposal to expand the co-chairmen seemed such an inherently good idea and so obviously necessary if we were to grow that none of us questioned, in Mr. Gross's terms, our "right" to do it, nor did we question whom we were representing by doing it. It just needed doing, so we did it. We ran a certain risk: most of us had only met Mr. Beluso the night before and Taylor and I were not exactly old hands.

But from their previous words and actions, and from the amount of time they planned to devote, Taylor and Mr. Beluso seemed the logical choices. I don't even think we talked about Charlie's relation to this new leadership; it was just understood that they would all work together for the common goal of a McCarthy victory. Also typical of later meetings, we never bothered to take any minutes, which meant a loss of continuity for anyone who was not there – a real problem – but we were usually all too busy thinking and listening to be taking notes.

Mrs. Grayboff's home is located well out of the city; it hugs the ground in a quiet suburb and is surrounded by tall trees. Upstairs that night, a live trio was playing, and Mrs. Grayboff was mixing punch. We talked with the twenty or so guests, all of whom were connected in some way with Georgians For McCarthy. Mary Beth arrived after about ten minutes; she is a tall good-looking brunette with an easy smile. She struck me immediately as being both friendly and a real professional politician, a mixture of college student and campaigner with a knack for doing the right thing and for putting people at ease. I poured her some punch and we sat down to talk with each other and with the other guests.

She said that she had dropped out of school during the spring to help her uncle and had been at work in all the later primaries. She and most of the other students had been exhausted by the end of the California campaign, and she had been badly upset by Kennedy's murder. Like all the other students, she had been sent home to rest in early June by the national organization, which no longer was in need of its mass army, but which did badly need local action groups started all over the country. The trip to Atlanta was Mary Beth's first outing since California.

After about an hour we decided to go downtown to the YDC-YDR Charity Ball. In typical college student fashion, I had borrowed my father's car for the event, and as we pulled out Taylor and Cathy left to go make final preparations for the next evening's reception. The ball was being held in the grand ballroom of the Regency Hyatt House Hotel, Atlanta's newest hotel and a really spectacular place, with a 26-story indoor lobby and a revolving restaurant on top. The ball itself was a mixed bag, with about a thousand people, two bands (one young, one not so young), and booths along the walls proclaiming the merits of every political candidate in the city and the country. As we entered we surrendered our tickets by "voting" with them in appropriately marked boxes for McCarthy, Humphrey, Rockefeller or Nixon.

Mary Beth and I immediately went around to the McCarthy booth, manned by two students, and said hello. We were quickly found by the black president of the YDC, and as Mary Beth was the only visiting national political dignitary, he had photos taken of us. The photographer struck on the idea of using me as some sort of a barber pole, on which Mary Beth struck McCarthy For President bumper stickers. What could one do, when involved with national politics, but swallow one's pride and try not to think about the comments at work which were sure to follow, and did?

That ordeal over, we then began meeting people. Rev. Morris was there with his wife; he was wearing both HHH and McCarthy buttons. We said hello to Charles Weltner, Atlanta's liberal Democratic former congressman, who was running again for the House of Representatives. Mary Beth proved the good-natured politician I had thought she was, politely thanking people for nice comments about her uncle and speaking confidently about his victory in August.

Following the somewhat labored introduction of every conceivable person of political note in the ballroom, including all the candidates for every post, and Mary Beth, we then got in a little dancing between conversations. It was apparent from the applause during the introductions that the Republicans were easily in control.

We were having a pleasant time until rather late in the evening, when about half the guests had departed. After a quick tourist trip up to the hotel's revolving restaurant, we returned to the ballroom for a final dance. At that point, John Wayne, who was staying at the hotel for the Atlanta opening of *The Green Berets* and a local radio station's traditional Fourth of July parade, made a guest appearance on the stage. I had never seen him before, live; but for my generation he was the hero of every celluloid war ever fought. The guests remaining, mainly young people, some of whom were dressed in Confederate costumes, pressed up close to the stage.

John Wayne staggered up to the mic, said hello and then proceeded with a short five-minute sermon of the election. If he were president, he said, he would go over and "kill every one of those goddamn commies" (cheers from the crowd). I asked Mary Beth if she wanted to leave, but she said that she would rather hear him out. I became uneasy as he went on, and as the crowd got more enthusiastic.

I wanted so much to tell them that the world is not like what they thought, full of good guys and bad guys and easy answers. As John Wayne yelled louder and the students in the Confederate uniforms pressed closer to the stage, their gray uplifted arms shining in the spotlights as they rebel yelled at the appropriate points, I had simultaneous feelings of rage and bewildering sympathy. I wanted to tell them that everything was all right; instead I finally yelled a reply to one of Mr. Wayne's more ridiculous remarks, and Mary Beth asked me to be quiet, as we could do nothing anyway.

In the end John Wayne said that what our country needed was "President Nixon, because he'd know what to do about Vietnam" - more applause from the crowd, especially from those dressed in Confederate uniforms, these being cheers for a Republican candidate which I thought would have given Abe Lincoln a start, had he known. Mr. Wayne finished, and as we left there were more uproars as Nixon's landslide victory in our voting-by-ticket election was announced. Obviously we had a lot of work to do if the McCarthy campaign was to make an impact in Georgia.

In the basement parking lot we found ourselves in one of those short sketches of life which are difficult to live through, or to forget. We wound up surrounded by Confederate soldiers and their dates while we waited for our car on the crowded traffic island. We--the two of us—had on our McCarthy badges. We were being pressed on all sides by Nixon buttons and cavalry swords. The hostility was complete.

No one around us said anything, but from the periphery there were remarks about having shown them tonight. I wanted to say something, but I didn't. I just looked around. We knew, and they knew, and we all knew what each other knew. One car arrived and a group of soldiers piled in, laughing and joking; they pulled away with a screech, their university sticker glaring on the back window. A minute of silence. Finally our car arrived. We got in quietly and drove off, smiling a strange sigh of relief at the parking lot door. We drove home a little disturbed; Mary Beth had overheard several unfriendly comments about her uncle following Mr. Wayne's speech. But by the time we reached Dr. Evans' home, where Mary Beth was staying, we had refound our good spirits, and I made plans to pick her up the next morning to go to the storefront opening.

The Georgians For McCarthy Storefront was located at 563 Peachtree Street in downtown Atlanta, about two blocks from the theater where *The Green Berets* was opening.

The storefront itself was just that – an empty store. In what would have been the front display case were all sorts of McCarthy paraphernalia, and one could hardly see out through the big glass window because it was so covered in posters. Along the wall to the left of the entrance was a long table filled with a sparse stock of relevant literature in little piles. The pay telephone was on the wall opposite. In the back was a small "office," partially partitioned off by a long cupboard which housed the storefront's supplies.

The rest of the room was empty, but there were folding tables and chairs which could easily be set up for doing mailings, drawings, or typing. The decoration on the walls increased with the passing weeks, limited in early July to a large map of Atlanta and some of the better campaign posters. On the sidewalk in front of the store there was always a table set up, manned by students, giving away McCarthy buttons and literature, and accepting donations in our big bucket.

Neither the storefront nor the McCarthy material had come free, and over the next seven weeks the storefront paid for itself with collected contributions. For the "opening," the place was full of balloons, home-made punch and cookies and the young people who were the shop's keepers, usually under the control of either Mark Evans or Page Miller.

Mary Beth and I arrived a little after ten: it was a hot, damp, cloudy July Fourth, not a good day for a parade. To anyone passing by the place, it must have seemed the cradle of the "children's crusade," because one was immediately struck by the absence of older people "in charge." Mary Beth and I waded in: Dr. Evans and family were there, as were other older members of Georgians For McCarthy, for whom this must have been a really grand day.

Mary Beth was immediately drawn into conversation by our female student workers, and I tried to make myself useful with whatever needed to be done, taking turns running the outside table, stamping "Georgians For McCarthy" and our address on the national literature, or talking to Les Leopold, whom I think had been put temporarily in charge of the storefront and Atlanta operations in general. This meant that he got every question ranging from "Where are the McCarthy buttons?" to "How can we get something organized in Decatur?" Les handled the responsibility well, but he should have been three people. Since both of them must have been involved with several such operations in the past, I could not help wondering what he and Mary Beth thought of our first storefront attempt at political mass communication.

After what seemed a short while it was time for us to go on to the television station for our "talk show." We arrived along with Dr. Evans, Marilyn Grayboff, and a carload of supporters. Although I had been on a taped show before, this was my first go at live television; but I don't think that either Mary Beth or I were particularly nervous, armed as we were with at least an hour full of facts, figures, impressions and experience.

Our MC put us both at ease in the beginning, and we actually had fun answering the questions from him, from the small audience present, and from viewers at home, who phoned in questions. Mary Beth did most of the talking, and she was asked mainly about past and present campaigns and her uncle's stand on the war. One gentleman phoned in and wanted to know if we had read *Mein Kampf*, the *Communist Manifesto*, and *The Rise and Fall of the Third Reich*, which we had, in part. I answered a question about youth involvement in the campaign and communication with the older generation. The hour was quickly over, and Mary Beth was interviewed for a later newsreel. Then we hurried into an office to listen to a radio because, in what must have seemed a super-saturation campaign, Marilyn Grayboff had also persuaded a local "talk" radio station to interview Charlie Negaro for an hour that same afternoon.

After the TV show we went back to the storefront for an hour, then I took Mary Beth for lunch at a famous old Atlanta restaurant and treated her to real "Southern fried chicken." At the storefront I made arrangements for Charlie to pick Hans up at the airport, and as Mary Beth wanted a rest before the reception, I drove her back to Dr. Evans' home. During the drive we started talking about Gene McCarthy's concept of the presidency, and Mary Beth said that she believed he saw the presidency much more as the leader of a team than as a one-man affair.

He believed, she thought, that cabinet members should be given both more say and more responsibility in public, more in line with the European system. With such a system the president could be seen as what in fact he was anyway: an arbiter of different policy possibilities, not the man who initiated all national policies himself. Such a system would allow for greater public understanding and debate on issues, instead of policies seeming to appear like a computer print-out from the little white box on Pennsylvania Avenue, without the arguments for and against a particular policy being widely known.

She also believed that a President McCarthy would actually do more to decentralize the over-bureaucratic federal decision-making process than any of the populist "states' righters." Apparently, within broad guidelines of federal responsibility and control, McCarthy believed that people should make as many decisions as possible at the local level.

I could not help recalling Mary Beth's words the next week while watching our weekly half hour "George Wallace for President" television show, in which our neighbor from Alabama talked endlessly about the evils of the federal bureaucracy and the need to return to good old Americanism. But I always had the nagging suspicion that, if elected, Mr. Wallace, though he preached "States Rights," would actually do more than any of the other national candidates to centralize the government and its control over our lives, in a last-ditch effort to ensure that we were somehow all good Americans behaving in "the proper American way."

That afternoon I used the peace and quiet Dr. Evans' house provided, located on a quiet tree-lined back street in the Emory University academic community, for a quick nap, since I was exhausted from the last few days' events. In a short while, though, Hans arrived, immaculately dressed in a three-piece suit. Whatever Hans lacked in height he easily made up for in dress, and one need only look at him to know that he was a "New York businessman." Hans was genuinely interested both in helping us for a few days and in sizing up the Georgia situation in order to argue persuasively for funds back in New York.

It turned out, however, that most of his help came to me in the form of criticism of people and the ways things were being run. I suppose that some of his criticism was well founded; but, after all, we were amateurs trying to do our best; and one could not wave a wand and suddenly produce a hundred experienced political workers. It also turned out that, for whatever reasons, no money ever came to us from New York, except $400 which Les coerced Hans into loaning us himself in order to pay the deposit necessary for two badly needed regular telephones at the storefront. But Hans meant well, and he did offer a ray of hope for crucial financial help at a time when we needed desperately to think big.

Mary Beth, Hans and I, after a quick snack at the Evans', drove over to Cathy's former home where she and Taylor had done an excellent job of getting the reception ready. Taylor was busily mixing his secret formula rum punch and Cathy was arranging chairs. We held a brief caucus. Cathy had only been able to invite two couples of the type we had hoped to have several of: those with money. This probably sounds crass, but we were still hoping to run our newspaper challenge poll, which we knew would cost over $5,000, plus the whole Georgia McCarthy campaign, which could use as much money as we could invest: therefore we were rather concerned that the reception go off well and that we make a good impression.

The majority of guests at the party were, in reality, people already involved with Georgians for McCarthy, including some of the storefront students, plus Mr. and Mrs. Walsh and Taylor's parents. There I first met Mr. and Mrs. Tom Lyman: he is an artist and art teacher at Emory, she is a former Chicago model. Tom was later to spend long hours designing our

McCarthy signs, and both of them were on the delegation at the Democratic National Convention. Mr. Walsh told me that he thought his injunction case against Lester Maddox's delegation would be coming up in court fairly soon and that he was optimistic about a favorable hearing.

Shortly our real financial "guests" arrived, and we were all reintroduced. After the first five minutes, Taylor and I relaxed; the party was going well and people seemed to be enjoying themselves. Forty-five minutes later we "brought the chairs around" and listened to Taylor talk briefly about the McCarthy campaign in Georgia and our proposed challenge delegation; Mary Beth was given an official welcome, and she gave a brief talk about the future and what a job it was going to be to organize Georgia. Then Hans put in a pitch for funds; I had to persuade him not to use the "Who'll pay for a month's rent on the storefront?" approach, since it would have been embarrassingly obvious to whom he was referring, though he argued that if what one wanted was money, one put the point across bluntly.

In the end we collected about $200 in direct donations, largely from people who had previously given. But one of our important guests seemed pleased – he took a pledge card and said he would send us a check in the mail; he also seemed particularly interested in the challenge and said that if we really got anything going to let him know. Unfortunately, we never heard from him again, as he and his wife left for a long vacation in Europe shortly thereafter.

I stayed behind for a while to help Taylor and Cathy clean up; we had mixed feelings about the evening. We certainly had not received the big pledge of help we had hoped for, either from Atlanta or from New York, and the financial picture was looking dimmer. On the other hand, we had had a pleasant evening and had provided a chance for people to meet and to discuss plans informally; we also had raised a few hundred dollars, all of which was badly needed.

More importantly, and this was the feeling that kept us going in similar situations later, we had taken a vital first step toward interesting the Atlanta business community: possibly through skillful follow-up work during the next week we would at least have more names suggested to us of people who would be willing to make that one much needed big contribution. Hans had gone home with our friends, the Pendergrasts, with whom he was going to stay. For the next day Richard Ramseur had arranged for Hans to meet another of the "right people," an old friend Mr. Ramseur had met in earlier campaigns. I said goodbye to Mary Beth, who went home with Dr. Evans. She was leaving early the next morning and she certainly could not have been a better emissary for her uncle's campaign. We all thanked her for coming and for giving the McCarthy campaign in Georgia a real boost. The only time I was later to hear about Mary Beth was when she and others were forced downstairs from the fifteenth floor of the Conrad Hilton during an early morning raid by the Chicago police on McCarthy's Headquarters, the Friday following the convention.

———

That next weekend our activity centered on the storefront, where Les sought to establish a city organization. As we were trying to get as many people involved as possible, I brought my good friend Rives Chalmers with me to the storefront that Saturday morning, hoping that he would "get the bug' and pitch in to help us. The evangelical spirit on our part showed itself whenever anyone new walked into the shop; over the course of this summer many people wandered in who were obviously just curious passers-by who wanted to get a button, a piece of literature, or "just look." But often someone would walk in who seemed to have come with a purpose, someone wanting to help. In those early days we immediately co-opted anyone we could.

After a long talk and a look around, most people would willingly leave their name and address to do future work, and our list of potential helpers grew both from these names and from the petitions which we were circulating in support of Senator McCarthy. The petitions were a national effort, but they included a space for the signer's address and we copied this information before sending the petitions on to Washington. People who came in were told that soon we would be needing help with different tasks: mailings, phoning, "block captains," further storefront organization, etc., etc. Their names were taken and they were told that we would call back shortly.

Looking back on the summer, I think this phase of our operations was the weakest. Probably there was no other way to have done it since the manpower and the resources just were not available before July. But the storefront and that sort of basic organization should have been begun in March or April, not June. By July, when our potential manpower could easily have been swollen, we were still in the "we'll call you back" stage. Instead, there should have been a long, specific list of tasks which had to be done, from relatively simple jobs like mailing to the much more complex job of area coordination, with broad instructions already prepared for the task.

As it was, we never did build up that kind of organization; by the time we could have handled it, it was August and we had to divert our manpower to other things. This lack of initial organization in the early stages probably discouraged people who otherwise would have helped. When we finally did ring them back, they were usually either too busy with something else, or they also felt that it was by then too late. But all of this criticism comes from hindsight; at the time we were quite optimistic and believed that somehow the whole state would suddenly become "organized."

That Saturday did, however, see a contradiction to this general rule in the person of Jim Sundberg, who came in obviously willing both to give a hand and also to help do the organizing. Jim is young, a hard worker, and a born field man. He said that he had been a SNCC block organizer back in the "old days" and that he knew east Atlanta and Decatur in and out. He talked with Les and me for a long time that Saturday, and we were convinced of his ability and his sincerity; he was made our "coordinator" (whatever that meant) for the mentioned area, and we judiciously marked it off on our big map, as if that really organized anything.

Meanwhile Les, who was not a small thinker, was appalled by the relative lack of McCarthy literature in the place. He was on and off the phone with Washington, ordering thousands of whatever he could get, especially buttons and bumper stickers. Here was a case of something needing to be done and someone doing it without asking – typical of the kind of actions which caused friction in the organization. Les said that the national headquarters hoped to be paid for these items, but that payment was not completely necessary. He ordered some items to be put on an "emergency" basis and to be shipped air parcel post (collect); the rest were to follow.

The good thing about new people in the campaign was that they brought in fresh ideas, new ways of doing things. Les' picture of what needed to be done had probably never dawned on our academic organization—he wanted to saturate the entire town with McCarthy literature, McCarthy buttons, McCarthy stickers, one under every windshield wiper at shopping centers and one in every mailbox. The continual problem with such new ideas was that, almost inevitably, they involved a bill at the end of the month, and most bills we could not pay.

In a larger sense, I think that the division within the organization was over the whole philosophy of the campaign. Throughout the summer this division caused several heated, personal diatribes. To those activists like Les, with whom Taylor and I generally agreed, it seemed that the only way to start a financial income was first to make an impression to let people know that we existed and that we were effective. To others, a minority in our group, the overall question was one of financial responsibility; that is, we should not spend money before we had it, and we should not be seen to be running an irresponsible campaign.

In the end, luckily, I think the forces balanced out, with enough of the latter so that the bills were not too big. But on July 6th, Les went ahead and ordered his material, and he also talked Hans out of $400 for the phone deposit (the current payphone system being worse than useless) on his "personal guarantee" that Hans would be repaid—a bit of a gamble.

Late that afternoon I picked up Hans and took him out to the airport. He had been on the radio that morning with Mr. Pendergrast talking about the "Businessmen for Peace" organization, to which they both belonged, another broadcast arranged by Marilyn Grayboff. On the way to the airport Hans related his experience of the day before, when the businessmen to whom he had been introduced by Mr. Ramseur flew Hans (in his own private airplane) up to a smaller town in the north of Georgia, so that Hans could talk to a few of his friends and get the feeling of a state which was "clearly for Wallace."

Hans there experienced a phenomenon which I was later to sample several times, especially at work, and which even showed up in the national polls by the end of the summer. The men to whom Hans talked were planning to vote, first, for Wallace; but if anything happened to him, they would vote next for McCarthy! While such a combination of political views seems strange, I think that it was widespread in the South; and it showed that voters wanted not only a particular candidate, but also, at least as importantly, a *change*.

This mood throughout the nation, which had shown itself elsewhere in the primary results, took a strange form in the South, but it was unmistakably present. People just did not want the same old policies and people running the country. Though voters disagreed with these policies for totally different reasons, perhaps, in Massachusetts and Georgia, this national mood for change was definitely at home in the South. One man even thought that Wallace and McCarthy should run on the same ticket, Wallace to handle national affairs, McCarthy to take care of international problems. It seems incredible that the Democratic establishment could not just lean out of any handy window and sense this mood, for change; or perhaps some of them eventually did and overreacted to crush it.

I said goodbye to Hans at the airport and thanked him for coming; he replied that he had enjoyed his first trip south; and, though he had not been able to elicit any financial aid, he promised to try again in New York to get us some money. As I drove home to get ready for a date, I found it hard to believe, after a month of inactivity and several days of immediate involvement, that Taylor and I had been back from Chicago less than one week.

3

MCCARTHY VISITS "WALLACE COUNTRY"

Many of the exact details of our meetings during the rest of July and August are difficult to reconstruct precisely, in terms of the precise dates of meetings, and who was at each one, and what was decided on each separate occasion. There were many meetings and many decisions which had to be made. Basically there were four major events for which we had to plan: McCarthy's visit on July 18th; a local rally at the Wheat Street Baptist Church on August 4th; the Democratic Party Forum's Challenge Convention on August 10th; and the nationwide M-Day rally on August 15th.

As the weeks went by we shifted our emphasis to whichever event was coming up next, trying to make contingency plans for later events whenever possible. Interspersed between these four major events were greater and lesser events, crises, and organizational problems, all requiring time and attention. The storefront also needed manning twelve hours a day, a job done well by the student volunteers. Though none of us had had any previous political experience, we somehow managed to operate fairly well.

Early that second week in July the new State Headquarters opened in the Dinkler Plaza Hotel, the hotel in downtown Atlanta which more than any other had seen such organizations come and go over the years. The hotel itself is spacious, well carpeted, and good looking; but it is definitely of a previous generation, and the elevators are tortuously slow. But such was really of no matter; the important thing was that, thanks to Mr. Beluso, we had our own three-room corner suite on the fifth floor, consisting of two bedrooms separated by a larger drawing room. The decor was institutional, like any other hotel. The bedrooms contained chairs, lamps, tables, and mirrors, while the sitting room had two long modern blue sofas, a few tables, and a large picture window facing a parking lot across the street. The beds were soon removed to make room for more tables and chairs. Extra phones were installed and a reception desk set up. A shiny new Coca-Cola machine made it all official.

Our new headquarters was small; later we could have used twice the space, but it was spacious compared to the backroom of the storefront or the Evans' living room. Charlie was staying only one floor below, and the hotel was ideally located in the center of the city. Two big signs outside and one in the lobby proclaimed our existence. Charlie, who by then had given up on the idea of being anything like a "Southern Coordinator," used the office daily; and it became the nerve center for all of our later operations.

Also early that same week national headquarters confirmed that Senator McCarthy would attend the Fulton County Democratic Dinner the following Thursday, in ten days, and that he would spend the night in Atlanta on a swing through the South. We were supposed to come up with proposals for the senator's itinerary while in Atlanta on that Thursday afternoon and evening. These proposals would be reviewed by an advance team which would be arriving shortly. We never could have made the decisions necessary nor run the operations involved with his visit had it not been for the larger facilities provided by our new headquarters.

Taylor and I were still very much interested in Georgians For A Democratic Convention and the prospect of our newspaper poll. We set up a meeting that week with Jack Spalding, the editor of *The Atlanta Journal*, to talk about the GDC and the possible use of the newspaper. On Tuesday, July 9th, Taylor wrote up a one-page GDC "position paper," which he ran off on the school mimeograph machine. We planned to give several copies to Mr. Spalding and to leave the rest at the McCarthy storefront. The first paragraph read:

Georgians For a Democratic Convention, a group of concerned citizens, has been organized to give the people of Georgia an opportunity to choose their delegates and express their presidential preferences for the Democratic National

Convention at Chicago. We have set three specific tasks, all of which require funds and manpower. First, we shall support legal efforts to challenge the constitutionality of the delegates chosen by the machine, "crony" politics of Lester Maddox. Second, we shall support the efforts of the Georgia Democratic Party Forum to select a challenge delegation at an open state convention, and we shall support the Forum's challenge before the Credentials Committee of the Democratic National Convention. Third, and most important, we shall seek to provide the people of Georgia with a preferential primary among the Democratic candidates for President of the United States.

The mentioned group of "concerned citizens" at that point consisted of Taylor, Mr. Walsh, and myself; but we were thinking big.

Since Taylor was a co-chairman of Georgians For McCarthy, I was made chairman of GDC. Sometime during that week Taylor and I also finally bought address books to save ourselves from the mountains of pieces of paper with important names and phone numbers which were beginning to overflow our desks and get lost.

One rainy afternoon that week the three of us went to call on Mr. Spalding: I took a three o'clock lunch break to be able to make it. Mr. Spalding was generally in agreement with what we were trying to do, but he was rather pessimistic about the newspaper poll. It would have to be considered a political ad, for which the paper charged much higher rates than regular ads. The price he quoted for a full-page ad plus a slipped-in return envelope sounded far beyond our means unless we suddenly inherited a very rich patron.

But he genuinely encouraged us and said that he could remember times in Georgia when change had seemed much less possible than it did that summer. Like so many meetings, we really accomplished very little, but we felt encouraged nonetheless, as if we had to go ahead and hope that a rich patron would come along making all of our plans possible, perhaps the next day.

At some point during those ten days before McCarthy's visit we arranged to get our fund-raising letter written and the mailings sent out from the storefront. As more planning was needed for the McCarthy visit, Les shifted his activities from the storefront to the Dinkler Plaza Headquarters, and Jim Sundberg took over the storefront operations. He, Mark Evans, Page Miller, and about twenty part-time student helpers did a magnificent job throughout the summer: there just should have been twenty more storefronts.

As the literature which Les had ordered started to come in, Jim and his crew set up make-shift booths at shopping centers, provided there was a car available and the shopping center authorities were agreeable. The front of the storefront soon became a warehouse filled with boxes of literature for envelope stuffing and distribution. Occasionally someone would come in from out of town and leave with a few boxes of campaign material for distribution in his home area.

We were starting to have some effect: I saw more and more cars on the expressways with "McCarthy For President" bumper stickers, though probably not as many as there were Wallace stickers (I was not that sure that Humphrey and Nixon even had stickers – it seemed that I never saw them). The storefront group regularly solicited extra help by telephone; and whenever there was a specific event coming up which needed publicizing, they did a good job of saturating at least the downtown corners. Though we could easily have used a hundred more volunteers and a hundred times the amount of literature, it always did my heart good to have someone I did not know give me a piece of McCarthy literature as I left work in the afternoon.

During that week in July, I first met John Tillman, a large "black radical" who could come on like a firebrand if he thought he was being messed with, but who was also one of the nicest of all the people involved in the organization. I really am not sure of John's background: various rumors had it that he was then with SNCC, that he had been with SNCC, that he had been to Cuba and China, and that he was nineteen. Though later, and especially at the convention, I was to grow to like John very much, my first impressions were not the best, which with John was rather easy since he had a habit of fixing little "Burn Baby Burn" stickers to the telephones, furniture, walls, and the Coca-Cola machine in the state headquarters.

He seemed to be in the headquarters continuously, but to have little interest in doing anything. I'm sure, however, that he felt the same way about us, and he was symbolic of a weakness of both our own campaign and of the national McCarthy campaign: a failure to win and to direct the support of large numbers of black people. On neither level was this failure intentional; in our case it just seemed to happen.

By August it was painfully clear to us that one of our first priorities in

July should have been to establish at least one storefront in a black neighborhood. Until late July there were no black people as co-chairmen of Georgians For McCarthy. We knew very early that this absence was a weakness, but it was difficult for us to do anything about it, other than to invite the few black leaders we knew to our meetings and to hope that they would be interested. Many potential leaders were already deeply involved in the campaign of Maynard Jackson, a young black lawyer, in his bid to upset incumbent Senator Herman Talmadge in the state Democratic Primary. And, as we invariably made decisions on a day-to-day basis, there was little master strategy on black involvement; had a black person simply walked in offering a storefront or offering to find one, we would have jumped at it.

As it was there was neither enough manpower nor funds to do everything, and one of the jobs which seemed to slip from day to day was the establishment of such a storefront. By August John Tillman would be given the go ahead and the funds to set up a two week storefront near Paschal Brothers Hotel on the west side of town, but it was pitifully too little and far too late. Though we tried, the key break just never came, the right man never walked through the door. Had it been April instead of mid-July we would have been all right. As it was we had to do what we could, eventually follow John's suggestions, and hope.

Late one afternoon that week, while at the storefront, I typed up a one page paper on why I thought a challenge delegation from Georgia was crucial both to Georgia's future and to the national McCarthy campaign, essentially outlining both the good it would do the state and the corner it would put Humphrey in unless he supported it, owing to the national image of Lester Maddox. My main point was a plug for funds for Georgians for a Democratic Convention; I gave the letter to Les, who said he passed it on to Washington, but we heard no more about it.

No response, in fact, came from McCarthy Headquarters until the first week of August, which did not really bother us, because we had more than enough to do anyway. And though our detractors were later to "accuse" us of planning with "outsiders" for a month before the Macon convention, in fact Charlie Negaro was to remark during the last frantic week before our Georgia convention that, had he to do it all over again, we would have paid more attention to the importance of the challenge delegation.

Also during those early weeks of July I first met Julian Bond, though the occasion was not particularly memorable. One afternoon right after lunch I was walking through the huge lobby of the bank where I worked when I saw Julian Bond just leaving a teller. Like all public figures about whom I had read, Julian aroused in me a certain amount of awe and curiosity. One always feels, I suppose, that such figures are larger than life, that they must have had more interesting experiences than the rest of us.

I had followed Mr. Bond's fight to win his seat in the Georgia legislature while I was in college; and, though at that earlier time my views on the war were not one way or the other, I certainly admired Mr. Bond's courage in fighting his case up to the Supreme Court. I also admired his willingness to fight even harder in a legislature which was obviously dominated by whites and which, until quite recently, had been all white itself. The only other time I had seen him had been at a Ray Charles concert in the summer before, when someone had pointed "Julian Bond" out to me in the crowd. I remember then being struck by his incredibly boyish face and his appearance of friendly sincerity. Now I saw him again, and I wanted to say hello. I walked up to him, introduced myself, and told him that I was proud of what he had been doing. He smiled, looked a little embarrassed, and thanked me. I then went back to answering credit references on our customers.

All these events were, however, taking place only on the periphery as we concentrated on the main event of those mid-July days: McCarthy's visit to Atlanta on July 18th. As with the later Macon convention and M-Day, we responded fairly well to the challenge of his visit. But I was impressed by mid-August by how lucky we were to have had a national organization and the Georgia Democratic Party Forum, both of which forced us to react to events decided outside of our own group. We were no top level political organizers craftily conceiving a grand master strategy for a Georgia campaign.

By July it was too late and we were too few. I think we met the challenges well, and often the decisions we made were crucial to success. In a larger sense, however, we always operated knowing that there was some new major event about to come up which needed a response from us. But this passive situation was, I think, good for us; what arguing we did was more or less over details and methods, not over broad strategy, on which we would have had trouble agreeing.

We received the go ahead for the McCarthy visit just as we were moving into the new state headquarters. We began that week with a meeting on Monday night in one of the "bedrooms." At this point, the only phones installed were the ones which came with the rooms, and we had not yet worked out our later system with the switchboard to divert all incoming calls to the reception room; therefore about every five minutes the phone would ring with a message or conversation for someone, causing the meeting to be delayed for long periods.

We still were not sure at what time on Thursday the senator would arrive or where he should stay. Mrs. Grayboff was definitely in favor of his doing either a live or taped television show, so that we could get the widest coverage out of a unique event. Mrs. Eliza Paschall, a white woman who was deeply involved with civil rights work and who joined us when she had time, said that the senator must take a walk in a black area and must meet with black leaders if he or we were ever going to make a strong appeal to the black community.

A rally was also crucial: the best location was Hurt Park, across the street from the old Atlanta Auditorium in the middle of the city, easily accessible to both nearby black residents and to Atlanta's thousands of downtown office workers. We thought that a lunchtime or 5 p.m. rally would be best to allow for maximum attendance. It would then be a short ride from there to the Southern Christian Leadership Conference's headquarters on Auburn Avenue for a talk with black leaders.

The Fulton County Democratic Club's dinner was scheduled for 7:30; there would be speeches by Senator McCarthy and by former North Carolina Governor Terry Sanford, representing Vice-President Humphrey. Following those speeches we hoped to have a reception sponsored by Georgians For McCarthy, to which we would invite a large number of friends and community leaders, hoping also to raise funds for local use. In typical fashion, we divided the responsibilities for all of those suggested activities between the people present at the meeting.

Another urgent matter at that meeting was financial reorganization: Georgians For McCarthy had quickly outgrown Judy Besdine's attempts to keep track of financial matters from her home, and she was the first to recognize it. During the previous week Ken Martin had learned that we could be registered as an "unincorporated non-profit organization." He suggested that we so register ourselves as quickly as possible and that the authority to disperse funds be transferred to two unpaid "fiscal agents," who would write checks but who would technically not have the same responsibility as the officers of a corporation.

The legal details seemed hazy to me; but Ken made sense, since as we were then organized I suppose that the four co-chairmen could have been personally liable for any debts or accidents. The co-chairmen present voted to have Ken so register us and for him to try to make a complete review of our financial situation (since both bills and contributions were turning up here and there at the storefront and at the headquarters); good banker that I was, I suggested the services of my employer bank, located about two blocks away, as the most convenient for our needs.

At this meeting the subject of Mr. Gross' checking account came up, really for the first time at a full meeting when he was present. One of the most irksome things about the whole situation was that Mr. Gross refused to tell anyone exactly how much money was in the account. In the end it turned out to be only a few hundred dollars, which was still more than we had at that time anywhere else; but his adamant silence did not help matters. When someone asked him if he would not consider merging his account with the new one to be opened under the joint control of the co-chairmen, he stated that he would consider doing so when he was convinced that the organization exercised sound financial responsibility, which he did not feel at the time.

Mr. Gross always had a knack for saying things in the least diplomatic way possible. I suppose we just shrugged that barb off, and I'm not sure what Mr. Gross expected us to do short of giving him complete financial control. One of Mr. Gross' problems was that he wanted people to listen to him and to follow him, but the way he went about things made people eventually do just the opposite. I think that Taylor and I stuck with him longer than several others, who fairly quickly wanted to vote him out of the organization completely.

Having made our tentative decisions regarding the senator's visit, we adjourned the meeting and decided to meet again on Wednesday night. The real nuts and bolts work necessary for the visit then began at the headquarters at about 10 a.m. on each of the following mornings, with Charlie usually there to handle the crises and decisions which came up.

At about that time Nancy Schwartz, a former friend of Charlie's, arrived. She was to stay the entire summer; and slowly the work of the headquarters came more under her control, with the daily help of Pat

Madsen and Jo Ann Thomas, two students who were always willing to type or to help in any way possible.

These four people, plus Dr. Chico Thomas and Les Leopold, became the unofficial full-time core of the headquarters, trying to make sure that the decisions reached by the co-chairmen were carried out, allowing for exogenous factors which sometimes required radical changes and quick decisions, usually made by Charlie. Inevitably Charlie and his decisions were then criticized by Mr. Gross, especially when the decisions involved spending money.

Stephen Mitchell, chairman of the national McCarthy campaign, flew into town on Tuesday to announce the senator's proposed visit and to sound out local Democratic leaders on the Georgia delegation. Few of us had any real hope of ever persuading any of Maddox's delegation to vote for McCarthy, but Mr. Mitchell had to perform the courtesy of trying, and I suppose that miracles do happen. He was unable to see Governor Maddox, but he did visit Joe Sports, Executive Director of the state Democratic Party.

Always optimistic in public, Mr. Mitchell said at a news conference that he had heard of the Maddox delegation's support for Humphrey but that he felt most of the delegates had not had a chance to meet Senator McCarthy nor to hear his views; he hoped that the senator's planned visit would both remedy this situation and also demonstrate to the Georgia delegates his strong public support, even in the South.

Taylor and I set to work immediately on our own personal responsibility: the post-dinner reception and fund-raising speeches. Taylor called the appointments secretary at the Dinkler Plaza Hotel and set up a meeting for us for later that week.

Richard Ramseur agreed to print formal invitations and envelopes, but he would have to know the exact quantity needed and the precise wording within three days if we were to have them in time for mailing on the weekend. Therefore Taylor and I called everyone in the organization's leadership and asked them to be making invitation lists, preferably including addresses. Mrs. Evans and Mrs. Lyman volunteered to address envelopes as soon as they were available.

At our Wednesday night meeting we had progress reports. Mrs. Grayboff could probably get TV time, but she needed to know exactly when the senator was arriving, which we would not know until the weekend. Taylor and I impressed everyone with the need to get their invitation lists in quickly. The major problem was the outdoor rally. Les and Chico had contacted the Atlanta police, who said that Hurt Park was no longer available for such events because the grass would be ruined. Besides, it appeared that the senator probably would not be arriving until after lunch, making a 5:15 rally necessary, which would create both a massive traffic problem and run the risk of being rained out by a late afternoon thundershower.

We considered an airport rally to be the best alternative. This was appealing because it greatly reduced in-town transportation problems. It would, however, require busing to get large numbers of people the ten miles out to the airport. As there seemed no alternatives, Les and Chico were given the go ahead to check with the airport and the transportation authorities.

Were an airport rally held, Mrs. Paschall pointed out, a conference with black leaders could easily be held at Paschal Brothers Hotel (no connection with her), a well-known integrated hotel in the black community, with easy access on and off the airport expressway. The hotel would be much more suitable than the SCLC headquarters, and facilities could be provided for a news conference afterwards; if there proved time for no other press meeting, we could thereby accomplish two goals with a minimum of wasted time and movement.

That Thursday at 5 o'clock Taylor and I met with the man in charge of organized activities at the Dinkler Plaza. He showed us, first, the large ballroom where the dinner itself would take place. We then went up the elevator (walking would almost have been faster) to the "Rainbow Roof," a large, partially mirrored meeting room on the top floor, which would serve our reception perfectly. There was a small kitchen adjacent, and we discussed the relative costs of punch and mixed drinks, plus cookies, catering, and set up costs. We then traced out the best route for the senator to take coming up from the ballroom to avoid running into a crowd. Taylor and I were shown the kitchen elevator, which was easily accessible from the back of the ballroom and which opened into the kitchen area on the top floor.

As we traced out the route, passing through a narrow corridor lined with kitchen tables and equipment, I thought of California and Bobby Kennedy. I suppose that I sensed for the first time the possible personal danger which men like Senator Kennedy and Senator McCarthy place themselves in almost every minute. We hoped that there would be no trouble in Atlanta.

Everything seemed in order: obviously we were dealing with people who had done such receptions many times before. Taylor and I then drove home for supper; I'm not quite sure how Taylor's wife Cathy and my parents were taking our new nightly activities. Cathy, who was a great sport about it all, really, must have been wondering after all the late-night meetings and quickly canceled plans whether Taylor had married her or the McCarthy organization.

My parents, who also were patient with my constant comings and goings, probably would have liked to have seen more of me, especially as it seemed that I would be leaving in the fall for a year or two in England. But they never said anything, and I suppose they felt better about what I was trying to do politically than if I had decided to leave the country, go to jail, or just let my feelings stay inside. My father had been involved in a somewhat similar battle twenty-five years earlier with the then Governor Gene Talmadge, who was trying to pack the state Board of Education with his cronies, so I hoped that he understood some of the feelings that I was having.

That night I drove over to Taylor's apartment right after supper. Mr. Ramseur required the printing details for the invitations, and we therefore had to come up with a master of ceremonies in whose name the invitations would be issued. We very much wanted to be able to print "Mayor Ivan Allen requests the pleasure of your company..."; and even though he was a known Humphrey supporter, we decided to call him.

Unfortunately he was not in at the moment, so we left our number and went back to thinking. In the course of a very frustrating three hours we thought of everyone we possibly could who might be willing to perform such a task, including Albert Bows and Jack Spalding, but everyone we called was either out or turned us down. We also called Hans Reinisch in New York, hoping for good news on his money raising efforts; he had no such news but said he was still trying. In the course of the conversation we told him of the senator's upcoming Atlanta visit, and he volunteered to fly down again and to help us with the fund raising at the reception. Though we had some doubts about his effectiveness, we could not refuse, so Hans said that he would be down on the following Wednesday.

It eventually became too late to call anyone else, so we just decided to begin the invitation with "Georgians For McCarthy request the honor of your presence..." Cathy, who is an expert at such things, drew up the correct form, while Taylor and I considered how to intimate that we were trying to raise money, so that people would not be shocked when we started, without being so forward that we deterred people from coming who did not know as yet whom they supported. After another long period of trying different phrases, we finally decided that "Donations Voluntary" would be printed at the bottom of each invitation.

Late that night we drove out to Marilyn Grayboff's where Mr. Ramseur had left the installment of a few hundred envelopes. We picked these up, plus Mrs. Grayboff's invitation list; we had arranged with Mr. Gross for him to leave his list in his mailbox. So we next drove downtown to his house, then over to Dr. Evans' where we left the envelopes, the two lists, plus our own lists, so that Mrs. Evans and Mrs. Lyman could start addressing the next day. Home about 2 a.m., then up for work at 6:30; but at least things were getting done.

Perhaps we should have realized by then that by all of us becoming so completely involved in the details of one specific event, the larger task of organizing a state campaign was irreparably crippled. But we did not. We were so short of manpower that no one could be spared to do strategic planning, even if we had thought of it. At the time Senator McCarthy's visit *was* the state campaign. Had we already possessed a statewide network, more could have been accomplished. And we did not even have time to solicit help. I never questioned our lack of significant growth as an organization; I just did what we were all doing: working hard and hoping that the senator's visit would be a big, boosting success.

That Sunday we had more progress reports. The airport seemed the only possible place to hold our outdoor rally, if we could get the national organization to help pay the cost of the buses needed. Paschal Brothers were willing to house the meeting and the press conference, and Mrs. Paschall, John Tillman, and Otis Cochran, another black organizer, were contacting participants.

It didn't appear that there would be any time for a taped television show, unless it was done in the Dinkler Plaza Hotel after the senator arrived from Paschal Brothers and before his dinner speech; this news disappointed Mrs. Grayboff, who was a convinced believer in the power of the media. Richard Ramseur, whom none of us had seen for a week, had been delayed in printing the invitations (he was also doing the mailings and the envelopes), and they would not be ready until the next day, Monday, in the afternoon. Because of this delay, and because we were still receiving late invitation lists and suggestions (many without addresses), Taylor and I called an emergency invitation addressing and envelope stuffing meeting for Monday night at the storefront.

At that meeting Ken Martin also made his financial report, which showed us almost even on receipts and payments. I had already opened our new checking account, and Ken and I were elected as the organization's unpaid fiscal agents. We were not to write checks for more than ten dollars without the approval of the co-chairmen. As Ken went through his list itemizing our bills, it became clear that, in the past, Charlie or someone other than the co-chairmen had been authorizing expenditures for printing, phone calls, etc., without the co-chairmen's prior approval.

I don't think that any item involved was particularly expensive or delinquent, but Mr. Gross seemed to delight in taking every possible opportunity to remind us all that we were financially irresponsible and that we must consult the co-chairmen if the organization was to function properly. I absolutely agreed with Mr. Gross, in theory. The problem was that the co-chairmen were usually difficult to find when an unforeseen expenditure decision was necessary. We patched over what by then were becoming Charlie's ragged nerves and assured each other that with our new fiscal system everything would work more smoothly. But still Mr. Gross kept his own checking account.

That Sunday night the national advance team arrived, led by Bill Holtzman, a McCarthy staff man who was extremely competent and energetic, characteristics necessary for someone constantly on the move and confronted each week with totally new problems requiring quick solutions. With Bill came Rose Davis, a young black woman, and two advance press men. There were several such advance teams with the national McCarthy campaign, and they were rotated constantly so that one was always about four days ahead of the senator at his major stops.

At the meeting in Charlie's room, Taylor, Charlie and I outlined to Bill the plans as they were progressing so far. He agreed with everything we had prepared, but he was against taping a TV show in the late afternoon. His major concern, he said, after earlier mistakes, was to allow the senator enough time to rest; otherwise, as had happened on occasions in the past,

Senator McCarthy would just announce that he was too tired to do a planned event and would leave, causing some embarrassing moments for the local people involved.

Bill called Washington and confirmed that the senator would be making airport stops earlier on Thursday in Raleigh and in Charlotte; with all that, plus what we planned, Bill said that we would have to allow plenty of time for rest if we expected an appearance at our after-dinner reception. All this news was not too encouraging, but Bill seemed to know what he was doing, so it looked like we would have to be content with a news conference at Paschal Brothers.

As Thursday drew nearer, more details had to be settled by Bill and the national advance team. They gave the go ahead on the airport rally and agreed to pay the bus bill if we could not. The plan was to run the buses from the parking lot of the Atlanta Stadium out to the airport and back. I hadn't seen either Les Leopold or John Tillman for about a week, but they were apparently doing a good job organizing for the rally.

We had secured the services of a fairly young, inexpensive band for entertainment at the rally; they would come in particularly useful if the senator's plane was delayed. We also had fliers printed up, urging people to come out to the airport, and Jim's team set about handing them out in downtown Atlanta. On several occasions during the summer, when we were desperately trying to arouse interest in one of our events, I wondered to myself whether George Wallace had to have advance men and crowd builders.

For a new note of professionalism, Bill also authorized a newspaper ad and several radio spots. Bill and Charlie spent a few hours with the leaders of the Fulton County Democratic Club, trying to prepare them for the near certain possibility that Senator McCarthy would want to stay in his room to rest and to read over his speech during the dinners and that he might not appear downstairs until dessert was being served. Taylor and I had hectic nights on both Monday and Tuesday, as still more "must" invitation suggestions kept coming in, mostly unaddressed. Midnight found us in the main post office, looking up every invitation's zip code, praying that the invitations would get speedy handling.

Charlie and Mrs. Paschall were organizing the meeting with black leaders, to take place between the airport rally and the senator's arrival at the hotel. One of the crucial factors was Julian Bond. Charlie had been in almost daily contact with Julian, urging him to publicly endorse Senator McCarthy. Julian, whose anti-war views and history in the Georgia legislature were known nationwide, would have been a big asset to either Democratic candidate. His own preference had been Robert Kennedy; by July he agreed most with Senator McCarthy, but he still seemed to be hesitating over a public endorsement, possibly weighing the benefits to be gained from staying with the Humphrey establishment against the problems arising from Humphrey's constant commitment to a war policy which Julian opposed.

At any rate, early that week, *The New York Times* reported that the Humphrey camp was claiming Julian's endorsement, which he had not given. Julian told Charlie that he would be at the meeting on Thursday and would talk over his endorsement with Senator McCarthy personally.

By Wednesday all the plans were made and we were more or less ready. Hans arrived on Wednesday afternoon. Chico and the advance men were handling last minute news releases; and the local press was giving us good coverage, as this was the first presidential candidate's visit to Atlanta during that summer.

Since I had to work that Thursday until 5 o'clock, I was not able to be at either the airport rally or at the meeting at Paschal Brothers, but both went smoothly. Taylor was the master of ceremonies at the airport, where a large crowd did, after all, appear, though many in the crowd were too young to vote even in Georgia, where the voting age is eighteen.

My friend Rives Chalmers and my brother Steve volunteered to help Les and Chico with the buses, and that operation went off smoothly. McCarthy's plane arrived from Charlotte right on time – 2:30 – and the senator gave a brief talk which was well received. Bill had told us that first impressions were important to the senator, and if that was true, apparently he liked what he saw, because he was in very good spirits throughout his whole visit.

There followed a motorcade over to Paschal Brothers, where the senator had a closed-door, hour-long meeting with a group of about twenty community leaders; and it was apparently a very natural give and take session for all concerned. Besides Julian Bond, other members of the Georgia legislature also attended, including Representative Ben Brown and Senator Leroy Johnson. Most Southern civil rights organizations also had representatives.

At the news conference following the meeting, Senator McCarthy came across in his usual low-key manner, emphasizing his concern for shifting national priorities away from Vietnam and towards domestic problems, especially the problems stemming from a hundred years of racial discrimination. In answer to a question on civil rights support, he replied that his record spoke for itself. He did not make a special impassioned appeal for black support, preferring to maintain his more natural intellectual stance, which Taylor felt he might have enhanced just a little that once.

Nevertheless, many of the black leaders felt that their meeting had been fruitful; and two weeks later at a rally in Columbus, Ohio, Julian Bond did what we had all hoped and expected; he gave his full endorsement of Senator McCarthy in the senator's bid for the presidential nomination, and joined the senator's campaign.

I walked over to the Dinkler Plaza Hotel right at five o'clock; and, upon entering the lobby, I knew that the Humphrey organization, though it might be invisible in Atlanta, was certainly alive and well somewhere: the entire lobby was plastered from wall to wall, ceiling to floor, on every available column, with Humphrey posters, signs, and pictures. Not a single McCarthy poster was in sight, so I hurried upstairs to find the skeleton crew in the headquarters already trying to get a table out the door with the small amount of literature we had on hand. I phoned the storefront, where our larger stocks were kept, and within half an hour we had retaliated with as many of our few posters as we could find room for on the crowded columns, plus a table full of McCarthy literature. But we could not match those HHH straw hats!

Pat Madsen was one of the girls still left at the hotel, and she had a small yellow button pinned to her collar. She asked me where mine was; I confessed that I was without one and that I did not know what they were. Pat said, as we stacked literature on the table, that they were Secret Service pass pins and that without one you could not go anywhere near the senator or his group. Bill had apparently been giving them out that morning. I began noticing that many of the men in the lobby had different shaped red bars pinned to their lapels: these were the Secret Service agents themselves. Later, when Bill arrived (wearing a multi-colored pin like Pat's), we all got yellow buttons for our lapels.

While waiting for Senator McCarthy's arrival, I wandered in and out of the hotel. It was a brilliantly sunny afternoon, though it started raining later. In front of the hotel were several vans unloading all of the cases and cases of press equipment, both luggage and working gear for the representatives of all the major networks and wire services, plus newspapers and national magazines. Many of the cases had McCarthy "ricky-ticky-stickies" - white and blue McCarthy flowers – stuck on the outside; and I wondered how these men, who apparently followed the senator everywhere, compared him with the other presidential candidates they had also followed.

Across the street from the hotel there was a great deal of construction going on, and I noticed that someone had prepared a welcome: directly across from the hotel's front door, on the skeleton second floor of the new building, someone had stacked a load of lumber and painted on the side in big gray letters "Wallace Country."

I walked up the street to buy a quick hamburger supper, and when I returned there was a long train of cars parked in the side street beside the hotel: Senator McCarthy had arrived. Just inside the side door Rose Davis was handing out hotel keys to the incoming press men, who apparently also lived as a group. Activity in the lobby was starting to increase, and I walked over to a clean-cut student couple who were sitting behind the Humphrey literature table. I, of course, was wearing the McCarthy button which was always on my lapel (except during banking hours). I wanted to strike up a conversation with them to learn what sort of feelings motivated students to work for Humphrey because I honestly had never met any before.

After a moment or two fiddling with the Humphrey buttons and paraphernalia and trying to think of something to say, I finally asked what they felt was inspiring about Mr. Humphrey. The boy glanced up at me and my McCarthy button, looked me straight in the eyes, and, with an "I've been waiting to say this" look, countered, "I don't know: not all of us are trying to commit treason against the United States."

After first making sure that he was serious, I tried to convince him that my motives were otherwise. But he remained adamant, and I eventually gave up. I then walked back upstairs to our headquarters, via the "Press room," where there were tables, paper, and typewriters provided; someone on the advance team had taken care of this necessary detail.

Upstairs the "regular crew" was back in our headquarters, including

Taylor, whose face had turned bright red from the sun at the airport. All seemed quite elated by the way events had gone so far. I used the back stairs to go up to the floor where McCarthy, his daughter Mary, and his close advisors were staying. I was met by a Secret Service man at the stairwell door, but I got through and found Bill and Charlie, with several other similar young men, talking in the hall.

I noticed that Charlie had meticulously brushed his curly hair for the first time in a long time and that Bill was nervous but staying on top of the situation. It struck me that, as far as the national organization was concerned, he was personally responsible for everything going well in Atlanta; it must have taken a special kind of man to move into a new city every five days and hope to find local people on whom he could count to accomplish jobs which he could never do alone.

The timetable called for Senator McCarthy to pay a visit upstairs to the Fulton County Democratic Club reception at about seven; after returning to his room he would then go downstairs to the dinner at about 8:15 in time for dessert and Terry Sanford's speech. Following his own speech, he would then come directly up to our Georgians For McCarthy reception, which was scheduled to begin at 9:30. For the moment there was little to do but wait.

Cathy arrived in the rain a little before seven with Taylor's suit for the evening. A couple of us went up to the Fulton County Democratic Club reception, where I said hello to Terry Sanford. We had met once before at the University of North Carolina, and I told him how much I had admired a speech he had given at Chapel Hill earlier that year. I also expressed my sorrow that we were then on opposite sides for the night. He said that it was all right, that in a larger sense he and I were really both on the same side, which I think was probably true. Senator McCarthy then entered, surrounded by Secret Service agents. I was surprised at first by how tall a man the senator is.

Senator McCarthy plowed through the crowded room in a record time. As Secret Service agents cleared a path, the senator pressed forward, smiling and shaking hands. Governor Sanford went over to greet the senator, and I eventually worked close enough to shake his hand. He looked exactly like all his campaign pictures, though he seemed somehow larger and more internally energetic than I had imagined. Though relaxed, he was constantly looking around and pushing forward. He would shake a hand, look away, shake another hand, smile, say a little something, turn to his side, move ahead, and shake another hand. Any real conversation was therefore impossible; within ten minutes the senator had made one loop of the reception and left. We had hoped that he might talk with people and personally try to win support. I remember being disappointed, since one of our goals had been to influence those from Atlanta who later would be at the Chicago convention. I felt that, perhaps, we had missed an important opportunity.

Shortly everyone began moving downstairs for the dinner, and Senator McCarthy returned to his suite for a quiet meal and a talk with his staff.

As soon as the "Rainbow Roof" was cleared out, a small army of us moved up from the headquarters to get it ready for our reception. Tom Lyman and Jim Sundberg had, according to plan, rescued our large posters and signs from the airport rally, and these were shortly decorating the walls and the columns; behind the speaker's stand we had to maneuver one hinged sign around an eagle which wouldn't move.

All along there was a Secret Service man watching, and when I innocently put my camera inside the speaker's stand to give myself a free hand, he quickly made me move it: no small black boxes were going into a place so close to where the senator would be. We finished the decorations off with two long strings of WELCOME McCARTHY, in foot high letters, strung right across the central area of the room. Though one string broke twice, we were soon all prepared. I then went downstairs to see how the dinner was progressing.

The ballroom had a double tier of tables running all along the longest wall, behind which sat all of the Fulton County Democratic candidates for every post in the country. In front of these tables sat an overflow crowd of the faithful following, many more than had been expected. Governor Sanford was already sitting by the podium, and Senator McCarthy entered right on cue as dessert was being served. With the meal over there then followed a period of political niceties which threatened to turn into a filibuster and to ruin our timing, as each one of the Democratic candidates was introduced and something said about him. I could only feel sympathy for Governor Sanford and Senator McCarthy, who smiled politely throughout the entire ordeal.

Governor Sanford spoke first, and it was a very good speech, hard-hitting and domestically oriented, though I don't think he said anything at all about Vietnam, which bothered me, as I felt it was the most important thing that should be talked about. When Governor Sanford finished there was a loud applause, and Charles Weltner rose to introduce Senator McCarthy. None of the Democratic establishment, even at the level of Fulton County, had endorsed Senator McCarthy, and so there was no person who was a "natural" for this duty. All in all Mr. Weltner did a very fine, very tactful job, saying that Senator McCarthy had certainly made us all stop and think about our country; and he ended by adding that he could at least be sure of one thing, that the next President of the United States would be a senator from Minnesota, to which everyone could applaud.

One group did more than applaud. A large portion of the audience on one side of the ballroom, mostly younger members, stood up, some on chairs, and started shouting "We want Gene! We want Gene," all making the V for victory sign. Such spontaneity was a pleasant surprise and the chorus went on for a couple of minutes.

Senator McCarthy's speech seemed to take up where Governor Sanford's had left off – a short, almost total agreement on domestic issues and then a speech about foreign policy, about bankrupt ideas, and about a real need for change. It was still low key, but on the whole I thought it had more bite than the speech we had heard in Chicago. Senator McCarthy, when finished, also received a large ovation.

It was then almost ten o'clock. At nine-thirty I had made a quick trip up to the Rainbow Roof to check on the reception. A large number of guests had already arrived; there were contingents from Augusta and from Athens. Cathy, Taylor, and Dr. and Mrs. Evans were doing duty in the receiving line, and the punch was all set up. But the room was still largely empty, and I feared that many of our guests, entering the lobby and seeing that the speeches were still going on, had waited just outside the large open door and listened. With the hotel's tortuously slow elevators it would take at least twenty minutes for all of them to get upstairs. Back downstairs I found Bill, advised him of the situation, and asked him to give us twenty minutes after the dinner before bringing the senator up to the reception. We stood a chance of losing some of the guests already upstairs, but it seemed the only thing we could do. Bill agreed.

With the end of his speech and the formal end of the dinner, Senator McCarthy was rushed out to a "waiting elevator." I was standing nearby and asked if I could catch a lift up; the Secret Service man looked at Bill, who said it was OK. The elevator was crowded. Senator McCarthy stood at the rear, his daughter next to me in the front. There was silence as the elevator started up and Senator McCarthy's eyes glanced up to watch the floors count by. I smiled and said hello, and I told them how much I had enjoyed escorting Mary Beth around Atlanta and how fine a person I thought she was. Senator McCarthy smiled faintly and nodded with a "Hmm" of recognition. I looked down at his daughter, Mary, who seemed worried about something. But she smiled back and said that her cousin was a good campaigner.

I suppose I was a bit inane, but what is one to say to a presidential candidate with fifteen seconds in a crowded elevator? They got off for a twenty-minute break, while I went on up to the Rainbow Roof to help out.

Luckily we had been correct on our timing, because with each elevator load the room swelled with guests; it was fairly full when the senator came in, smiling and shaking hands on the way to the podium. I had been told five minutes before that I should introduce Dr. Evans, who would introduce Senator McCarthy. I tried to jot down some remarks about Dr. Evans and Hans Reinisch, whom I would introduce later. But there was not time to write anything before the senator was seated on stage and we were ready to start.

Though I have never really been afraid to speak before large audiences, I do often contract a nervousness which leads anyone who talks with me just before such an occasion to believe that I am not listening to them. In such a state I was trying to explain to Hans about the fund-raising timing; but then we had to begin. The senator was seated on the right of the platform, hands together, looking very relaxed and smiling. Dr. Evans came up and took a seat next to the senator. So I just swallowed hard and said something briefly about Dr. Evans being one of the original co-chairmen of Georgians For McCarthy; and then Dr. Evans, who got a well-deserved round of applause, introduced his former professor.

Senator McCarthy seemed completely relaxed and happy; Bill had warned us that he might just say a few words of thanks and leave, but he didn't (we had impressed on Bill that there were people in the crowd who were new to Senator McCarthy and who had not been present at the twenty dollar a plate dinner). Whether Bill had passed this on to the senator or not, I don't know, but Senator McCarthy gave another short speech, and he even threw in a few jokes.

Knowing what they must have known about the way nationwide delegate polls were going, it must have been difficult for the national staff, and especially for Senator McCarthy himself, to keep coming out day after day both optimistic and hopeful for the local faithful. But I suppose that they, too, had the hope of changing as much as they could along the road to the convention, win or lose in the end; so they kept going. Senator McCarthy seemed particularly optimistic late that night, and he wound up by saying that they had started out with nothing in the fall before, determined to move the nation, and that they were still confident of victory in August. I thought that he came across very sincerely, and he got a big hand at the end.

He then again shook hands and talked with people while slowly moving toward the door, and as soon as he was out of the room we began what we had known all along would be a big gamble: fund raising after the main speaker had finished and when people naturally wanted to leave. I immediately got up and asked everyone to stay; then I introduced Hans who I expected to give a brief, simple pitch. Instead, unfortunately, he began a proper speech about how much money they had raised in New York and how much was needed to come from Georgia. I'm sure that he didn't mean it, but he seemed to be almost talking down to "us people from Georgia."

I soon noticed that many guests were starting to leave, and I desperately wanted Hans to finish so that I could introduce Mr. Pendergrast, a home-grown Atlantan. By the time we eventually got to the fund raising itself, I noticed that our guests were hurrying out. We managed to collect about $450 which was badly needed; but we still lacked our wealthy patron, whom all of us had been hoping for, but who just would not appear.

When most of the fund raising was over, I went out to talk to my parents, who had been in the audience for the senator's speech; they seemed disturbed about something. My father asked me if I had not smelled the smoke while I had been talking. I said no, of course not. But then standing with them out on the floor, I did notice the smell of something burning. Two policemen and a Secret Service man arrived, and Dad led them just outside the Rainbow Roof and into the small elevator lobby where another policeman was standing watch at the door to a stairwell.

Just inside the door, on the concrete landing, right beneath a wooden ladder and the intake duct for the Rainbow Roof's ventilation system, someone had started a fire with a pile of rags and kerosene while Senator McCarthy was speaking. Traces of smoke had started filtering in through the ventilation ducts, located in the center of the room, just as Senator McCarthy was leaving. Dad, an engineer, and another man had gone to have a look as the smell got worse; they found the fire and put it out before it reached the ladder. But by that time it was too late; many guests had been frightened and, not wanting to be caught on the top floor of that hotel in case of a fire, had left rather quickly. Whatever the motives of whoever had set the fire, he certainly had at least deprived us of our audience.

The McCarthy staff people seemed unshaken by the fire incident; and I suppose that it was, luckily, a small matter. They were more happy that the whole day had gone so well, that the senator had come across so well, and that he had found support in Atlanta in the heart of the South. When one considered all that could have gone wrong, it did seem that everything had gone off amazingly close to schedule and in an encouraging way, from the crowd at the airport to the cheers at the dinner. Everyone in the local organization at the headquarters was also happy; and I guess that we really had done a pretty good job, aided by a large dose of outside help at the end.

Senator McCarthy was to leave early the next morning. Taylor and I went home that night fairly satisfied with his Atlanta visit, though I did not believe the senator's visit had changed the mind of a single Georgia delegate. And I had forgotten to take a single picture.

4

A RALLY IN THE BLACK COMMUNITY

After the high point of Senator McCarthy's visit, we all took a needed day's rest; the two weeks of July involved a lot of work, but we did not seem to get much further in our hope to swing the state over to McCarthy. It was at about this time that the organization stopped growing and stopped drawing in significant numbers of new people. Toward August we did, in fact, enlarge the number of co-chairmen greatly, including Ken Martin, Mrs. A. M. Davis (an extremely conscientious Atlanta black leader), Mrs. Paschall, Otis Cochran, Chico Thomas, George Blaugh (a local businessman), and myself.

But these were people who for the most part had already been involved with the organization and who were already helping to make decisions. Their increasing participation was part of the rationale for enlarging the number of co-chairmen, plus the fact that Dr. Evans was leaving shortly for Europe and that Mr. Beluso seemed to be taking less interest in the meetings.

If the swelling of the co-chairmen was supposed to make those people involved feel some new responsibility for the campaign's success and thereby motivate greater involvement, by late July it was really too late for new ideas, and we simply did not have the funds for ambitious new strategies. Instead we spent those two weeks shaking down our own organization, which proved invaluable in the end, but which ideally should have been done in May.

At some point during July we were visited by Dave Mixner, who had been given a job in Washington, instead of Atlanta. Taylor and I were both glad to see Dave, and he brought with him two of his friends and co-workers, Sam Brown and Frank McDonald. I was not sure of the specific structure of the national McCarthy organization, but I soon learned that Frank McDonald was Charlie's immediate superior: he was the "Southern Desk Man" in Washington, working under Curtis Gans, the man in charge of the entire McCarthy field operation.

Frank was one of several regional directors, and it was to him that Charlie reported and from him that he received support. Of all the McCarthy staff I met, I think that Frank could most easily pass for a football player. His job, like Curt Gans' and Charlie's, was far too much for one man to handle; I suspect he wound up doing more simple compiling of the events which were occurring in his own area rather than he did any actual directing of their outcome.

Sam Brown was also involved in the operations wing of the McCarthy campaign; Sam appeared to be much more soft spoken and easy going than Frank; but Sam was a veteran of civil rights work in the early 1960's (in fact the entire McCarthy campaign was reaping the first harvest of those young men and women who had graduated from college in those idealistic, optimistic, activist days of five years before). I later learned that Sam had been one of the masterminds of the first brilliantly successful McCarthy field campaign in New Hampshire. The same group was later to receive national attention as the leaders of the Vietnam Moratorium.

But that July Sam, Frank, and Dave had come down to Atlanta for a few days to visit Charlie and to evaluate the local situation. Though little was actually changed or planned, that I know of, as a result of their visit, they did get a firsthand glimpse of our people and our activities, which probably helped us to get some priority assistance a few weeks later.

During this period in late July, Mr. Walsh's injunction case went to court. With Toni Case, a young female co-worker in my office and a McCarthy supporter, I went to the Federal courthouse on the first day of the case to sit in for a short while. Mr. Walsh and his fellow lawyers were seeking to enjoin the Lester Maddox delegation from representing the people of Georgia at the Democratic National Convention, arguing that there must be a process of "one man one vote" in any such system which ultimately helps select the next president of the country. They were arguing in a rather gray legal area, because the founding fathers had not foreseen the growth of political parties and had not provided for their maintenance in the constitution.

After a long hearing, the three-judge federal court finally ruled that it could do nothing for just that reason: political parties were free, under the constitution, to use whatever methods they wanted in choosing delegates to their conventions. Mr. Walsh and the plaintiffs would have to look to the Democratic Party itself for redress of their grievances; the federal court could do nothing. Mr. Walsh planned to appeal, but by then it was too late to hope for an official state primary or state convention before the convening of the national convention, scheduled to start on August 26th.

During this same period, though we never officially buried it, Taylor and I realized that our hopes for the GDC and for a newspaper poll just were not going to materialize. The crucial donation of $5,000 never came: Hans went back to New York the Sunday after McCarthy's visit, still optimistic that we might find a contributor; but we never saw Hans again, and no money ever came. As the days went by, we realized that we were going to have to work entirely within the framework of the Macon convention being prepared by the Georgia Democratic Party Forum and slated for Saturday, August 10.

Concurrent with our other activities, Taylor and I were receiving overtures from Vernon Shell, a member of the on-going staff of the Coalition For An Open Convention, from the new COC headquarters in Chicago. He called several times regarding a Southern Regional COC to be patterned after the earlier meeting in Chicago and to deal mainly with the various Southern challenge delegations and platform recommendations on civil rights Vernon assured us that Al Lowenstein would be there and that several black leaders, like Hosea Williams of SCLC, involved with "Resurrection City," would also attend; these men would serve as the catalysts for what would also be a working meeting to decide on convention strategy.

Vernon wanted to hold the meeting in Atlanta; both Taylor and I explained our deep involvement in Georgians For McCarthy, and we regretted that there just were not enough hours in the day for us to also help very much with the COC. The date was also a problem, since Sunday August 4th was our own rally at the Wheat Street Baptist Church, and Saturday the 10th was the Forum convention in Macon. I doubted whether many people from Georgia, at least, would then give up both days of their weekend to come to the COC on Sunday the 11th. The next weekend would then be too close to the Democratic National Convention.

Vernon insisted that his people could handle the organization from Chicago, if we would just lend a hand whenever possible to help to include as many local people as we could. He also felt that Sunday, August 11th would be the best day, even though we might not get a good turnout from Georgia. Though neither Taylor nor I were really too keen for the Southern COC, because we felt that there was more work, that late in the summer, for each state to be doing at home, we nevertheless did not want to actually discourage what could prove to be a creative exchange of ideas.

Late in July, Toni Casey and I received an invitation, through a banking friend, to give a short talk for McCarthy at the luncheon meeting of a small service club in north Atlanta. Toni had been a debater, and she presented a good case. She had previously written a long letter to the editor of the *Atlanta Constitution* about McCarthy, and her letter had been published in full.

Toni was typical of the talent that we could have captured had we been better organized earlier in the summer. As it was, she was frustrated by our meetings and by our lengthy decision-making processes. She did not particularly care about being involved in these, but as it was, there was little for a talented person to do between the levels of storefront work and central policy making. Toni could easily have been the coordinator for a large area, but the plans for that kind of activity just were not made until it was too late to use them effectively.

Taylor and I did have some further success at a later speaking engagement, this time at a luncheon meeting at the Atlanta Junior Chamber of Commerce, arranged by Mr. Bows. It wasn't exactly a two-sided presentation: Taylor, who was always good at such things, gave a facts and figures account of the entire Vietnam situation, starting back in the early 1920's. I then gave a brief speech about the mood on campus and the involvement of young people in the Kennedy and McCarthy campaigns, spending some time on our own frustrations in Georgia. Whether the young businessman audience was listening or not, Taylor and I were finally doing the kind of communicating we had so wanted to initiate back in June.

When our talks were over we got a polite applause, and several members of the audience came up and thanked us for "saying so well what they had been feeling"; but there were no contributors of time or money. There was, however, an incredible response from the press. Three radio station newsmen had been on hand to tape our speeches, and afterwards they corralled us in the hall for interviews. They asked all sorts of fairly neutral questions about what we were doing, what we thought about the war, and what we thought about Georgia politics.

I remember that one of the reporters from a very large Atlanta radio station asked Taylor whether he thought there was any hope for a democratic government in South Vietnam. Taylor spent a long time answering "Yes." We were then both amazed when this newsman turned off his mic and said that he didn't think that there was any such hope for democracy in South Vietnam and that he was heartened by our optimism!

For the next two days portions of our speeches were broadcast on the local news, and one morning they were repeated almost completely on an "in depth" local news show. I was kidded by friends at work who had been awakened by their alarm radios only to find us talking about the state of the world so early in the morning. Taylor and I were pleasantly surprised that our speeches received such attention, and it only further confirmed a theory that I had developed the spring before while working on my roommate's campaign: in politics, it seems to me that acceleration is more important than velocity.

That is, from the point of view of press coverage and general attention, it is much better to have nothing but to seem to be heading somewhere than to already have everything. The McCarthy campaign in Georgia was *news* for just that reason, and since so seldom were speeches like ours given, they were news, too. The press is interested in that sort of new, different activity. I could not help wondering how much coverage and attention we would have aroused if we had given pro-war speeches and backed Vice-president Humphrey.

Of course, in the end, nationally, it could be argued that we received this coverage only because we were just a flash in the pan and that the real Humphrey support was devastating, whether it was news or not. This fact may be true, but I still believe that this kind of coverage is a big help to anyone trying to start a political movement. Had these speeches been made in March, and had we then had more time, perhaps we could have accomplished much more. At least we hoped that this coverage helped further one of our own personal primary motives, that of challenging people to think and to evaluate their own views on a significant national issue, such as the war in Vietnam.

Three major events were next coming up on the calendar, all of which required from our organization a great deal of partially simultaneous planning. The final plans for M-Day were being made in New York and were filtering down to each of the cities which were to participate. M-Day was to be essentially a massive McCarthy rally in Madison Square Garden in New York, including a "host of stars." The rally was to be broadcast live coast-to-coast on a nationwide closed circuit television network, with more big name entertainment, both national and local, supplied live in each of the cities. Such a simultaneous political broadcast would be the first of its kind, and the New York headquarters hoped to raise a great deal of "last push" funds. The tentative date was set for Thursday, August 15th; we were to secure suitable ballroom facilities and to do all of the local work, with the help of a single national coordinator who would arrive the week before M-Day.

Another of the coming events was the Democratic Party Forum's Convention in Macon, scheduled for the Saturday before M-Day, August 10th. We had been in constant communication with Mr. Kehrer and Rev. Morris, and the Forum's plans were going according to their schedule. Taylor, myself, and several of us had joined the Forum so that we could officially keep informed on the plans; I was urging everyone I could to join, because I was afraid that at the last minute the convention voting might suddenly be done by "members only." There was to be a final Forum planning session in Macon on Saturday the 3rd, and I asked Mr. Kehrer and Rev. Morris if I could sit in, as both a member of the Forum and as a representative of the McCarthy forces within the state. They welcomed me and said that they would be delighted for me to join in.

The third, and most immediate event was our first and final significant attempt to arouse interest for the McCarthy campaign in the black community. We planned a rally at the Wheat Street Baptist Church on Auburn Avenue, scheduled for Sunday, August 4th. Mrs. Paschall, John Tillman, and Otis Cochran, along with Les Leopold, had been the force behind getting the rally approved by the co-chairmen, and they took care of most of the planning. With Charlie's help, they managed to secure, as speakers, Fannie Lou Hamer from Mississippi, Mary McCarthy, the senator's daughter, and Julian Bond.

So it was for these events that we had to plan at our meetings during the end of July and the first of August, though it was difficult to take "first things first," since all required a lot of planning at roughly the same time. Eventually each of us had a separate responsibility for each of the three events, and we were supposed to do as much as possible on all three as the days went by. As stated above, the Georgians For McCarthy leadership stayed about static from this point on. The mailing had finally gone out and funds were beginning to trickle in through the mail, just staying about even with daily expenses, though not going far towards our larger fixed costs, like the headquarters and the Sunday rally.

Though we were awaiting details from New York about M-Day, we started investigating possible sites, one part of the event which we would have to pay for ourselves. Ken Martin was in telephone contact with New York regarding sites and stars. Most of us felt best about having it in the Dinkler Plaza, because the cost would be under $500. The only other location free from obstructing columns was the ballroom at the Regency Hyatt House, but the bill there (just for the use of the room) would be an incredible $1,200.

New York answered that they wanted the biggest and best place in town and that the Dinkler Plaza would be too small. Even though the location decision had to be made far in advance so that tickets and leaflets could be printed, we delayed it for a few days, hoping that with more information from New York we could better judge which location would be the best.

Taylor volunteered to be in charge of ticket sales for M-Day, while most of the rest of us were working on organizing for the Macon convention. We hoped to have a list of stars ready two weeks before M-Day so that we could get publicity and advance ticket sales going. We decided on three ticket prices - $20, $5, and $3 – based not on where the holder would sit but on how much he was willing to give. Each of us felt certain that we could sell a large number of tickets to friends who would come just for the sake of the entertainment.

Taylor put in an order for the tickets, and Ken kept the pressure on New York to give us more information. I personally felt very good about M-Day at that point, since it seemed that so many stars and so much talent was being put into it. I was certain that with its help we might at least pay our bills.

It should probably be pointed out that the whole M-Day extravaganza was being planned and run by the New York state McCarthy organization, not the national headquarters in Washington. The New York organization was by far the largest and most effective of the state organizations, and contributions from New York kept the national campaign alive. But there was friction at the top of the two organizations over autonomy: the Washington HQ never gave its blessing to M-Day, which most of its people considered to be a potential fiasco on a grand scale.

New York pressed ahead with its plans, though, and most of the Washington field men were allowed to judge local conditions as to M-Day's feasibility. In some places it was axed; but, in Atlanta, Charlie agreed with us that it was our one last chance to communicate with a lot of people and to bring in some much-needed revenue.

On Saturday, August 3d, the day before our Wheat Street Baptist Church rally, I got up early and drove to south Atlanta, where, as agreed, I met Rev. Morris, Mrs. Morris, and Al Kehrer in the parking lot of a motel just off the south expressway. I then transferred to Rev. Morris' cream-colored station wagon for the hour and a half trip to Macon and the final planning meeting for the Forum's Open Convention of Loyal National Democrats, a meeting which was to prove of great importance.

Rev. Morris and Mr. Kehrer were expecting representatives that day from six or seven of Georgia's ten Congressional Districts; the Forum had membership in all districts but one in south Georgia. At that point I really knew very little about the internal organization of the Forum, other than who the leaders were, that they had about $400 in the bank, and that they had 400 members throughout the state.

We made a quick trip into downtown Macon to the Dempsey Hotel, where the Convention was scheduled for the next Saturday and where our own meeting was originally supposed to be held. There we met Bob Griffiths and Steve Price from the University of Georgia at Athens – Bob a teacher and Steve a student – plus a couple of other Forum members from Macon and Columbus. Since none of us had on our buttons, I didn't know whether these were McCarthy or Humphrey supporters.

I soon learned, though, from conversation, that Bob and Steve were both involved in the Athens McCarthy organization, the most ambitious outside of Atlanta (they also had their own Athens storefront). We all soon left for a private dining room in a motel restaurant on the north side of town, where our meeting was then scheduled to take place; we left a note at the Dempsey in case anyone should come in late.

My purposes in attending this meeting were twofold: first, I hoped to contribute to the general discussion on rules and procedures for the convention. Second, I wanted to get a precise record of these procedures and take them back to our McCarthy Headquarters so that we would know exactly the rules and the operative procedure for the subsequent Macon convention. The Forum had been mailing out literature over the past month advertising the convention as being free and open to all "loyal national Democrats," specifying that once you had signed a pledge of your loyalty, you were then entitled to vote under a "one man one vote" procedure.

It sounded like a simple, open, democratic convention to elect a challenge delegation, but we still needed to know the details. Dave Mixner had arrived in town late that week, and our own group was just beginning to start "gearing up" for the Macon convention. We had a vague promise of financial help from Washington through Charlie; but to vote at the convention one had to be a Georgia voter, so money by itself would not be of much use. That meant, simply, that we were going to have to create a statewide McCarthy organization in all of eight days and then get as many supporters as possible to Macon on the following Saturday.

After ordering lunch we sat down around a long table in a partitioned-off part of the dining room, paneled very tastefully in mahogany. I was sitting about in the middle of the table; on my immediate left was a black minister from Macon; on his left, at the end of the table nearest the window, sat Mr. Kehrer. Then around the table across from me were Bob and Steve. Next was Mr. Herb Goldman, an AFL-CIO official in Cobb County, just outside of Atlanta. One other gentleman, I think from Columbus, sat beside him. Rev. Morris sat at the other end of the table, always exuding optimism and usually smoking a cigar. Next to me on my right sat Mrs. Morris.

We fairly quickly got down to business. Mr. Kehrer reviewed the highlights of the coming convention, why it was being called, and what its purpose was to be. Rev. Morris reported that work was proceeding well on the challenge brief, which would be centered mainly on the disloyalty of Lester Maddox to the national Democratic Party, as well as his inappropriate authority to select all of the Georgia delegates from a list submitted to him by James Gray, the state Party Chairman. The challenge brief had to be filed with the Credentials Committee, with a copy to the state party headquarters, by the Monday after our Macon convention; and Rev. Morris was sure that he could complete it on time.

We then had district reports, such as they were, on projected attendance. Bob and Steve said that they expected about fifty from Athens. I said about eighty at the most through the McCarthy organization in Atlanta. After everyone had reported, Mr. Kehrer deduced that there would probably be between 450 and 500 delegates present on the following Saturday.

When lunch was over we took up the proposed agenda for the convention. It would start at 11 am with the selection of a chairman (assumed to be Mr. Kehrer). There would then be an acceptance of the rules and the agenda. Mr. Kehrer would read a short speech of purpose and welcome. Since identical telegrams had been sent to both the Humphrey and the McCarthy national headquarters, requesting them to send observers, it was assumed that two such men would be present to be recognized. Congressman Mr. John Conyers of Detroit, who had accepted the invitation only the day before, would give the keynote speech.

There would then be a lunch break at noon, after which the delegates would reconvene at one o'clock in separate rooms, by Congressional Districts, for the election of four delegates and four alternatives from each district. Any unfilled places would then be filled by the convention as a whole when it reconvened. After a collection, the chairman would charge the delegation to represent the convention fairly in Chicago. The convention would then adjourn, leaving the delegation, which was to be a completely autonomous body, free to choose its own chairman and officials and to plan the details of the challenge ahead.

That all sounded fine to me, but I had pictured a convention as a place to give speeches for candidates and to pass resolutions on different issues; and I had not noticed any such place in the proposed agenda. When I broached the subject, Mr. Kehrer replied that the sole purpose of this convention was to elect delegates for the challenge delegation, not to play "partisan politics." This convention would be no place for partisan speeches or resolutions.

I was somewhat taken aback; and, while I was thinking, Steve asked about partisan literature and paraphernalia. No, that was out, too, as far as Mr. Kehrer was concerned. This was quite a revelation: a state convention called to elect delegates to a national party convention, where a man would be nominated for U.S. president, without anyone at our convention saying one word either about the candidates or about policies, nor even allowed to pass out literature! To hear Mr. Kehrer speak, one would have thought that what we were doing in Georgia was somehow taking place in a vacuum, not connected at all with events in the rest of the nation.

Over and over, both here and later, Mr Kehrer kept repeating that our purpose was to do something for the people of Georgia and not to play partisan national politics. He was so convincing that finally I agreed with him about the speeches, but we three young participants held out on the policy issues and the paraphernalia. We argued that we should *at least* pass a motion condemning the present selection method and pledging ourselves to change it. But Mr. Kehrer argued that the convention would drag on all day that way, and that the elected delegation could subsequently pass such motions, if it wished. We did convince him to allow posters and paraphernalia in the lobby outside the convention hall, but inside we would have to be limited to buttons.

If I had had previous convention experience, I would have pressed harder on these demands. I should have. But I considered myself to be there as a guest, and I was in a delicate position, I thought. We believed that through Mr. Kehrer's union connections, he could easily turn out between 500 and 1,000 Humphrey supporters at the convention. Mr. Goldman even made the comment that day that "his boys" (i.e. the union) were all ready for a 30-car caravan down from Marietta.

Mr Kehrer was a high official in a statewide organization with easy internal communication; and, even though he reported fairly low expectations, we were afraid that a few key phone calls could bring out hundreds of supporters in a matter of hours. On the other hand we had no state organization ourselves, at all – I hoped that we might be able to get 300 people, total, to Macon on the next Saturday.

Mr. Kehrer was still talking in terms of making sure that all candidates were represented; he even quoted figures like "70%-30%" and "60%-40%," and both he and I knew that that was more McCarthy representation than on the Maddox delegation. Given his apparent strength, it seemed foolish for me to argue long and hard from a power position which I did not have, thereby possibly ruining our so far cordial relations with the Forum leadership. I was also afraid that if I argued too strongly I might give the *impression* of strength, thereby triggering those key phone calls which, for all we really knew, had already been made anyway.

We then discussed voting procedure, which at first seemed simple, but then became complex. Mr. Kehrer proposed that, in each district meeting, nominations would be taken and then everyone would vote, the nominees with the four highest totals being elected. But I pointed out that, if he really did want a mixed delegation, this system would be disastrous; for, like it or not, people would probably vote for a nominee who would represent their candidate. Furthermore, they would probably vote *only* for the nominees who represented their candidate, meaning that whichever candidate had the majority in any one district, that candidate would receive *all* of that district's delegates. Mr. Kehrer and Rev. Morris took the point, and after about an hour's deliberation we finally mutually agreed on the following system:

If there were a quorum present when the district reconvened after lunch, a member of the Forum would call the district meeting to order. A District Chairman would then be elected by a simple majority. Nominations would next be made for delegates; the nominees would stand up and identify themselves. The nominees would then be voted on in turn; anyone receiving a simple majority would be a delegate. It would be up to the chairman to remind the district meeting as the process continued as to the changing composition of the chosen delegation (i.e. by race, sex, and political leanings, if known); and the District Chairman would ask that the voters keep these factors in mind as they voted for the remaining delegates.

This process would continue until four delegates and four alternates were elected from each district, providing that there were sufficient nominees. Anyone's name could be brought up again if he were defeated the first time. The District Chairman would report the election results to the convention as a whole when it reconvened, at which time anyone who had been present at the district meeting could offer any disagreement with the Chairman's report, and the convention as a whole would arbitrate any disputes. The total convention would then fill any vacancies in either delegates or alternates and would confirm the district nominations by electing those nominated as official delegates.

This system seemed the best to ensure both democracy and a fairly well-balanced delegation. Mr. Kehrer said that he would be responsible for getting the procedural rules and the agenda typed up. Both Bob Griffiths and I had been taking profuse notes, so I was not too worried about unexpected changes in the agenda. We thought we had covered everything, and the meeting broke up at about four. Mr. Kehrer and Rev. Morris said that they planned to arrive in Macon on the next Friday night to make any last-minute plans. I wanted at that time very much to talk to Bob and Steve about McCarthy activities in Athens, so they volunteered to drive home through Atlanta and to drop me off at my car. I said goodbye to Mr. Kehrer and Rev. Morris; I think we all felt that the meeting had been productive.

As we drove to Atlanta through a beautiful Georgia summer afternoon in Bob's Mustang, both Steve and Bob confessed that they had been taking the same passive role at the meeting that I had: with any luck they hoped to have one hundred McCarthy supporters from Athens, not fifty. Bob said that he was still sure, however, that we would be the minority. But, if there did turn out to be any way for us to win a majority of the challenge delegation, he believed that we should do so for the sake of the national McCarthy campaign. But I still agreed with Mr. Kehrer that we should not alienate the Humphrey National Convention delegates from whom we needed help and thereby ruin our chances of winning in Chicago; besides, the possibility of us having an overall majority seemed so remote that I gave it little further thought.

We did, however, discuss several points which would quickly become parts of our statewide strategy for the next week. One obvious point was the need for organization among the minority McCarthy delegates, if they were not to split their vote and fail to elect anyone. Another was the critical role of the District Chairman in the election process. His nomination and election, if we were organized, could be the first signal of our strength in each of the districts.

This fact brought up the need for internal communication: with the voting being done by district, it might take two hundred people to have a majority in the larger districts, while twenty might be a majority in one or two of the smaller districts. Therefore, if we were winning no delegates in the larger districts, it would be necessary to quickly communicate this fact to the smaller districts, where we might more conceivably have majorities, instructing them to elect majority McCarthy delegations. Both Steve and Bob seemed to have the situation well in hand in Athens, and the university could prove a great asset for the convention, since students with homes in the smaller districts could be organized in Athens both to call home for help and to swell the ranks of their home districts.

I arrived in Atlanta late that afternoon and went immediately to our headquarters, where I reported the results of the planning committee to Charlie, Dave, and Chico. Dave, who already was, of course, a veteran of many state conventions, could not believe that there were to be no partisan speeches and no resolutions. I explained my feeling of impotence in trying to change those decisions, and we went over all of the procedural details that I had recorded in my notes. Already several maps were springing up on the walls, neatly marking off each of Georgia's ten districts and pinpointing the few cities where we had known sympathizers.

I also reviewed the conversation held in Bob's car, and we all agreed on those points. Over that weekend and the following Monday our basic strategy for the convention evolved. First, we would assign someone in the headquarters to each of the ten districts, hopefully one-on-one. That person, mainly by phone, would follow every lead that we had in that district, always trying to get more leads from anyone who proved sympathetic. While we would try, obviously, to get as many McCarthy sympathizers to Macon as possible, we would also encourage anyone and everyone to come, as we genuinely wanted as many people as possible to participate (though hopefully not all from one union), and we wanted the convention to be a success.

By Wednesday we would try to have chosen ten "District Leaders," to whom we would send all of the literature we could spare about the Forum and the convention (most of it gladly supplied by Rev. Morris), plus a general set of instructions about holding a McCarthy district caucus, hopefully before Saturday if possible. At that pre-convention district caucus the McCarthy supporters would decide on a tentative list of delegate nominees and on a nominee for District Chairman.

At the convention itself, we planned to set up a central control point in the lobby to follow each district election as it proceeded and to send runners to any district where we had a majority, to be tested by the first vote for District Chairman, with instructions, depending on how the other district elections were going.

———

That Sunday afternoon our Wheat Street Baptist Church rally was to take place. Taylor and I arrived at the church right after lunch, with Taylor's mics and amplifiers, left over from his college band days, in the trunk of his car, in case we needed them. It was a hot and humid day, occasionally threatening to rain. The church was located on a corner (neither street being named Wheat Street) in an entirely black neighborhood near the SCLC headquarters. The church building was large, built from gray stone; behind the church itself there was a large Sunday School Building, which, we noted, had plenty of classrooms in case we wanted to hold working meetings afterwards. Between the two buildings sat the pastor's home, a pleasant white house with a high porch and a shady tree in front.

After looking around for a while, Taylor and I knocked on the front door and were immediately welcomed inside by one of the most outgoing people I have ever met, Rev. William Holmes Borders, who had volunteered to let us use his church for the afternoon. Following a few minutes of conversation, Rev. Borders commissioned one of the small boys currently occupying his living room rug to show us the meeting hall where the rally was to take place and the kitchen where we could mix lemonade.

The meeting hall was in the basement of the church building: it was no more than a large room, pleasingly cool, with a high roof and a wooden stage at one end, in back of which were the props for an annual Christmas play. There were small columns running the length of the room, and the walls looked like their painting had been a parish project. The floor was concrete, and there were rows of folded chairs already set up, with more available in the back. All in all, it was the perfect place for the kind of rally we hoped to have.

Taylor and I set to work testing the sound systems and setting in the middle aisle the one mic we brought, to be used for questions from the audience. Pat Madsen and Jo Ann Thomas soon arrived, and we sent them off looking for an open store with lemonade mix. We had had flyers printed announcing the rally; the flyers had supposedly been distributed by John, Otis, Les and Jim's people in the black community. From somewhere John Tillman had procured a car with a loudspeaker on top, and he had been cruising the black communities announcing the rally all morning long; now he was covering the area near the church. People started to trickle in, and we were surprised by how many new white faces there were, apparently drawn by our newspaper ad that morning.

As a light, humid rain started to fall, a car arrived with Fannie Lou Hamer, Mary McCarthy, and Charlie. Fannie Lou Hamer immediately strikes one as the archetype older black woman; but as soon as she begins to speak, you know that she is set on changing the world, fast, and not on playing any archetypal roles. We had all met Mary McCarthy when she had accompanied her father to Atlanta, but she had not been given a chance to say much in public on that earlier trip. Mary, like her cousin, is also a college student, another "drop out"; she is somewhat shorter than Mary Beth, and not quite as immediately striking. But she is easily just as persuasive in the arguments, and she was back in Atlanta to represent her father on her own. Julian Bond came in a little later; Taylor was to be the master of ceremonies, and he and Julian talked about the speaking order.

While I fidgeted with a loose wire on the amplifier lead the people kept coming in. As was standard operating procedure at all such events, we had a table of literature and buttons at each door; and most importantly, we had a "guest list" on which people were asked to sign their names and addresses. Pat and Jo Ann had finally mixed up some lemonade, which was badly needed to help dull the rising heat. Handheld fans were passed around, more wooden folding chairs were set up and set to creaking. Soon the basement had the odd flavor of a political meeting somehow happening in the middle of a church revival, or vice versa. It was a very heterogeneous group, and I was happy that we could bring such people together; though, as usual, I had hoped we would have more.

It took a while for the room to fill, so we delayed the start. When we finally began the room was nearly full, but it was painfully obvious that some of our efforts had been in vain: more than half of the faces in the crowd were white. Somehow either we were not communicating; or else the black community, after Kennedy's death, just did not seem to care anymore.

After a prayer from Rev. Borders, Taylor first introduced Julian Bond, who unfortunately had to speak quickly and leave to go to another meeting elsewhere. This was the first time that I heard Julian speak in person, and his presence and his sincere youthful appearance carried over easily in the way he spoke. He talked briefly. . . about the war, about how we had to have change; and he said that he was convinced that Senator McCarthy was the only man who could bring about that change by giving the Democratic Party a new, vital leadership. After finishing and apologizing for having to leave so quickly, he received a rousing applause.

As Julian left, Taylor introduced Fannie Lou Hamer, a woman who had been fighting the fight in Mississippi for at least eight years; she looked tired, but she looked eternal, as if she could go on fighting forever. Even though Mrs. Hamer had not endorsed either Senator McCarthy or Vice President Humphrey – none of the Mississippi challenge people, more or less sure of unseating the regulars, wanted to disturb the water – she nevertheless did recount their experience with Hubert Humphrey in 1964 as an example of how the political system was going to have to learn to change faster if it was going to keep the support and the respect of black people, who were tired of words with no action.

She blasted us for being a largely white audience and asked where the black people were. She talked about the poor black people she knew in Mississippi, about how they had been used, about how they had no jobs, no money, and no political power. Over and over she emphasized that the situation had to change, and change fast, whoever was elected president. She is a most moving and forceful speaker and at the end she received a huge ovation. I could not help wondering how often she had been cheered by a "white liberal" audience, which she had just blasted, but then found little real help when the push came to shove of actually helping to change the system.

Mary McCarthy gave a strong speech on her father's behalf, going back to the primaries, recounting how the people had voted for a change, but how the political establishment was nevertheless lining up behind Humphrey. She hoped that we could have some influence on our Georgia delegates, and she wished us luck with any challenge delegation that might be forthcoming from Georgia.

Once the three principal speakers were finished, we had questions from the audience; one man asked Mary what she really thought her father's chances were. She, of course, gave an optimistic answer: Humphrey did not have nearly as many delegates as the recent polls showed; there was a possibility of as many as seventeen different challenges; and if any challenges from the South won, there was the possibility of a large Southern revolt on the first ballot; so she was optimistic.

After about forty-five minutes of questions and answers, we had to cut the meeting short because our speakers had planes to catch. We took up the usual collection; Taylor reminded everyone of M-Day coming up in ten days; I announced that there would be a meeting immediately following in the church's education building for anyone interested in the Forum's challenge convention scheduled for the next Saturday; we would talk about both strategy and organization.

Before walking back to the education building, I said goodbye to Mary McCarthy and thanked her for coming. She remarked that she enjoyed being in Atlanta and that her father had been so impressed with his Southern tour that he had wished primaries could be somehow arranged in Georgia and throughout the rest of the South.

With that encouragement, about thirty of us began our meeting in what was a small combination gym and auditorium in the Wheat Street Baptist Church education building. We started by passing around a list for all names and addresses, and then I outlined briefly the background of the Forum convention, the procedures decided upon the day before, and our developing strategy. There was real, immediate, noticeable interest among everyone there. I think for them it was like the feeling that Taylor and I had experienced during the lawyers' meeting at the COC: here, at last, with this Macon convention, after a lot of talking, seemed a means of action which might actually accomplish something.

Everyone wanted more details, so I promised to mail them the copies of the Forum literature that I had. Besides representatives from three of the districts immediately surrounding Atlanta, W. D. Quesenbery of Augusta and Grace Watson of Thomasville also were there, both hoping to bring a couple of carloads to Macon. Since Augusta is in the same district as Athens, I gave Mr. Quesenbery the phone numbers of Bob Griffiths and Steve Price, and I asked that he contact them regarding a district caucus.

After questions, we broke up; one black woman had asked for some

McCarthy literature which she said she could pass out in a shopping center near her home; so I drove to the storefront, picked up a mixed box of our dwindling reserves and drove it over to her house late that afternoon. That night I addressed thirty envelopes and mailed my Forum literature out to our afternoon's "guests," complete with a little exhortation about trying to bring a carload of supporters, each, to Macon the following Saturday.

5

THE DELEGATION OF LOYAL
NATIONAL DEMOCRATS

The ten days from Monday, August 5th, to Thursday, August 15th,
were easily the most exciting, most intense, and most nerve
racking ten days of the Georgia McCarthy campaign. We were
involved in two big gambles: a convention in which we might win some
McCarthy delegates on a challenge delegation from Georgia, and an
entertainment spectacular which we did not have the funds to back if it
flopped. Those were ten days of peak activity in the headquarters, when
the rising tension sometimes showed itself in our meetings.

Early that week Sam Brown arrived again for consultations with
Charlie, Dave, and the rest of us. We outlined our Macon convention
strategy, and Sam said that there might be some money available for ads,
buses, and gas so that our leaders in the districts could both rouse local
interest and then get people to Macon; but first we had to organize. Sam's
main concern, however, was with the challenge brief. There was apparently
a team of young lawyers in Chicago working under Mr. Joe Rauh, who had
been the lawyer for the 1964 Mississippi challenge delegation and who
therefore had the most experience in these matters.

This team of lawyers were broadly following Mr. Rauh's guidelines in
preparing 1968 challenge briefs for other states, especially those concerned
with a pro-McCarthy challenge. Sam wanted us to tap their experience and
understanding with our challenge brief from Georgia. He did not want us

to rely solely on Rev. Morris, who was conscientiously doing a good job but who had had no previous experience with the highly specialized subject of challenge briefs. Sam was not sure that Rev. Morris' attempt would be particularly inadequate; he just wanted us to have all the help possible.

So during that week he had lunch with Rev. Morris and Mr. Kehrer, and though they would not agree to changes in the brief from outside - this was a "Georgia matter" - they did promise to delay its submission until after the delegation had been elected and its own members had decided on a course of action, since the brief was to be submitted by the delegation itself and not by the Forum.

That Sunday and Monday I had word from Vernon Shell at the COC that their plans were going ahead for the Southern Regional COC, scheduled for the next Sunday in Atlanta's Henry Grady Hotel. He read me a list of potential participants, with phone numbers, in four surrounding states; and he requested, if I had time, that I call them. I explained that I probably would be already loaded that week with responsibilities in Atlanta but that I would try my best.

At our Georgians For McCarthy meeting that Monday night we still were not sure if M-Day was going to take place. We were starting to get a little uneasy about all the bills coming in, so we decided to use the Dinkler Plaza. We could not sell as many tickets for its smaller room, but the financial risk of a total flop was not as great. Ken Martin was commissioned to relay our decision to New York, along with an urgent plea for the names of the stars involved, as we desperately needed to print advertisements and send them out.

At that same meeting I announced the plans for the Southern Regional COC. Most of the co-chairmen were neutral on the matter, but Mrs. Grayboff was upset because she had been planning a "Citizens' Day" at the Fulton County Courthouse for that same date, hoping to invite many of the same people as participants. She was planning to hold an all-day hearing on the Democratic Platform, urging citizens to come and to express their views on what should be included. Armed with this local information, she would then ask for a personal appearance before the Platform Committee, also meeting the week before the convention; or she would at least forward the recommendations to the committee chairman.

I agreed with her that hers was also a worthwhile activity and that to hold a challenge convention, the COC, and Citizens Day all in the same weekend could only hurt all three. But as there were only two more weekends left before the committee hearings began, I did not think that we had much choice. I did promise, however, to relay her concern to COC in Chicago.

It was during this week that our headquarters really came into its own as the nerve center for a statewide organization, made possible only because of the long, self-sacrificing, hour-to-hour work of so many people. As far as planning for the Macon convention was concerned, the state was quickly carved up and responsibilities assigned. We hoped that most of Atlanta could be handled by a mailing.

Mrs. Paschall, Les, John, and Penny Micklebury, a young reporter from *The Atlanta World*, who had joined us about the time of Senator McCarthy's visit, set to work to organize in Atlanta's black community. We also felt that, between the McCarthy leaders in Athens and Augusta, their district needed little attention, just coordination. Everywhere else we assigned responsibilities for organization, to be carried out mainly by telephone. I was assigned to two of the geographically larger districts in the southern part of the state.

The people in the storefront and in the headquarters set to work compiling lists of known and not-so-known supporters in every city in the state, culling their information from our McCarthy petitions, guest lists, and even old list of supporters for Ellis Arnall, who had run against Lester Maddox in the 1966 primary. Each name had to be checked for address, city of residence, and district, hopefully also turning up some indication of the person's known political leanings. In many instances our city-by-city process wound up being little more than asking "Who do you know who is liberal?" Someone compiled a list of all the colleges and university campuses, district by district, hoping to find the right kind of student leaders. Whenever one of us got a "lead" in someone else's district, we immediately passed it on, and daily visits to the headquarters usually produced new names to be added to my lists.

The headquarters appeared, on the surface, to be in constant chaos; but slowly a pattern of organization was developing. Whenever anyone located a particularly interested person in a new locality, we immediately mailed him, by special delivery, as much Forum and McCarthy literature as we could spare, plus the names and phone numbers of any other known "leaders" in his or her district. Each of us was individually responsible for doing this mailing, and we had reports on our progress and on our disappointments throughout the state. Meanwhile we got out a separate mailing about the Forum's convention – plus another appeal for funds – to our "regular' mailing list, consisting mainly of people in the Atlanta area (but that could include four or five different Congressional Districts).

We had originally hoped to use the Wide Area Telephone Service (WATS) line at my bank, after hours, for our long-distance calls. For two nights Nancy Schwartz and I stayed in the Credit Department until 9:30, while the cleaners went about their work, phoning our leads. But that system proved impractical, both because there were too many calls that had to be made which could not wait until night and because I was a little nervous about what my boss might say if he found out. By Wednesday a little money had arrived from Washington, so most of the calls were done from the headquarters, though I personally continued to "work late" and to use our WATS line for my own calls.

Those first two days I also tried doing some calls for the Southern Regional COC. I called Rev. Bill Coats, who had been at the original COC, in Chapel Hill. He didn't sound too enthusiastic. As far as he was concerned North Carolina was locked up for Humphrey, and he did not believe that Dr. Reginald Hawkins' challenge delegation would do very well, since it was only challenging the percentages of black people on the official delegation, not the selection process itself.

I also called Mr. John Cashin, chairman of the National Democratic Party of Alabama: he was more enthusiastic about the COC, but pointed out that the MFDP was having its convention in Mississippi on the same day, so we could count them out. After trying to call other names which I had been given and finding no answers, I finally decided that our Georgia work was of greater priority at the moment, if we were going to have any challenge delegation at all, so I went back to my Georgia calls altogether. Later I advised Vernon Shell and he assured me that they could handle all of the calls from Chicago.

Typically I would have on my two district lists the names of twenty possible leads in each district, with only half of the names including phone numbers. At first I spent long hours with the out of town operators trying to locate the phone numbers; but as this was wasting valuable time, the volunteers in the headquarters started doing as much of this checking as possible for all of us during the day, since the information service was free.

I called on Monday and Tuesday nights to lay the ground work (trying to get our known supporters first, where possible).

Though I was sitting in the bank's Credit Department, I would start off "Hello: I'm calling from McCarthy Headquarters in Atlanta; I don't know if you already know about the open state convention being held by the Georgia Democratic Party Forum this Saturday in Macon to elect a challenge delegation for the Democratic National Convention, so I'm calling just to find out if you plan to be there and if you need any help getting to Macon."

Responses, of course, were varied. Some people were already very much planning to attend and they seemed to be probable candidates for our District Coordinators. Others were hearing about the convention for the first time; to them I mailed our literature, special delivery. Still others were already Forum members, and also Humphrey supporters, and they were a little bewildered by the call.

Several of the people whom we contacted throughout the state were ministers with backgrounds in civil rights work and they were not committed to either Humphrey or McCarthy. This did not matter to us – we sincerely wanted the largest representation possible from throughout the state – and we made the same vague offer to them of financial help for renting buses or for running local newspaper ads that we made to anyone else who seemed at all enthusiastic. We still were not sure if we would receive any substantive help from Washington, but we promised to call back later in the week.

Even with all of this sudden activity, however, our organization was not too complete nor well-functioning. There were huge holes in our state map, especially to the north of Atlanta. Even in the districts where we were "organized," that usually just meant that we were in telephone contact with three to five people whom we had never met and about whom we knew little more than that they "planned to attend." Much of our initial exuberance wore off as, towards the end of the week, plans started to fall through, local people were having problems raising support, and our projected attendance started to be scaled down. Even by Thursday and Friday we had no real idea of how many people would actually turn up, nor in many cases whom they would support.

We also had no idea how many delegates the Forum was going to muster; we just assumed, as we felt it was natural to do so before a state convention, that Mr. Kehrer and others were doing the same kind of organizing among Humphrey supporters, with, we thought, much easier access to large numbers of people through years of contacts throughout the state.

By Wednesday we received the go ahead from Washington to pay for a few buses, some local radio and newspaper ads throughout the state, and a half hour Friday Atlanta television show, consisting mainly of tapes already used elsewhere around the country with an appeal at the end for supporters to come to the Macon convention the next day and to use that unique opportunity to show their presidential preference. We got this budget go ahead in a rather interesting way, though Sam Brown said that it was standard operating procedure among the field men. Sam would make a commitment to spend the needed money, personally, then call Washington and claim that he would be thrown in jail if headquarters did not back him. He said that this was the only way the man with the money would know that he was really serious about something. And the system did seem to work.

About that time Nelson Schneider arrived to handle the radio and TV tapes; Nelson was a duly elected McCarthy delegate from New York who had experience with this kind of media communication and who had come along to give us a hand. We felt, in doing our advertising, that we were not only furthering our own cause, but that we were also enhancing the credibility of the entire convention, however it turned out. We hoped that our advertising would ensure a truly open convention which had received mass attention, not limited simply to the people on the Forum's mailing list and their friends.

By Wednesday we realized that our original plan to have organizational district meetings prior to Saturday was not going to be feasible; these meetings would have to be held in Macon on Saturday, sometime just before the convention itself. This situation was true except in DeKalb County, adjacent to Atlanta, where we did have a meeting early Wednesday evening in a church near Emory University, planned by a student organizer, Steve Mills.

Mr. Walsh, who lived nearby, had agreed to stand as a district delegate, if he was wanted, and he was there at the meeting. The attendance was discouraging; only about twenty people showed up. But it was the same night that Richard Nixon was being nominated in Miami, and we hoped that the coverage was keeping people away. We outlined all of our plans to date and elected a tentative district coordinator and tentative nominees, including Mr. Walsh; but we hoped that this group would be a minority of those attending the convention, and we recognized that another meeting would have to be held in Macon when all were present. It was not exactly encouraging.

There was one interesting sideline to this meeting, though, for me. Someone at Headquarters had told the press about our meeting, and a local television team was on hand to film our near-empty room. They also wanted an interview with "someone who was organizing" the McCarthy forces for the Macon convention; of the people there I seemed to qualify, so I went out on the church lawn and in the fading sunlight a reporter asked me several questions, including how many McCarthy supporters we hoped to have in Macon and whether we would also take Humphrey supporters. I had to skirt the first question and answer that I didn't know, since I really did not know, and since I felt that either too high or too low an estimate could be disastrous. To the second question I answered an honest "yes."

Later that week I saw an old family friend, to whom I had remarked earlier in the summer that it did not seem to me that politicians ever really answered questions. Our friend had seen my interview on a news broadcast, and now he congratulated me for being a "real politician" and for learning how to "not answer questions as well as anyone." He was half-joking, but I was somewhat upset, because I didn't *feel* like I thought a "politician" should feel. I guess I was coming to realize that maybe all those "politicians" are just as honest as I had been, and that possibly in an area that is as much an "art of the possible" as politics is, there just are not easy, cut and dried answers all of the time.

On Wednesday we also got bad news from New York: they insisted that we hold M-Day in the Regency Hyatt House Hotel. As we had to make a quick decision if we were going to have any tickets available for advance sales, we decided to go ahead with the larger location. We probably should have pressed harder for the Dinkler Plaza, but we had so much else to do that we just gave in; we could not cancel the whole show, as it was our last hope to balance our budget.

The Regency Hyatt House wanted, at minimum, a $500 deposit by that Friday for the ballroom's use the next Thursday. As we did not have that much money, we had to find someone to stake us on the faith that we would at least take in $500. By Thursday one of the girls had persuaded a well-known Atlanta architect to put up the $500, provided we would write him a postdated check for $500 for the Friday after M-Day. Ken Martin, the other fiscal agent, would not do it; he already thought that he could see the financial handwriting on the wall, and he was starting to talk about resigning.

Ken had been doing an extremely good job with a very difficult problem; our finances. Thanks to him we had accurate records of all our bills and our receipts. But I think he finally felt that we might not be able to pull it out in the end, and I did not blame him for worrying, since he was an older businessman and well known in Atlanta. I, however, had faith that we could bring in $500, and I saw no alternative way of raising the money. On Friday I went ahead and signed the postdated check. Early the next week Ken resigned as fiscal agent, though he stayed on to help; I asked him to give health reasons to the bank so as not to raise undue alarm. This whole maneuver was certainly putting us out on a limb; but I knew that, in a real bind, Taylor and I could put up $500 between us. It was a gamble, but we knew we could cover, and we both felt that M-Day was our last financial chance.

By Thursday night we had phoned back all of our district coordinators and made all of the pre-Macon plans that we could. We asked that either they, or a representative, be in Macon on Friday night, when we would take final reports and make our last plans, depending on our expected relative strength, the layout of the hotel, and any last-minute changes by the Forum. There was not much else we could do.

I drove home that Friday night immediately after work. A friend of mine from Chapel Hill and Miami, Buck Goldstein, was in town for the weekend, and I had invited him to come down to Macon with us. Taylor arrived about six; the three of us, all of our lists, and a couple of small suitcases then headed south, stopping at Globe Ticket Co. off of the south expressway just long enough to pick up our M-Day tickets, which we hoped to sell and distribute at the convention.

We arrived in Macon at about 7:30, and after a quick hamburger we drove to the Dempsey Hotel in the center of the city. The Dempsey is another of those almost dateless hotels, neither particularly old nor particularly new. The lobby occupies most of the ground floor. Since I had taken a quick look around the Saturday before, the geography of the hotel was familiar to me. Diagonally opposite the counter in one corner of the lobby were the elevators and the stairs, the latter going down one flight to the bar and up to the mezzanine level assembly hall where the convention was to take place.

After ascending these stairs to the mezzanine level, one finds a small lobby, with a passageway leading to the convention hall straight ahead and two fairly large meeting rooms on the left. The convention hall itself seats 800 to 1,000 people, with a small addition in the back to handle any overflow. The ceiling is fairly low, and the walls are a sort of institutional pale yellow. As one enters through the main door in the back corner of the room, the speaker's platform is forward and on the left, and a small corridor on the right leads to a set of tiny conference rooms off to the side.

Taylor, Buck and I entered the main lobby to find Cathy, who had found a list of names on Taylor's desk in their apartment and who, thinking that Taylor had forgotten something important, had borrowed a friend's car and driven frantically all the way to Macon. The names were, in fact, not important. She was a little crestfallen, but Taylor soon had her cheered up; the worst part was that she had brought no suitcase with her and would have to drive home that same night.

Though neither Charlie, Sam, nor Dave had yet arrived from Atlanta, they had phoned ahead and reserved, besides personal rooms, two large rooms to use as our offices. We asked for the keys to these and went to have a look, accompanied by three students from Americus who had been waiting in the lobby: our first McCarthy District Representatives.

The upstairs floors of the Dempsey are shaped like a squared-off horseshoe; our largest "McCarthy room" was at one of the corners on the third floor. The room was quite spacious with two double beds and a large conference area: this would be our headquarters. The smaller room, located in the other corner down the hall, already had the beds removed and two long tables set up with electric typewriters on top. We hoped to get a mimeograph machine the next morning, and one of my first duties was to make a call to ensure that it would arrive on time. "We" were expecting the machine; but it, the typewriters and these rooms were not being paid for by Georgians For McCarthy: they were part of Charlie's budget from Washington. Compared to other state campaign expenses, it must have seemed a fairly good investment for the small amount of money involved.

The many events of that Friday evening were complex, exciting, and, in a few personal cases, saddening. By 8:30, on schedule, more of our district coordinators were arriving, checking in, and finding their way to our headquarters. Taylor was starting to get his M-Day ticket consignments sorted out, while I checked with the manager about the availability of the hotel's several meeting rooms for the next day at noon. Some of our older district coordinators were also members of the Forum, and several went in search of Mr. Kehrer; he was not registered yet at the desk, but someone had seen his wife in the lobby. Everyone else stayed in the headquarters, talking about their experiences in trying to organize for the convention.

About nine o'clock Charlie arrived, accompanied by Joe Rauh, Frank McDonald, and Curt Gans. I had understood that Mr. Rauh would attend the convention as the McCarthy representative, but I had not known that he would arrive that night nor that he would be accompanied by Frank McDonald or Curt Gans, the thirty-year-old chief of the entire McCarthy field organization. We were, of course, very glad to see them in Macon.

Mr. Rauh, the lawyer for the 1964 Mississippi Freedom Democratic Party, is tall, with gray hair, glasses, and an expression which has to strain to seem unsmiling. He immediately introduced himself around and started listening as we more or less small talked while waiting for everyone to get up to the room. Curt Gans is short, and he looked thin and tired, as if he had been without enough sleep for a very long time. That night Curt almost always looked like he was deep in serious thought; his words came out somewhat slowly, without any emotion, as if he was trying to choose each one precisely. His job must have been almost impossible; and the strain showed, physically, though his mind seemed always at work.

After the week's long work of organization, I was in a mood of constrained expectation, not very given to creative thought or direction. One of the problems with such political activity is that one too often winds up in a mental rut. For one becomes so tied to a particular course of action that alternatives are never imagined. And one is so caught up in details that there never is time to reflect. I was in such a state early that evening, intent upon fulfilling my specific responsibilities as an area coordinator for our minority delegation. Shortly we got down to business, which consisted, at first, of going around our now packed "headquarters" room, letting each person introduce himself and give his own assessment of his week's activity and of our current position. This was not only for the sake of our new visitors, but also so that all of us would more or less understand "where we were at." By the end I personally estimated that we would have about five hundred "McCarthy" delegates there the next day.

At some point in those first few minutes it was mentioned that, contrary to his earlier promises, Rev. Morris had gone ahead that afternoon and sent his just-finished challenge brief into the Credentials Committee office without waiting for a delegation to be selected, or for the merits of the brief to be judged by that delegation. Except for this fact, the significance of which I did not yet fully understand, I felt pretty happy about what we had accomplished that week, and I looked forward to us legitimately winning our 40% of the delegation.

Curt, who had been standing silently by the curtained window while the reporting was going on, now started asking questions. Had we seen a final copy of the convention agenda and the rules for election? Did we want the whole convention to get by without passing a single resolution? If we had the power to unseat him, did we want an avowed Humphrey man in the critical role of convention chairman, able to recognize speakers and to judge votes? If Mr. Kehrer and Rev. Morris had gone back on their word regarding the brief, how did we know that the rules or the agenda had not also been altered to restrict voting eligibility? What was our assessment of the Humphrey strength?

These questions seemed to me, since I was still thinking in terms of Mr. Kehrer's arguments about not alienating Humphrey delegates in Chicago, a little too partisan and too distrustful of Mr Kehrer and Rev. Morris, whom I thought, if nothing else, meant what they said about an open convention and mass participation.

At about this point there was a knock on the door, and in came Mrs. Kehrer and her friend, Mrs. Johnston, neither of whom most of us would have recognized had not some of the older Forum members said, very loudly, "Hello Mrs. Kehrer." There then followed a rather embarrassing silence, as they came in and sat down in the middle of the room, seeming not to know what was going on but interested in participating. Finally one of the older Forum members explained that this was a "McCarthy meeting" and asked if they would please give us another half an hour by ourselves.

This request seemed only fair to me; I assumed that there was probably a similar "Humphrey meeting" going on somewhere else. I was, of course, looking forward to seeing them, Mr. Kehrer and Rev. Morris, later to talk about final plans, as we had agreed to do on the previous Saturday. Though I was sure that they would understand, they looked suddenly very hurt, and as they left they gave us all angry glances and muttered about "not being wanted," and about "what could be the purpose of such secret meetings?"

Alone again, Curt went on with his questions, to which some of us answered that we thought perhaps he was being a little too cautious. Curt then talked for about ten minutes, and in that time my concept of our Macon convention and of our McCarthy delegate goal changed completely. Curt recounted the events of the 1964 Democratic convention, when Lyndon Johnson's forces had been in complete control and when no reforms had been possible.

In 1968, however, the national McCarthy and Kennedy primary victories ensured that there would always be the required eleven signatures for a dissenting minority report from either the Credentials Committee or the Platform Committee. Also, this year there would be the eight state delegations necessary to request that a motion first be debated on the open floor before being voted on.

These McCarthy, Kennedy, and McGovern delegations had, if not a majority, at least a large enough minority to force issues into the open and, thereby, hopefully, to force change. Without these delegations, Humphrey would be in the same total control as Lyndon Johnson had been in 1964. And once again not one of his supporters on the key committees would dare to dissent against the status quo for fear of alienating delegate support which Humphrey needed.

I had always recognized the advantage to the McCarthy campaign of having a pro-McCarthy delegation elected from Georgia, because it would put Mr. Humphrey in the embarrassing position of having to support either that challenge delegation or else the pro-Humphrey delegation chosen by Lester Maddox. But I had accepted Mr. Kehrer's argument that to elect a majority McCarthy delegation would sour our relations with the majority of convention delegates and spoil our chances for success. As Curt spoke, however, I realized an absolutely crucial fact for the first time, a fact which Mr. Kehrer realized neither in Macon nor later in Chicago. The truth which Curt showed us was that, not only for the sake of the McCarthy campaign, but also for the sake of *Georgia's success*, we had to elect a majority McCarthy delegation, if at all possible.

A pro-Humphrey challenge delegation would be a disaster, because it could too easily be persuaded into a political compromise which only patched over the issues but which really changed nothing: i.e., a handful of the "most disloyal" delegates on Maddox's delegation might be unseated, or else a few of the "most loyal" of the challenge delegation might be added. But, with two essentially pro-Humphrey delegations, the challengers would too easily be susceptible to the "let's not rock Humphrey's boat" argument, and nothing would really happen either to change the national convention election rules or the state of Georgia's Democratic Party.

Such a pro-Humphrey delegation would probably never agree to an eleven man minority report, no matter how badly they were dealt with, persuaded that such an open convention debate would upset their own candidate's needed Southern support. A few members of the challenge group claiming to be more "loyal," would, at most, quietly be added to the already chosen Maddox delegation, and that would be the end.

With a majority McCarthy delegation, on the other hand, the delegation would be immune to such partisan persuasion, and complete assistance could be expected from the minority of the members on the Credentials Committee, if a suitable settlement could not be reached which substantially changed the old system. This help would assure a floor fight on national television, which, even if the challengers lost, would do more toward dramatizing Georgia's incredibly undemocratic process than a compromise which was worked out quietly in the background and quickly voted through.

For all of us who had never had any experience with a national political convention, Curt's assessment came as a revelation, but one which was immediately obvious when pointed out. He was saying, in effect, that it was fine to talk about a 60%-40% Humphrey-McCarthy delegate split, if such a delegation had any chance of actually being seated. His point was that such a delegation would never be seated, since partisan pressure could be used to force acceptance of a nearly meaningless token compromise, as was the case with Mississippi in 1964.

The importance of the challenge brief, who controlled its presentation before the Credentials Committee, and on what grounds the brief was based, started to become painfully clear. We all agreed with Curt that, for the sake of our own success, we had to try to elect a majority McCarthy delegation. And Curt's earlier questions about the agenda, the rules, and Mr. Kehrer's role as chairman suddenly became much more relevant, if we were going to try, not just to participate in the convention, but instead to actually *control* its outcome.

For me, at least, the importance of our actions, our decisions, and our timing increased a hundredfold. We were no longer there just for the ride; we were going to try to take over the convention. This was a completely different matter, requiring, quickly, a whole new approach to our role, since our group was then, possibly, the one hope for ultimate success. Suddenly the success of the entire Georgia Challenge seemed to be on our shoulders, and this responsibility required some careful, tactful, unforeseen decisions.

We first decided that I, as the one who had been present at the arrangements meeting the previous Saturday, should try to find Mr. Kehrer and secure a final copy of the convention agenda and the rules. We would then look them over and make sure that all was in order. Meanwhile Mr. Rauh, as the official McCarthy observer, would also try to find Mr. Kehrer to say hello and to talk about, in the light of Mr. Rauh's experience, any changes in the convention agenda or the challenge brief which might ultimately help our case in Chicago. The rest of our state coordinators would talk about the best ways to handle their district meetings and our internal communication, while Taylor was to give our consignments of M-Day tickets to anyone who thought he could sell a few.

After about an hour of checking around the hotel for Mr. Kehrer, Mr. Rauh and I wound up in the lobby talking briefly with Curt and Frank. Down the stairs from the mezzanine walked Mr. Kehrer, Mr. Goldman, Mr. Johnston and their wives. We immediately walked over, and I made an attempt to introduce Mr. Kehrer to our guests. It was obvious, however, that Mr. Kehrer was quite emotionally upset. After introducing Mr. Rauh I tried to go on to Curt and to Frank, standing unobtrusively in the background. But Mr. Kehrer interrupted with "Yes, I know who *they* are and why *they're* here," in a tone which sounded both angry and hurt.

Mr. Rauh then tried to ask if they could get together some time that night to discuss the convention and the brief; but Mr. Kehrer, after quickly saying "No, we don't need to discuss anything," then produced from his satchel a small ad from a local paper which we had run, proclaiming the convention and the one opportunity for Georgians to vote for Gene McCarthy. He handled it as if it were a piece of fingerprinted evidence in a criminal case, waving it at me and saying, "What do you mean by these? Are you trying t ruin this convention?"

I was terribly embarrassed by Mr. Kehrer's manner and the glowers that we were getting from all of those with him. From then on he just gazed straight ahead, shaking his head, not listening to Mr. Rauh's requests for a rational discussion, and kept saying, angrily, almost to no one "No, we don't need to talk. The whole convention is probably ruined. We said no partisan politics. You may have ruined two long years of work." No amount of rational, good-natured pleading would change his mind; and as our voices got louder and the whole lobby started to be interested, we decided that there was no point in going on. The confrontation broke up; we went back to our headquarters. I had been completely unprepared for Mr. Kehrer's attitude: he was now "blaming" us for taking the Forum at its word and simply organizing as many delegates as we could to come to Georgia's first and only open state convention. What else were we supposed to do?

Back upstairs we unhappily reported our meeting with Mr. Kehrer, and Curt asked the obvious question, "Do you want a man as emotionally upset as Mr. Kehrer now is to be chairman of something as important as this convention?" Since we still did not even know how the final agenda looked, most of us were a little afraid of what might be in store the next day, with a possibly too-flexible procedure and with Mr. Kehrer doing all the interpreting of the vague portions. I felt perhaps that we had not really given him a proper chance on the rules, so I went upstairs to Mr. Kehrer's room, where I found him with the same group of people.

As quickly and as diplomatically as possible I asked if there was any business left over from the previous Saturday which still needed discussing and if I could see a final copy of the rules and agenda. Mr. Kehrer repeated that there was nothing which we needed to talk about and that he would not give out any copies of the rules and agenda to anyone until ten o'clock the next morning, one hour before the convention was to start. As he seemed adamant, I said all right and returned downstairs.

We then began to make contingency plans for the possible need to change chairmen. We all realized the risk involved – that it might blow the whole convention apart within the first ten minutes, leading to bitter debate, accusations, and lost time in full view of the press. We still were not sure of our action, but we had to prepare. Meanwhile, however, some of the older members of the Forum went upstairs to try to smooth things over, and at about eleven-thirty we got word that Mr. Kehrer and friends were willing to talk to Mr. Rauh. Several people pointed out that "someone from Georgia' ought also to be there, and since Mr. Rauh also wanted Curt along, he asked the two of us to accompany him upstairs.

After Mr. Kehrer agreed to see the three of us (there was no problem with me, but Curt's inclusion took a little persuading), we all sat down in a circle in Mr. Kehrer's room. I was sitting in a straight back chair by the door, with Curt and Mr. Rauh similarly seated to my right. Mr. Kehrer was in a chair further on the right; sitting on the bed to his right was Mr. Johnston, then around the room were their wives, and, on my left, Mr. Goldman.

Mr. Kehrer seemed to have regained most of his composure, and he apologized to Mr. Rauh, saying that he had long been one of Mr. Rauh's greatest admirers for the work which Mr. Rauh had done with the civil rights movement. But though he seemed emotionally more in control, he still refused to let us see the final combined copy of the rules and the agenda; and, he wanted to know, what did we need them for anyway? Mr. Rauh, who really did a remarkable job of remaining good-natured, said that there probably would be no differences of opinion on the agenda, and that he certainly did not want to dictate any changes, but that in such matters it was usual to give everyone an equal opportunity to contribute. Curt, who suffered several personal barbs during the meeting, was exerting even more self-control, slowly choosing each word in a rather labored manner. He agreed with Mr. Rauh and pointed out that if there were any differences of opinion it would be better to start talking about them then, rather than letting them first boil up on the convention floor.

Mr. Kehrer answered that I had been at the previous planning session, that I knew what had been decided, and that there had been no changes. He asked what we wanted to change. Mr. Rauh pointed out that until he had seen a final draft, he could not possibly say what might need altering but that probably there would be nothing. We went on like this, in absolutely fruitless discussion, for over an hour, interspersed by repeated thoughtless emotional attacks on Curt and his field men who had "come in from outside" and who were trying to "ruin our convention."

Though I tried to argue that it was impossible to have a political convention without some sort of partisan loyalties, Mr. Kehrer kept insisting that the purpose of the convention was simply to elect a challenge delegation, and not to "play partisan politics." We would hear that statement many times later, and eventually it struck me that whenever Mr. Kehrer said "no partisan politics," what he really meant was "we need to be pro-Humphrey"; for it was obvious that he was being just as "partisan," if not more so, than we were. I'm not sure whether he used this semantic smokescreen intentionally or not; perhaps he actually believed that being pro-Humphrey was the same as being non-partisan. At any rate, for the next two weeks, we would be charged with playing "partisan politics," apparently meaning that he and his friends were not.

In this meeting it also began to dawn on me that perhaps there were not the long convoys of union workers and the tight Forum state organization which we had assumed. Maybe, just maybe, that had all been a myth; perhaps we really were to dominate several of the districts: why else would Mr. Kehrer be reacting the way he was?

In the end we accomplished nothing that night. Mr. Kehrer pointed to a box in the corner, said that the finished agendas were inside and that he would give no "one group" an "advantage"; everyone would get them at ten o'clock the next morning. We didn't even bother to point out that 'one group" already had them. We finally bid them goodnight: everyone tried to be diplomatic, and we left with a "may the best man win" attitude all around.

By the time we returned downstairs, several people had gone to bed. We did the only thing we could and planned to hold a meeting at 10 o'clock the next morning to spend our final hour reviewing the agenda and deciding on what to do about the chairmanship. Mr. Rauh, Curt, and Frank were very tired and headed for the sack. I heard that Rev. Morris had arrived while we were upstairs, so Sam Brown, Taylor and I went up to his room to welcome him to Macon and to find out where he stood in this situation.

Since it was late, we knocked on Rev. Morris' door quietly; he quickly answered and led us into the large suite which he had reserved a week before. His wife was already asleep in another room, but he was glad to see us and had us sit down in his huge "sitting room," decorated rustically with heavy wooden beams and thick furniture. On the walls were replicas of nineteenth century newspapers and bullfight posters. He offered us drinks, and then we sat down to talk.

Rev. Morris was always the good-natured optimist, which at times later on led him to believe almost innocently that things would all somehow "work out for the best" without much work on our own part; but which that night was a welcome change from the views expressed during the last three hours.

After an inquiry by us, Rev. Morris eagerly showed us a copy of the challenge brief which he had just finished and mailed off that afternoon. He said that he had gone ahead and mailed it because to have waited any longer might have caused it to arrive too late. I had never seen such a document before and I wanted to take a good look. The cover page stated that the brief was being submitted by the Georgia Democratic Party Forum on behalf of the Georgia Delegation of Loyal National Democrats, and it was "respectfully submitted" by E. T. Kehrer and Rev. John Morris.

The document itself consisted largely of copies of newspaper articles, some going back several years, documenting State Chairman James Gray's leadership in "Democrats for Goldwater" and also Governor Maddox's sentiments for George Wallace. There was then some documentation on other members of the Maddox-selected delegation, allegedly showing their activities in prior Wallace and Goldwater campaign activities. On the whole I thought that Rev. Morris had done a remarkably good job of presentation and documentation.

While we passed the brief around we talked about everything from Sam's work in New Hampshire to Rev. Morris' position regarding the Macon convention. On the latter Rev. Morris was prepared to let either of the national candidates win a majority of the delegates, as long as they were loyal national Democrats and willing to serve the interests of Georgia, first, at the Democratic National Convention. Rev. Morris' concept of the purposes of an open state convention seemed refreshingly similar to our own.

As we later said good night at about 3:30, Rev. Morris was just starting to prepare the Forum's signs and posters for the next day; and while we walked back to our rooms we remarked that, if it finally did become necessary to challenge the chairman, Rev. Morris would make a good choice as a genuinely neutral replacement. Taylor and I found Buck already asleep in our room; we racked at about four, and I was in one of those expectant moods which almost made sleep impossible. But I knew that we would have to be up early the next morning and that we had a lot to do, so I tried to relax.

————

After what seemed like ten minutes, the alarm clock went off at eight. Finally, quickly, after five weeks of planning and a single week of organizing, the day of the first open Democratic convention in Georgia had arrived. Taylor, Buck and I roused out of bed, shaved, dressed, picked up our by-then familiar pads of paper and lists of names, and headed off to make sure that everybody else was also up.

Immediately following breakfast it was my job to see the hotel manager and to book every spare meeting room in the hotel from twelve until one, when we planned to hold our "McCarthy caucuses." Though there were not ten such rooms available, we thought that some of the less-represented districts would be able to double up. That taken care of, I went up to our "printing room," where Pat Madsen and Jo Ann Thomas, having just arrived, were trying to type mimeograph stencils for a "McCarthy Delegate Instruction Sheet." This was to include a list of our different district caucus rooms, the tentative chairman of each meeting, and a few points about trying to ensure an evenly balanced district delegation. Though the mimeograph machine had yet to arrive, we portioned out the caucus rooms by districts, and I left the final typing and running off in their experienced hands.

Next, several of us went to the mezzanine lobby where Rev. Morris (who I don't think had been to sleep), his wife, and Mr. Johnston were busily putting up the Forum's signs. I offered to give them a hand, which they accepted, and soon the entrance way was adorned with a home-made sign of large hanging letters, proclaiming the Convention of Loyal National Democrats. Inside the convention hall itself, a similar, larger banner was hung behind the speaker's platform.

As we were setting up the sign-in table, I saw Mr. Kehrer approaching with two more boxes of paraphernalia. Since it was only 9:30 I didn't ask him about the agenda, but he immediately struck me as a changed man. Well fitted out, he seemed happy, almost jovial, as if the events of the night before had never occurred. I said hello, and he asked me if I would like to be the one to move acceptance of the rules as the first order of business when the convention started: here was a seemingly new security! I agreed, of course, and he said that he would recognize me first off, once he was elected chairman.

The ten o'clock McCarthy meeting had been called for our room, to avoid any unnecessary intrusions by enthusiastic supporters during our last hour of decisions. I made a quick trip up to the room, where many new and old faces were already assembling: Taylor, Curt, Frank, Dave, Charlie, Mr. Rauh, Dr. Finn from Carrollton, Dr. Quesenbery from Augusta, Phinizy Calhoun, McCarthy chairman from Athens, Dr. and Mrs. Ross Clark from Savannah, Mr. Medway from Americus, Dr. Albert Bond from Macon, plus several organizers for each of the districts.

With everyone now assembled we went over the final plans for our noon district caucuses and read out the room assignments. It was up to each district "team" to make sure that all the McCarthy supporters from their district knew about their caucus and the proper room. We repeated the plans that each district should quickly elect a "McCarthy chairman," whom they would later, as the first order in the larger official district assembly, attempt to elect as District Chairman. They were also to decide among themselves a balanced slate of "McCarthy delegates," and we reviewed the need for constant communication with our central table, where a running count of the delegates would be kept and quick decisions made if it appeared that the delegation was becoming too lopsided, one way or the other. This central table would be set up in the lobby and manned by Curt and Sam, since they could not participate in the convention itself.

Just before ten I went back downstairs to ask Mr Kehrer for copies of the agenda and rules. In an almost nonchalant manner, he said "Oh, yes," walked over to a large box by the sign-in table, and pulled out a handful. "How many do you want?" he asked, and I took about twenty. In the mezzanine lobby itself there were huge Humphrey posters going up, a Humphrey literature table out, and what seemed to be like an overwhelming number of new arrivals, all sporting HHH buttons. A quick check downstairs showed that Jim Sundberg had not yet arrived from Atlanta with our McCarthy paraphernalia.

Back upstairs our room was now absolutely packed; George Walsh had arrived, and more people knocked on the door as we talked. Quickly we passed around our too-few copies of the agenda, and we took five minutes out for everyone to read and to study it. The document was, to my relief, little changed from the notes which I had taken. It combined an agenda with the rules regarding nominations and election, both for the district meetings and for the larger convention proper. There was, as we had agreed the Saturday before, no allowance for partisan speeches nor for resolutions.

Dave Mixner spotted only one procedural problem which he thought needed to be tightened up. In the clause regarding the presentation to the reassembled convention of the district, results by the District Chairmen, the procedure stated that anyone could challenge what had happened during any district's meeting. As this might lead to endless challenges by a losing side, Dave suggested that we ask for this section to read that such a challenge must be made only by someone who had actually been at that district's meeting. This suggestion seemed fair enough, and I noted it as a possible amendment.

Nothing else in the agenda itself seemed to need alteration; but the question of speeches, resolutions, and a challenge to the chairman had yet to be settled. The first two were decided negatively almost immediately largely because of the time they would have involved at the convention. Curt, however, still pressed for a new chairman, hopefully Rev. Morris. I think that most of us from Georgia opposed this move. I pointed out that Mr. Kehrer seemed much more in control of himself that morning and not as likely to do anything irrational. Someone else said that the agenda and rules were really quite tightly arranged, with little room for interpretation or alteration.

All of us felt that, since we still could not know our own relative strength, an overt move to change the chairman which we might easily lose, would create unneeded hostility before the convention even really started. Furthermore, many of the older McCarthy members of the Forum would not know about the events of the night before and might take such a move as just an unprovoked vindictive assault against Mr. Kehrer, an old friend.

As eleven o'clock was drawing close and we still had all of our district organizing yet to do, we prevailed upon Curt to risk letting Mr. Kehrer stay as chairman for the sake of a united delegation once the convention was over. By quarter to eleven we had carried the day; we then quickly emptied the room, and our district coordinators went to find out if their people had arrived as scheduled.

When we arrived downstairs, the mezzanine lobby was filled with people and activity, and I remember being depressed by the seemingly countless number of new people with Humphrey pins, hats, and buttons. Finally Jim had arrived with our McCarthy "stuff," and several girls were giving out McCarthy buttons to whomever asked. The convention hall itself was three fourths full. Since we were sitting in no official groupings, and since so many people were "button-less," it was still impossible to tell who was in the majority, but Humphrey buttons seemed to be sprouting everywhere.

Our district coordinators were doing a good job of passing the word among their people about their caucus at noon. In the hubbub of the lobby, a couple of us had a little trouble restraining John Tillman, who had just arrived from taping up large posters showing Vice-President Humphrey with his arm around Lester Maddox, taken during Humphrey's visit to Atlanta the spring before. We thought that this was playing a little dirty and finally persuaded John to take the posters down. Just before eleven our buses from Atlanta, organized by Mrs. Paschall, finally arrived.

At about this same time Julian Bond and John Lewis, formerly with SNCC but then director of the Southern Regional Council, arrived by car. Julian went into immediate consultation with Curt, Frank, and several of us about taking the role as our McCarthy District Chairman for Fulton County, which he quickly agreed to.

A little after eleven the opening gavel sounded; by then the hall was overflowing its thousand seat capacity and spilling back into the smaller room opened in the rear. A small roped off area near the door was marked "visitors," for those under eighteen or those from out of state. To be allowed into the convention area proper, one had to show a pin he received when he signed the loyalty pledge at the check-in table. The press was arranged in the front row on the speaker's right, with several TV movie cameras present. Three microphones were standing in the center aisle to take points from the floor. Everything was ready.

Mr. Douglas, a black Forum member from Macon, began as temporary chairman. Following a per-arranged plan, he asked for nominations for chairman, and several people rose to nominate Mr. Kehrer. Then someone else rose to move that nominations be closed. The vote was unanimous, so Mr. Douglas stepped down and Mr. Kehrer assumed the chair. He gave a brief speech about the history of the Forum, about the Maddox-selected delegation, and then added that he hoped we would accomplish something that day which would change Georgia politics forever. Without further ado, he asked if there was a motion to accept the proposed agenda, of which everyone by then had a copy.

I raised my hand by the rear microphone, and Mr. Kehrer recognized me. I pointed out that before I made such a motion, I thought it would be best if we actually elected a chairman, since in the excitement we had only voted to close the nominations; and I therefore moved that we accept Mr. Kehrer as chairman by acclamation. This move got a unanimous vote, and I hoped that we had thereby helped ease any ill feelings which might still remain. Mr. Kehrer then recognized me again, and I moved that we accept the agenda with the one "friendly amendment" which Dave Mixner had proposed. Mr. Kehrer accepted the amendment as a good one, and the agenda was unanimously accepted as amended. Those hurdles were finally over.

Mr. Kehrer next recognized Mr. Rauh as the official representative from the McCarthy National Headquarters; Mr. Rauh got a very big hand, but we still could not tell our relative strength. Kehrer announced that unfortunately the Humphrey national office had not seen fit to send an observer. We then took up a collection for our as yet unelected delegation, to help with the unknown expenses of challenging at the national convention. We collected about $400 and as Mr. Goldman was put in charge of the money, I asked Jim Sundberg to help him get it to the hotel safe.

There then followed the speech by the Guest of Honor, John Conyers, who recounted his early days in Georgia and his confidence in our success. Just before noon Mr. Kehrer outlined the nomination procedure contained in the agenda. We were to reassemble at one, by districts, for nominations; we then recessed for lunch.

But very few of the McCarthy delegates had lunch that afternoon. Despite the confusion caused in some new people's minds by the fact that there were "two caucuses" in two different places – one "McCarthy," the other "official" - our plans went off almost like clockwork. Hundreds of people, most of whom we had never seen before, got up from their convention hall seats and went straight to the proper meeting room arranged for their McCarthy delegate caucus.

Taylor, Curt and I had a quick look around to make sure that everything was running smoothly; in every instance our coordinator had taken over immediately and most caucuses were in the process of electing their chairman. Taylor and I then returned to our own Fulton County caucus, one of the largest, where Julian was immediately and unanimously elected chairman. Though Julian had been in on none of our planning sessions, he knew what had to be done. Our caucus took place in a rather long room, one wall hung with draperies. A blackboard stood on one of the "wide" sides near the curtained wall. About a hundred of us sat around this blackboard while Julian asked for nominations for delegates to the Democratic National Convention and Taylor wrote the names on the blackboard.

Our district, like all the rest, would eventually nominate four delegates and four alternates; the convention itself would finally elect them. Julian was our first McCarthy nominee, then John Lewis. Soon the list grew to include Al Horn, an Atlanta lawyer, Mrs. A. M. Davis, Dr. Chico Thomas, Penny Micklebury, even Taylor and myself. As we soon had more than eight nominees, all of whom came to the front of the room to introduce themselves, Julian suggested that we simply decide on our first four choices, then see how things went in the larger meeting before proposing any order of nomination for the others, since we would have to judge the overall composition of the delegation. We then voted on all of our nominees, and the four selected as the "top four," in order, were Julian, John Lewis, Mrs. A. M. Davis, and Al Horn.

Our business quickly and happily concluded, Taylor and I went downstairs for a candy bar and Coke lunch while Julian took the results of our caucus to the "central table," now set up in the mezzanine lobby on the side opposite the convention hall entrance. All of the other McCarthy caucuses were similarly as successful, and all the other chairmen reported in on time. Most of us were a little hungry that afternoon, but that hour of organization was a crucial factor in our favor.

A little after one the official district meetings to nominate Georgia's challenge delegation began. Our Fulton County meeting, the Fifth District, was held in the area to the speaker's left in the large assembly hall, while the Fourth District (DeKalb County) met to the speaker's right. There were

150 to 200 people at our meeting, several of whom we recognized as McCarthy supporters who had missed our earlier caucus: we passed the word to them regarding our first four delegate choices.

We quickly got down to business, with Ben Brown, another black representative in the Georgia House and long-time Forum member acting as temporary chairman. He took nominations for District Chairman and both he and Julian were so nominated. The final vote was overwhelmingly for Julian; and we seemed to be in complete control of the Fifth District!

Julian then took nominees for district delegates, and we soon wound up with about twenty, including all of our earlier caucus nominees, plus several "Humphrey" delegates. Since it was a little confusing as to exactly who had been nominated, all the nominees came to the front of the meeting and introduced themselves, adding a little about their qualifications. Then, so that we could more easily adjust for the composition of the delegation as it was elected, Julian proposed that we not take the nominees in order, but instead that we hear motions from the floor regarding who should be voted on first.

We counted the total number of people at the meeting and decided that anyone who received a majority of the vote would be declared elected, while if someone lost once, his name could come up again as the delegation was filled out. Julian was a very patient chairman, explaining the system in detail several times until everyone understood it and there were no more questions. A group of tellers, including Taylor, myself, and several Humphrey supporters, came to the front to help count the votes.

With everyone ready, Julian now took voting motions. His name came up first, and he won a near-unanimous vote, which was duly counted and reported to Mrs. Johnston, who was acting as our secretary. Julian then quickly thanked everyone and recognized another member of the meeting, who motioned for Ben Brown. This motion presented somewhat of a "crisis." Ben was not one of "our" nominees, but he is a well-respected and capable black leader, whom, of all the possible non-McCarthy delegates, we hoped most of all would join the Fulton County delegation. After a quick consultation with Julian, when the vote came, Taylor and I, who were already standing at the front of the room, raised our hands "for"; and though we had not foreseen this particular bit of communication, many of our other delegates, who also wanted to vote for Ben anyway, got the message and voted "yes." Ben won a majority and was elected. Next came John Lewis' name, and he, too, was elected.

This situation then presented another crisis, for Mrs. A. M. Davis was our own next choice; and, sure enough, someone nominated her. The problem was that we had already elected three black delegates, and Mrs. Davis is also black. I walked over to Julian and advised him of our racial imbalance; he then pointed out to the meeting, as the District Chairman was supposed to, that the Hughes' Call to the Convention asked for delegations representative of all racial groups, and we were about to elect an all black one! When the vote came, Julian's warning and the fact that Taylor and I did not vote "yes" was enough for Mrs. Davis to lose. We then elected Al Horn as our last delegate nominee, followed by Mrs. Davis as our first alternate.

We sent someone out with the news of our elections so far, and I looked across to see Mrs. Paschall in charge of the Fourth District meeting. Word came back that all was going well; the elections were all happening so fast that it was going to be difficult to influence the final make up anyway. I suppose that Sam and Curt, realizing how well things were going, just sent out the word for all the districts to try to maintain some political balance.

In our district, Taylor's name came up next and I was really happy for him, since I felt that he would have a great experience if he got to go. To my delight, he was elected as an alternate delegate. We then elected Rev. Austin Ford, a politically neutral white Atlanta minister, and my name came up for the position of last alternate. It had never occurred to me that I might be elected; I felt that there were many other people who were obviously better, more important choices than myself; but, despite that fact, I was elected.

Julian congratulated our district on its patience in using a complex, but necessary, election process, and he promised them that we would represent them well in Chicago. After a great applause we broke up, and shortly most of the other districts also finished their duties. Back out in the lobby, Curt, Sam, and Julian were looking at the results as reported so far. It seemed apparent that we had a slight McCarthy majority of those already elected, but there were five delegate vacancies from the less populated districts; and we hoped to use those to add very important people, like Mr. Kehrer and Rev. Morris, who, in the excitement and the confusion, had not been elected in their own districts!

We also hoped to make a more rounded delegation in the vacant alternate positions, of which there were seven. I'm sure it must have been a bit of a pleasure for men like Curt, Sam and Dave, always in the minority at previous state conventions, to suddenly wind up in the position of trying to ensure that more Humphrey delegates were elected! For the first time I even detected a bit of a smile on Curt's otherwise emotionless face.

As the agenda had outlined, all the elected District Chairmen next met with Mr. Kehrer in one of the small conference rooms next to the large hall, while the convention reassembled. Though this meeting was supposed to last only five minutes, it went on for forty-five, while the people in the hall got more restless over the unexplained delay. Outside the conference room stood Mr. Johnston and Mrs. Kehrer, and no one else was allowed into the meeting. When the door finally opened, Mr. Kehrer walked out in the convention hall. Julian, coming out, said in a low voice, "Mr. Kehrer is going to resign."

After bringing the convention to order, Mr. Kehrer said that he could no longer continue as chairman of the convention for reasons which he felt sure that we would all understand. Everyone instead felt that this was an entirely pointless act, destined only to ruin the convention and its chances of electing a united delegation to represent Georgia at the Democratic National Convention. One of the older Forum members asked for an explanation, but Mr. Kehrer would not give it; he just resigned. Joe Jacobs, who had been appointed parliamentarian, felt no such scruples for diplomatic silence. He too resigned, but he took the opportunity to give a completely out of order sermon about "outside partisan forces" and the "planned sabotage of this convention for the sake of a national presidential candidate," while the press cameras rolled. This diatribe over, we were then left without a chairman at a point half-way through our convention business.

The convention started to flounder: Rev. John Morris was nominated for the chairman but he declined. Then Julian was nominated, but he also declined. Finally, Rev. James Hooten, a McCarthy supporter from Savannah, was asked if he would chair the convention, and he accepted. I had only met Rev. Hooten briefly before; he was not one of our "organizers," but he was an old Forum member and well respected within that organization. Nearly forty, Rev. Hooten, with short brown hair and glasses, is both persevering and determined to do what he thinks is right.

These were the qualities most needed at the time, and Rev. Hooten did an extremely good job of chairing a difficult meeting. George Walsh was elected to be the new parliamentarian, and Taylor took over the post of the secretary, who had also resigned.

While Mr. Kehrer and Mr. Jacobs were out in the lobby holding a press conference and denouncing us all, we got back to the business at hand, after nearly an hour's delay. We then spent two hours receiving the district reports and the nominees from each of the ten districts. All nominees were elected, without change, by the convention as a whole. We then had to fill the delegate vacancies; Mr. Kehrer was the first nominee. By this time he and his closest friends had assembled in the corner on the speaker's left, watching the proceedings. He declined the nomination. He was renominated, but he declined again. Then Rev. Morris was nominated, and he agreed to stand. After another long and tiring hour and a half, we finally completed the election of all the delegates and all 'the alternates', and Rev. Morris was among them. Then Rev. Hooten briefly charged the new delegation to represent well the Democrats of the state of Georgia at the Democratic National Convention. He called an immediate meeting of all delegates and alternates in the largest of the conference rooms; and, at about six o'clock, the convention was adjourned.

Curt and Mr. Rauh had to fly back to Washington immediately; Taylor and I said good-bye to them in the mezzanine lobby, which by now had a well-used look. All of us were disappointed by the actions of Mr. Kehrer and Mr. Jacobs, and we hoped that their resignations would not affect our standing in the state or with the Credentials Committee. Despite this one disappointment, on the whole we were all very happy with the way everyone had carried out their tasks. The day had been a success because of hundreds of individuals, and we especially needed to thank our district coordinators for the fine work they had done on little notice. By the time Curt said good-bye he was actually smiling, and we all parted with "See you in Chicago."

Next came the final meeting of the day, and the first meeting for the newly elected Georgia Delegation of Loyal National Democrats. The eighty of us sat around in a large semicircle in the same room where earlier our Fulton County McCarthy caucus had taken place. Many familiar faces had been elected as either delegates or alternates, including Mrs. Paschall, George Walsh, and Dr. Finn, but by far the majority of people were new to us and probably new to politics. We first elected Julian and Rev. Hooten as our delegation's co-chairmen. Next we decided that, since we were strung out all over the state and not in easy communication with each other, only our co-chairmen should speak to the press on the official business of the delegation.

Ben Brown was elected vice-chairman; Rev. Morris turned down a similar nomination. Mrs. Paschall agreed to be secretary. While we talked, we passed a list around getting everyone's name, address and phone number. We had no idea how or when we would go to Chicago, but everyone was asked to indicate on the sheet whether he could partly or completely pay his own way; only a few could. Al Horn and Mr. Walsh were then elected our legal counsel.

As most of the delegates had to leave shortly, all of the arrangements for the Chicago convention, the hearing before the Credentials Committee, and the delegation's physical accommodation were left in the hands of the "officers," with all of us volunteering to help if asked. Mrs. Paschall agreed to type up the lists, and the officers said that they would communicate with everyone as soon as definite plans were made.

The meeting was adjourned, but a rather short man with glasses who had been sitting quietly near the front asked urgently that Julian, Rev. Hooten, Al Horn and Mr. Walsh please stay for another fifteen minutes and have a word with him. As I had been talking with him before the meeting, I also stayed behind, and we were soon joined by Taylor. He introduced himself as Al Harris; he was a young lawyer from Chicago, one of those working on the team with Mr. Rauh. He had just flown in that afternoon from Chicago, and he wanted to talk about our challenge brief.

"If you want to win in Chicago before the Credentials Committee, you will not do it with the brief prepared by Rev. Morris. You need a whole new brief," were his first words. We all thought such a task was impossible, since the brief had to be in by Monday. Al Harris, undaunted, went on to say that he had been studying the Georgia case and that a brief based solely on disloyalty would not be enough. This same lawyer team was preparing, in fact, to argue a case against a "loyalty challenge" being brought by Robert Vance of Alabama against all the McCarthy delegates.

Instead, said Mr. Harris, the brief should be based on four points: the undemocratic selection method of Maddox delegation; the under-representation of black Georgians on that delegation; the systematic discouragement and exclusion of black participation in the affairs on the Georgia Democratic Party; and, only lastly, the disloyalty of some members of the Maddox delegation. Furthermore he was prepared to fly back to Chicago that night and to start writing the brief. He would work all day Sunday and would, if necessary, have the briefs flown to their destinations by personal courier, to meet the deadline.

The problem of Rev. Morris' brief having already been submitted came up, and Al suggested that Julian and Rev. Hooten immediately wire a telegram to Governor Hughes, chairman of the Credentials Committee, asking that the brief submitted by the Forum be withdrawn and stating that a new brief, to be the one officially submitted by the Georgia Delegation of Loyal National Democrats, would be in his hands on Monday.

Mr. Harris obviously seemed to know what he was talking about, and Julian and Rev. Hooten agreed, with the approval of Al Horn and George Walsh, to everything that Al Harris had suggested, provided that he remained in communication with Al Horn, who would also be given a chance to inspect the brief, if at all possible, before it was submitted. Al Harris agreed, and pointed out that even if the latter were not possible, the main thing was to swap the briefs: additions or subtractions of detail could be made later as long as the major substantive issues were contained in the original brief. With the problem of the brief decided, we all then headed home for Atlanta.

It was already dark when Taylor, Buck and I got in Taylor's car and drove to a nearby Macon restaurant for a celebration steak and a beer. Quite unexpectedly, both Taylor and I were now alternate delegates on a challenge delegation to the Democratic National Convention! We were obviously happy, not just because of that, but because the whole convention had gone so well and so according to plan. We talked for a while about Mr. Kehrer, who was to be quoted in the Atlanta papers on Monday as saying "The Georgia challenge to the Maddox delegation is now a lost cause."

We decided that it was perhaps understandable that Mr. Kehrer had not appreciated Curt Gans' arguments of the night before; he had not been at our meeting. His resignation as "chairman," though, since it threatened to ruin the convention, was a little less understandable, as was his refusal to even help make policy by becoming a delegate. But, thinking back on our overwhelming total majority and our earlier overestimation of the Forum's strength, one fact soon struck us which I'm not sure Mr. Kehrer ever really appreciated. If it had not been for us and for our organizing, there would not even have *been* a Macon convention, unless one could consider a "convention" to be a limited number of Forum members electing each other as the delegation's forty delegates and forty alternates; and we doubted that the press would have seen the meeting in exactly that light.

According to Mr. Kehrer, the challenge was "ruined," and we were to "blame"; but that was not how the three of us felt. We believed that we had elected a delegation representative of all moderate and liberal Democratic elements in Georgia. Although a majority of the delegation was probably pro-McCarthy, we believed that we fairly accurately represented the anti-administration feeling among Georgia's liberals. Moreover, should Curt Gans prove correct, our non-Humphrey orientation might be a great benefit. And we were also glad, then, that men like Julian Bond, Rev. Hooten and, in fact, 90% of the delegation, had *not* actively participated that summer in our state McCarthy organization, for there were thereby included on the delegation new people with new ideas.

The Georgia Democratic Party Forum and Georgians For McCarthy had been the midwives, but the Georgia Delegation of Loyal National Democrats was a new creation, with much broader representation and much greater strength than either of its predecessors. We felt good about the delegation and its chances for success under the leadership of men like Julian Bond, the other officers, and Al Harris. And soon we were on the road toward Atlanta and a long sleep.

6

CHALLENGE COORDINATION AND MCCARTHY DAY

The following day, Sunday, August 11th, was scheduled for the Southern Regional Coalition For An Open Convention. Though the meeting was supposed to start early in the morning, I just could not get up before ten. I remember being exuberant that morning about the way everything had worked out the day before, and I suspected that the COC would prove anticlimactic. But I felt obliged to attend anyway. Since there was a Georgians For McCarthy meeting called for that night, and since Taylor did have a wife, he had said that he could not go to the COC. Rives Chalmers, who had been at the convention the day before, and Buck Goldstein, who was still in town, agreed to go; so we drove down about noon.

The Henry Grady Hotel is seemingly of a little earlier vintage than the Dinkler Plaza Hotel, with a much more spacious lobby. The COC was taking place in a large, tastefully furnished assembly room on the ground floor. As the three of us entered the room at the rear, Al Lowenstein was just starting his speech; there were only about forty people in the audience. An NBC news crew was there, though, filming his every word. I'm sure that, by this point, Al could give such speeches in his sleep; though this Sunday, given the time and the place, he talked more specifically about Chicago and the hope that the Southern Challenge Delegations held out for changing the old political system.

Al was followed by a large black man with a short beard, who seemed to be dressed in fatigues. I was later to learn that he was Hosea Williams, of the SCLC and recently with Resurrection City. Mr. Williams gave a speech not unlike the one Fannie Lou Hamer had given the week before, though he, too, laid more specific emphases on the Democratic National Convention and his hope that the platform would contain measures which black people could believe in and vote for.

While Mr. Williams was speaking, Frank McDonald and Sam Brown walked in and sat down beside us. The official McCarthy organization had always been somewhat skeptical of the COC as a ploy to win support away from McCarthy and for McGovern, and I supposed that Sam and Frank had come along to see what was up.

After Mr. Williams' speech there was a break for lunch, to be followed by workshops upstairs on topics such as "The Platform: War and Peace" and "Pre-convention Strategy." As we were getting up, Rev. Bill Coats from Chapel Hill entered through the rear door; he was glad to see us, but he said that the whole day had been, so far, a total waste and that nothing new had been said or done. I felt badly about having been one of the people to have persuaded him to come, and I guess it was just a bad weekend for such a meeting, with so much else going on.

We went over and said hello to Al, who, typically, had to leave soon to catch a plane. He did, however, spend some time talking with Frank and Sam about the COC and the McGovern campaign. Al said that he saw McGovern as a "halfway house" for former Kennedy delegates who did not particularly like McCarthy but who needed some place to go besides Humphrey if the convention was to be kept open for anyone else, be that someone else, in the end – McCarthy, McGovern, or even Teddy Kennedy. We talked on for another half an hour, but then Al said he was about to miss his plane.

Buck offered Al a ride to the airport in his cousin's car, and shortly the four of us were on our way. We talked for a while about the Macon convention, about Al's latest experiences, about McCarthy's chances (fair), and about the National Student Association, which Al had helped found and in which Buck was then involved. Their NSA convention was the week before the Democratic National Convention, and Buck asked Al if he could come and speak. Al agreed, even though he was, besides all else, trying to run his own campaign for Congress in New York.

When we got to the airport the parking lot was full, so I went inside with Al to make sure that he caught his plane, while Buck and Rives drove around. All was in order and we were saying goodbye when I asked him if he thought that there was anything more we should be doing. With the insight gained from years of political involvement, Al quickly answered, "Yes, I think you ought to go back to the Henry Grady, get together with Hosea Williams, and announce some sort of a committee to coordinate the challenges from the South; that's the kind of leverage we need to keep the convention open. Get on the NBC films with it, if you can." I expressed my complete inadequacy at such an undertaking, but he said to go ahead and give it a try. I finally said I would, and we parted.

Back at the Henry Grady I sought out the "Pre-Convention Strategy" workshop, already in progress. It consisted mainly of students and was led by Ken Guido of the COC staff. They were talking about a huge rally originally planned for the Sunday before the convention in Soldiers Field, Chicago. Mayor Daley had apparently blocked the rally by reserving Soldiers Field during the whole week for the Democratic National Committee, though they had no use for it.

While they discussed whether or not to hold the rally elsewhere, I sat down and drafted a long motion calling for the establishment of a Southern Challenges Coordinating Committee, which would serve as a central coordinating body for the various challenge delegations, "uniting them in their mutual goals for a democratic state election process and fair representation of all minorities within each state."

My resolution stated that the Southern Challenges Coordinating Committee would not require nor impose on the various delegations any unanimity on political preferences; all of the delegations would remain completely autonomous in all of their own affairs. The SCCC's purpose would be to serve as a larger platform both for expressing the delegations' common goals and for soliciting large scale physical and financial aid, which any one delegation might find difficult to raise on its own: after a few alterations my motion was passed by the workshop, and I left to try to find Hosea Williams.

I got to Mr. Williams just before the meeting reconvened; I explained to him my conception of the SCCC and said that Al had asked me to seek his help in getting it off the ground, to which he agreed. Gaining in boldness, I then sat at the speakers' table and told the COC staff man acting as MC that I wanted to speak about the formulation of a Southern Challenges Coordinating Committee, hoping that the NBC news crew would turn on their cameras. I tried to put on my most serious face, and I quickly wrote out a five minute speech. My fingers tapping on the table and my foot beating out rock rhythms on the carpet reminded me that I was nervous.

When I finally was introduced and got up to speak, NBC did take notice. And so there I was, approximately an hour and a half after Al had thought of it, standing in front of national television cameras and boldly announcing the formation of the Southern Challenges Coordinating Committee! Though I don't think the footage was ever used, it was an amazing example of the right thought at the right time, for the SCCC was later to be of great importance; and, if for no other reason, the Southern Regional COC was a rousing success.

Mr. Williams gave me his home phone number and said to call him; he suggested that we get together for lunch on Tuesday, with the Georgia challenge leaders, to discuss just what the SCCC could do to help. Ken Guido gave me the names and phone numbers of the leaders of challenges from North Carolina, Alabama, Mississippi, and Texas. That night I called Julian in Atlanta and Rev. Hooten in Savannah. Rev. Hooten was already planning to be in Atlanta on Tuesday, and we set the luncheon date. Julian said to try to add John Lewis, which I did.

Early that evening we had a Georgians For McCarthy meeting at the Dinkler Plaza. Everyone had been in Macon the day before, so that particular activity needed no further exposition. We had no time to rest on our laurels, however, but instead had to shift the same sort of maximum organizational energy into McCarthy Day, which was scheduled for that Thursday evening. Gail Stern had arrived the Friday before; she was to be our New York coordinator, though I'm not sure about her previous experience with such events.

Taylor had passed out several hundred tickets on consignment in Macon, and he then made consignments to all of us. The tickets were numbered, and Taylor kept exact records of where each ticket went, expecting either the ticket or the appropriate receipts returned on Thursday night. All of us took a stack of tickets and most of us felt certain that we could sell quite a few.

At that meeting, using money which John Tillman had received as a specific donation while on a trip to Washington, we gave the go ahead for our first and only storefront in a black area. John had located a suitable unused shop near Paschal Brothers Hotel, and we would only have to pay a small salary to the two people John had found to run it. This storefront was to stay in operation for two weeks, until the Democratic National Convention, with an option for longer in case McCarthy's fortunes went well in Chicago.

There was, however, also the usual bad news. First, Mr. Beluso, who was not at the meeting, was refusing to guarantee payment on the headquarters any longer. So that same afternoon Charlie had guaranteed payment for our one final week, until the next Friday, hoping that we would make enough money on M-Day to cover. Then, more or less as an outgrowth of this discussion, Joe Gross, who had only just found out that we had been forced to move M-Day to the Regency Hyatt House, launched another of his sermons on financial irresponsibility.

In the end he proposed a motion that Georgians For McCarthy should refuse to take any financial responsibility at all for what happened at M-Day. Such a motion was pointless, since we could not then stop M-Day if we had wanted to (as the Regency Hyatt House would still demand its $2,200), and his motion did not pass. But then, for the sake of his own conscience, I guess, Mr. Gross said that he wanted us to know that, as far as he was concerned, he was not personally responsible at all.

We did pass a motion, however, making George Blaugh the new second fiscal agent to take Ken Martin's place. Against my wishes, Mr. Gross also got the motion passed that our two signatures would therefore be required on all checks. I was to make the proper signature card changes on Monday.

With Dr. Evans gone to England, Mr. Beluso pulling out, Mr. Gross refusing to take responsibility, and Ken Martin's resignation as fiscal agent the next day, it might sound as if Taylor, with all of the tickets, and myself, with a postdated check, were being left holding a very large bag. We were, along with the rest of the organization, and we could not have pulled it off, had it not been for the absolutely unending work of Charlie, who could have left for Washington by then, Nancy Schwartz, Pat Madsen, Jo Ann and Chico Thomas, Jim Sundberg's teams, Augustine Ochoa and Tenent Neville.

The latter two Atlanta men, along with John Thompson, who arrived from Washington, spent every working hour of that week on the phone, calling every conceivable large donor we knew, asking them to buy as many tickets as they could. We set up a system whereby any tickets bought by a large donor but not used would be distributed to people at the new storefront who otherwise could not afford to come. As usual, we never did get the really large donor we were looking for, but those long hours of phone work did in the end produce a great deal of revenue.

Nelson Schneider also stayed behind, gratis, to help with publicity. Gail Stern coordinated our activities with New York, including the closed-circuit television hook-up. The final "list of stars" - limited to Carl Reiner and Harry Belafonte in New York – came out too late to help us much, but we did receive a shipment of heavy cardboard kiosks, brightly decorated, which Jim and his people set up all over town to sell tickets on the streets. While Mr. Ochoa and Mr. Neville concentrated on trying to find "large donors," Nancy, Pat and Jo Ann went down our lists of local supporters – compiled over the summer – calling and asking for either sales in advance or at least an assurance that they would attend on Thursday night.

I'm afraid that I personally sold only a few tickets. I was soon involved with the SCCC – but I did sub-consign tickets to Toni Casey, who used her feminine charm to sell several within the bank. And, of all the means we tried, these ticket sales proved the best way to raise money, because people felt that they were "buying something," whether they eventually used them or not. But it took a great deal of very hard work to sell $2,000 worth of tickets at $3 each, and by Wednesday night we were still a very long way short of the $1,200 we needed just to pay the rent.

On Tuesday at noon I made my first visit to the Southern Christian Leadership Conference (SCLC) headquarters on Auburn Avenue, where the sign outside still read "Rev. Martin Luther King, Jr., Director." The office building itself had only one floor and was obviously overcrowded with work. Hosea Williams' office was just inside the front door, where a receptionist tried to keep track of the innumerable phone calls and visitors incoming for members of the staff, who usually were on assignment somewhere else. From the brief visit I paid to SCLC, I felt as if the whole operation combined the zeal and the idealism of a church with the responsibility and bureaucracy of a corporation, stirred well by the chaos and activity of a campaign headquarters.

Mr. Williams was late that day, which seemed to concern no one; all of the SCLC staff were badly overworked, and during that week Mr. Williams was often in the office until after midnight. I knew nothing about Hosea Williams other than what had recently been in the papers regarding the ill-fated Resurrection City. Even after four days of working with him I still find it difficult to describe him, except to state that he seemed a militant idealist accustomed to making the quick decisions necessary when one has taken on the work of four men. He could seem, at exactly the same moment, both the compassionate listener and the hurried leader. When he finally arrived he was immediately surrounded by aides and visitors needing a word with him, and even as we walked the three blocks to our restaurant meeting place, he continued to be surrounded by three or four people, planning various activities as they waited at traffic lights and dodged cars.

Inside the dimly lit side dining room of our restaurant rendezvous, we were soon joined by Julian Bond, Rev. Hooten, John Lewis, and Chico Thomas. After ordering, Mr. Williams picked up a pencil and piece of paper and started by saying "O.K., now what do you people need in Chicago? Let's start with food, housing, transportation, an office, secretaries, banners and money. How much of this do you have?" We admitted that we had none. While Mr. Williams started writing these and other necessities, it really struck me for the first time what a massive logistics – not to mention political – operation we were undertaking, needing accommodations for our eighty Georgia delegates in a city in which all the hotel rooms were supposedly long-since booked and with a budget approaching zero. And besides us, there were also all the other Southern challenges with similar needs and similar budgets. My fingers started tapping on the table.

Mr. Williams said that Jesse Jackson of SCLC in Chicago could probably be counted on for some help with things like food and staff, but that we had better start to consider sleeping in churches. He added that we could use the facilities of the SCLC in Atlanta to set up the Southern Challenges Coordinating Committee, which would hopefully find easier going in arranging such things and raising money than any one of the delegations alone. But to be effective the SCCC would have to include the leaders of all the challenge delegations for the South and would have to be set up immediately. Mr. Williams proposed a conference call, to be arranged by SCLC, for seven a.m. Thursday morning. He further proposed that the

SCCC be composed of the chairmen of all the challenge delegations, plus John Lewis, me, and himself.

Julian and Rev. Hooten thought that the SCCC was a good idea and they agreed to the conference call. I was to contact the other leaders, except in Mississippi, which Mr. Williams said might be a problem, since they might not want to "rock their winning boat" by joining something like the SCCC. The Mississippi challenge was bound to win, and they apparently had all the money and support they needed. But for just this reason we felt that Mississippi's inclusion was critical, to show that Mississippi's problems were not unique and that the Democratic party could not get away with tackling Mississippi 1968, Georgia in 1972, Alabama in 1976, Texas in 1980, etc. John Lewis, who knew the leaders there personally, volunteered to call Mississippi.

Neither then nor at any time after did it seem unusual to me that I was working with well-known figures like Julian Bond and Hosea Williams, perhaps because both of them so naturally and instinctively put one at ease. We were suddenly just working together, no questions asked. Looking back, I have, on occasion, wondered who or what they must have thought I was; but at the time it seemed we might have been friends for ten years. Few men I met that summer could handle responsibility so humbly.

That night, between calls trying to sell M-Day tickets, I returned to the SCLC headquarters to use their WATS line, for a change, to call North Carolina, Alabama, and Texas. Using the numbers supplied by Ken Guido of the COC, I had very good luck and got through immediately to Ed Cogburn and Mrs. Billy Carr in Texas. They responded enthusiastically to the SCCC proposal, and said that they were willing to participate in the conference call on Thursday.

I got the same response from John Cashin in Alabama. Dr. Reginald Hawkins in North Carolina agreed to the conference call, but he was a little skeptical about the SCCC, fearing that it was an attempt to tie the challenges to a particular political banner, which he would not accept. I discussed the problem with him for a long time, and in the end I think he felt better about the sincerity of the SCCC's political neutrality.

After these calls I went back to our headquarters, where the last efforts at pre-M-Day ticket sales were still being made. We were not looking good; but a couple of really large sales were in the air, about which we would know more the next day, on Wednesday. Nelson Schneider was working on the few radio ads we were gambling on to bring in door sales. Taylor, Mr. Neville and Mr. Ochoa were doing a good job keeping track of every ticket, exhorting phoners to still make more calls, and driving fresh blocks of tickets to anyone who thought he could sell more. Meanwhile Gail Stern was handling the physical details for the Atlanta show. John Tillman was pushing tickets near the new storefront, usually at reduced rates, selling them for whatever people were willing to pay.

Lunch Wednesday consisted of a quick trip to headquarters, where the disappointing news had just come in that the hoped-for large sales to two businesses had not come off because ours was a "political" rally. I also called John Lewis, who was having difficulty locating Aaron Henry in Mississippi, but he said that he would keep trying. I phoned SCLC and left all the names and numbers for our conference call with Hosea Williams' secretary, who would then call the special operator in charge of such calls and give her the details.

Thursday morning, M-Day, I got up a little before six and drove downtown to SCLC, where the night watchman let me in. I called the conference call operator, who plugged my line into our call right at 7 a.m.: on the line were Rev. Hooten in Savannah (Julian was campaigning with Senator McCarthy and could not be included), Dr. Hawkins in North Carolina, John Cashin in Alabama, Mrs. Billy Carr and Ed Cogburn in Texas, and Hosea Williams at his home in Atlanta (he had left SCLC only three hours before). We talked for about half an hour, and there was almost total unanimity in everyone's minds concerning the purposes of the SCCC. Dr. Hawkins expressed his apprehensions concerning political affiliation and its possible harm to our larger purposes, with which we all agreed.

Once everyone had also agreed to serve on the SCCC, Hosea said that we would handle a press release from Atlanta. He then volunteered me to go to Chicago the week before the convention to try to coordinate the SCCC's activities. By this point in the summer I was becoming impervious to such suggestions, so I did not even protest (I had been told, besides, that I could count on the help of SCLC in Chicago). Though most of the participants knew nothing about me and my lack of qualifications, they agreed that I should go. We further decided to have a meeting early the next week in Chicago to put the SCCC into operation with myself to handle the time, place, and necessary communication.

That morning at work, during my coffee break, I drafted a press release on the SCCC, which I dictated to Hosea Williams' secretary over the phone – to the interest of my friends in the office, who were mostly Nixon and Wallace supporters. The plans were for Hosea and his secretary, with more experience at such things, to reword my rough factual draft and to make it into a real "press release," which they would then send out through their usual channels under the name of Julian Bond. Julian had earlier agreed to this arrangement, because we had learned during that week that if one wanted the national press to notice a release, Julian's name was a very good way to get that attention. John Lewis had reported that Aaron Henry, though not included in the conference call, had agreed to the SCCC "in principle," so Mississippi was included in our press release, which appeared as the lead on the second page of Friday's *Atlanta Journal*.

This article also contained an announcement by Senator George McGovern that he was supporting the Georgia challenge delegation. In the body of the story there was also the news that Mr. E. T. Kehrer had called an executive meeting of the Georgia Democratic Party Forum for Saturday afternoon to "determine what the future role of the Forum will be with regard to the challenge." Most of us were afraid that Mr. Kehrer was going to try to persuade the executive committee to pull the Forum's support out from under the Georgia Delegation of Loyal National Democrats, a move which would cripple the delegation's standing before the Credentials Committee. Rev. Hooten, a member of the Forum's executive committee, was therefore making sure that the entire committee would be present on Saturday, giving Mr. Kehrer less chance of pushing through such a motion.

Thursday at lunch I again visited headquarters, where the situation for that evening was looking grim. We still did not even have the $1,200 necessary to pay the rent, much less any of the other local expenses; but we had sold enough tickets to ensure, if everyone came, that we could probably raise the difference when a collection was taken up. Taylor was already at the headquarters (his teaching duties had ended the week before), making sure that all the consigned tickets were accounted for and back in our hands for the door sales.

I returned to the bank for a four hour "work break," then it was back to headquarters at five, where the operation was already starting to shift up the street to the Regency Hyatt House for our last Atlanta event of the summer. Every available piece of paraphernalia we had left was brought in from the storefront by Jim Sundberg, who was also in charge of our

"McCarthy girls," teenagers in bright colored uniforms who would pass the donations buckets.

Pat Madsen and I walked up to the Regency Hyatt House, inside and down to the same large ballroom in which Mary Beth McCarthy and I had attended the YDC-YRC Fourth of July Ball. Now the room was filled with a sea of chairs, all facing the stage where a large screen was set up. Near the front of the center aisle sat a huge video machine plugged into several large cables: our closed circuit TV equipment. Several familiar helpers, Chris Ware and Mark Evans among them, were already busy setting up tables and pinning posters to the curtained walls.

By then it was about six o'clock: M-Day was scheduled to start at eight locally, with the cable TV entertainment coming on at eight-thirty and Senator McCarthy's speech a little after nine. In a last attempt to raise money, several of us took tickets and an M-Day kiosk upstairs to the crowded main lobby where we actually did a pretty good job of selling tickets (I sold a $20 ticket to one man from out of state who was amazed to learn that there even was a McCarthy organization in Georgia).

As Taylor and Gail Stern had to handle all of the last-minute physical arrangements, I volunteered to oversee the door sales. There was a long counter area just next to the main ballroom door, ready-made for such activity; Jo Ann, Pat and I set ourselves up there at about 7:15 with all of the tickets we had left. At 7:30 I was greeted by a man who said that he was in charge of hotel security, and he showed me a letter from the manager requiring him to collect $1,200 in advance before he would allow the show to start! This was a new condition to me, and so I sent him off with Pat looking for Taylor, while Jo Ann and I sold tickets. I even remember "hiding" all of the larger bills we took in so that our security friend could not easily tell how much we had.

The door sales were going well: from somewhere, somehow, just like in Macon the weekend before, the people came, largely as a result of the work at the headquarters, and the individual persuading by hundreds of supporters whom we had urged to "bring a friend." But many of our audience were students, to whom we sold tickets at one dollar each, if they could not pay more; and by five until eight, we *still* did not have the $1200 in cash which the security man was demanding. He was now stationed right next to us and watching our every move.

With $1,200 in rent, $800 in other M-Day expenses, and over $600 in our

Georgians For McCarthy bills (not counting the headquarters rent), it was no time for this gentleman to start talking about cutting off the electricity to the ballroom unless he got his $1,200. My logic finally prevailed on him that the only way either he or we were ever going to get any more money was during the collection period halfway through the program, which meant, obviously, that he had to let us start. He finally agreed, and the show went on, with the ballroom then over three quarters filled, and Taylor and myself very anxious young men.

As our local MC, Cleveland Amory, kicked things off just after eight, another young man introduced himself to me as a member of the nationwide accounting firm handling the finances for the evening; he requested that he be allowed to watch the counting of the collections. He was then to split any amount over and above the local costs and forward half to New York. While the first of the local entertainers went on singing folk songs, I gave the "McCarthy girls" a pep talk and told them to bring any funds collected only to Jim, Taylor, or myself.

At 8:30 the live show from Madison Square Garden flashed miraculously on the screen. Gail, who was in telephone contact with New York, reported that both the image and the sound were excellent. Carl Reiner was the MC, and Harry Belafonte sang while Taylor and I got more and more nervous. At a little before nine the critical moment came: the first live nationwide fund-raising campaign was about to begin. The plan was for appeals to be made both in "the ring" in Madison Square Garden, and in each of the tuned-in cities. Announcements of large donations, either in New York or elsewhere, would immediately be relayed across the network. We had arranged for our house lights to be turned up partially, and while Carl Reiner and others in New York exhorted the faithful coast to coast, Taylor took the microphone in Atlanta and made our plea for donations, acceptable by cash, check, or pledge.

Though there were several immediate pledges of thousands of dollars in New York, the best we could do locally was a couple of pledges for a hundred dollars. While the buckets and the pledge cards were being passed out, Taylor continued his plea. Then from New York Joe Rauh appeared on the screen, making a national appeal by stating "There is a challenge delegation down in Georgia, led by Julian Bond, who desperately needs our support." This got a great applause from our audience and several more pledges. The buckets were, in fact, starting to fill with more money than we had seen in a long time, but it was impossible to tell how much we really had.

As a last desperation effort I went to the stage and identified myself as the fiscal agent for Georgians For McCarthy who was responsible if the bills were not paid. I told everyone that the summer's campaign had involved a lot of sacrifice by a lot of people, and I asked them not to let the campaign end in debt. If I sounded a little desperate, we were (Oh for that one generous donor of $1,000 who could have made the whole summer so much easier!). The people in the audience gave and gave, many several times. Mr. Gross gave $100. Taylor's parents again contributed. By the time Senator McCarthy started speaking, we were convinced that, even if we still could not cover our bills, the people there that night had given very generously and as never before.

Taylor, Ken Martin, the hotel's security man, the young accountant and I did not get to hear Senator McCarthy that night: we immediately went downstairs to count the money. After all the cash was stacked in neat piles, we gave the security man $1200 off the top; he agreed to tear up the earlier reservation check, thanked us, and signed a receipt. That hurdle was over. We then used an adding machine to total the rest of the cash, and we decided to total the pledges and divide by half, since many would probably prove uncollectible.

All together that gave us about another $1,200. Taylor and I quickly added up our other expenses, which came to just over $1,200, when we threw in every possible cost we could think of. We "padded" our expenses by about $400 in this manner for two reasons: First, most importantly, after an unpleasant experience at our earlier Dinkler Plaza reception, we were afraid that later that night or the next day we might suddenly be presented with bills which we had not known about; and we feared that, once any money had been sent to New York, it would be impossible to get it back to pay new local expenses. Second, we had just witnessed the New York effort raise what looked like well over $100,000; and we figured that, even if no new expenses actually did turn up, while the extra $200 our "padding" might cost New York would not make much difference there, it might made the critical difference as to whether we finished in the black in Atlanta or not. At any rate, our local accountant was happy with our cost estimates, so we kept all of the money in Atlanta.

We returned upstairs to find Atlanta's M-Day drawing to a close.

Everyone said that Senator McCarthy's speech was the finest he had ever given, finally lashing out in an attack on Vietnam and Humphrey's policies. Our audience had apparently reacted quite actively, and at that point they were listening to the final number by a local soul group. M-day was at last over, and all of us were very, very relieved. Most of us had been running at full speed by then for over ten days; but then suddenly, unless the Chicago convention was a McCarthy success, our campaign in Georgia was largely over. After sticking around to make sure that everything at the hotel was in order, most of us went back to our Dinkler Plaza Headquarters where, for the only time during the entire summer, we relaxed and had a party.

We were all terribly happy with the way the summer had gone, bar a few minor difficulties and close calls; and there was a bit of fraternal spirit among us that night, for it really was the first time that we had all been together without the immediate need to plan something. Taylor, Charlie, Nancy and I went around thanking many of the people without whom none of our small successes would have been possible. I invited Charlie, Nancy, the Besdines, Taylor and Cathy over for a quiet supper at home on Friday, before we all split up and went off to Chicago. Ken, Taylor, Charlie and I also agreed to meet at lunch the next day to sort out our bills and to pay as many as we could. Taylor took the cash home with him for safe keeping.

The next day, Friday, was my last day of work at the bank, and in a way I hated to leave the people who had been so patient with my politics and political phone calls and who had even managed to teach me a lot about bank credit. By the end of the summer Nixon and Wallace stickers adorned the outside of many trash cans, and we finally had some heated lunchtime discussions. Earlier that week I had screwed my courage up and made an appointment to see our bank's president, Mills B. Lane, who was quite well known throughout the South for his good works. I wanted to ask him about financial help, either for M-Day or for the challenge delegation. At our meeting, early on Wednesday morning, he had been most attentive to my pleas and had said that he would let me know. I never heard from him again, which was understandable, because I had not really expected any significant help.

At noon on Friday I went across to the headquarters. Ken, Taylor,

Charlie, and the money were already there. All during the week I had been purposefully delaying the change over to the new fiscal agent system, with George Blaugh as cosigner; Taylor, Charlie and Ken had agreed with my delay. Taylor and I felt that a few of us had, in effect, been left with the total responsibility for M-Day. We therefore felt that we had the right to disperse any funds raised without interference from those who had opted out of responsibility for that particular event but who might then have different ideas about where the money should go. So we sat down in the headquarters with every bill we had, and I started writing checks.

With the money from M-Day and the pledges that Mr. Ochoa and Mr. Neville had begun immediately to follow up on the phone, we paid every bill, except the earlier headquarters bill, part of which we still considered to belong to Mr. Beluso, and the phone bill, which Ken would have to ask the phone company to prepare. We put all the checks in envelopes, and while we were working, the phone men came in to take out the extra telephones, as we had asked. I then walked around to the bank with our sack full of money, made the deposit, and only then picked up the signature cards to make George Blaugh our new fiscal agent. It had been one hell of a way to run a campaign, and I doubt that we would want to do it that way again; but I could at least leave Atlanta knowing that we had done our part to make sure that, unlike any other campaign that I knew of, almost every single bill had been paid.

All summer long I had felt badly about Charlie and Nancy having to spend all of their time in the Dinkler Plaza Hotel with few breaks; but there had been no opportunity until that Friday night to have them "out to the house." My mother had consented to cook us supper. Early that evening Nancy and July Besdine watched the Besdines' baby daughter while Taylor, Charlie, Richard Besdine, my two younger brothers and I played a little touch football before supper.

But even that night we were not free from phone calls: Rev. Hooten called from Savannah and said that he had received a telegram from Al Kehrer canceling the Saturday executive meeting of the Georgia Democratic Party Forum. Rev. Hooten was afraid that Mr Kehrer had become aware that a majority of the Executive Committee would not vote to withdraw support from the challenge delegation and that he was either sending spurious cancellation telegrams to a few of the members or else he had decided upon some individual action. None of us knew anything about the situation. Rev. Hooten still planned to come to Atlanta the next day to attend a morning meeting of the delegation's officers and lawyers, and he could then check on the Forum meeting.

The next morning Taylor and I drove downtown to the delegation's officers meeting in Al Horn's office. I had never met Al before the Macon convention, but I found out later that he had done a great deal of civil rights case work. His law firm was located in a small but adequate office in one of Atlanta's older office buildings. We were met there by Al, George Walsh, Rev. Hooten, Ben Brown, Mrs. Paschall, and Rev. Morris, who, like us, was not an officer, but had some interest in the plans to be made since he had written the first challenge brief.

Al Horn had a few copies of the new brief which Al Harris had written the previous Sunday and delivered to the proper authorities just in time. All of us, including Rev. Morris, agreed that the new brief was much stronger, much tighter, and much more "legal." We were glad that we had listened to the young attorney.

One of the main items of business that morning was finding suitable witnesses to testify before the Credentials Committee. Julian, who was still campaigning with Senator McCarthy, was obviously the delegation's key witness, and it would be best for him to talk about the system under which the Democratic Party of Georgia then selected its delegates, plus the composition of the Maddox delegation. Ben Brown agreed to talk about the exclusion, in general, of black people from state party affairs. Rev. Morris was our expert on the loyalty of some of the Maddox delegates and would also talk about the Forum's earlier fruitless efforts to change the party from the inside.

But we needed a witness who could give a firsthand account of discrimination within the party. Ben said that he thought he knew a couple of black leaders in Athens and in Americus, who might be willing to recount their experiences. He and Al planned to phone that afternoon and, if necessary, to drive anywhere in the state they needed to, asking for help.

The other pressing matter was transportation to and physical accommodation once in Chicago. It was possible that the Credentials Committee would turn us down, but with a minority report almost guaranteed we would still have to spend all the money necessary to get the entire delegation to Chicago. This expense would be required even though the delegation might never see the inside of the convention hall, if the minority report failed to pass.

We obviously needed an "advance man" in Chicago to start making arrangements, and as I was free that week and was already planning to go for the SCCC, I volunteered. Taylor then volunteered to help Mrs. Paschall with the transportation problem; each delegate and alternate had to be contacted, and from somewhere the money had to come in for either plane or train tickets.

Our final plans were set. I would leave for Chicago the next morning where, following the slim leads we had, I would try to find immediate accommodation for the seven or eight men who would be arriving on Tuesday for our Credentials Committee hearing on Wednesday. I would also start looking for accommodations for the 60 to 80 delegates we expected would be coming up the following weekend. I was also try to get the SCCC set up and functioning. Taylor would work with Mrs. Paschall on Sunday and Monday making travel plans, then he would come to Chicago on Tuesday in search of funds to pay for the tickets, plus helping me with accommodation arrangements. Meanwhile Mr. Horn and Mr. Walsh would work on the legal presentation, and Rev. Hooten would write and mail a letter to all of the delegates and alternates explaining what was happening.

Just before Taylor, Mrs. Paschall and I left to go to a Georgians For McCarthy meeting in a nearby church school building (our headquarters was, by then, closed), and before Rev. Hooten and Rev. Morris left to go make sure that there really was no executive committee meeting of the Georgia Democratic Party Forum, I typed up a short "letter of introduction" for myself, addressed "to whom it may concern," and signed by Rev. Hooten, asking that I be given all possible aid in finding accommodations and funds for our Georgia Delegation of Loyal National Democrats. I had no idea what I was getting into.

Since we were late, Taylor, Mrs. Paschall and I sped over to our last pre-convention meeting of Georgians For McCarthy, which we found already in progress around a large square table in a church school classroom. The Besdines, Mrs A. M. Davis, Mr. Gross, Ken Martin, Les, Otis Cochran, Charlie, Jim Sundberg and George Blaugh were all there. Unfortunately, a small argument had already started between Les and Mr. Gross, who had decided unilaterally to chair the meeting. A motion was quickly passed to give Taylor the chair; and, for once, we had no more arguments. Taylor asked for a financial report, which I gave, with my fingers crossed beneath the table.

I think everyone was so glad that the bills had been paid that no questions as to our "right" to pay them were asked. With some of the money which Ken reported had just come in that morning, we voted to pay Les enough expense money to get him out of hock with the Dinkler Plaza; we paid a few new bills; and we still had enough left to cover the phone bill which was due to arrive any day. Whatever difference was eventually left over from the original phone deposit, plus our final balance, we allotted to be divided between Hans Reinish, who still had only been partially repaid for his earlier deposit, and the remaining rent on the headquarters. We also voted to keep the original storefront open throughout the convention, and possibly even beyond, if everything went well.

Regarding future financial matters, since I would be staying near Chicago for a week following the convention at a graduate school conference and would therefore not be of much future help, both George Blaugh and Jim Sundberg were made the new fiscal agents. I passed over to them all the records I had, plus the new signature card forms. As a last matter, for those who would still be in Atlanta, a time, date, and place was named for a post-Chicago meeting to discuss whatever new developments the Democratic National Convention produced.

Our meeting that Saturday afternoon, chaired well by Taylor, was probably the most smoothly run meeting of the whole summer, and I think that all of us, including Mr. Gross, were happy with the way everything had actually worked out, considering all of the things that might have gone wrong. I said goodbye to Jim, the Besdines, Otis Cochran and George Blau, who were not coming to Chicago; both Mrs. Davis and Mr. Gross were alternate delegates, and Les and Charlie were planning to come to help the national McCarthy Headquarters in any way that they could. We all thanked both of them for their long weeks of help, which had been crucial for whatever small successes one could attribute to our summer for McCarthy in Georgia – our publicity for Senator McCarthy, our attempts to make Georgians reconsider both the Vietnam War and the state's Democratic processes, and our help with the new Georgia Challenge Delegation.

I told Taylor that I would see him on Tuesday in Chicago, and Ken

Martin drove me home to pick up some financial papers. After saying goodbye to him in our turnaround, I went inside to pack all of my worldly belongings into a trunk for two years in England and into a suitcase for three weeks in Chicago. I finished about ten that night and went out for a late date. The next morning I was up early and soon on my way for my second visit to Chicago in six weeks.

7

HOUSING, TRANSPORTATION AND
BAD NEWS

I arrived at O'Hare Airport late Sunday morning with twenty dollars in my pocket and a letter of introduction from Rev. Hooten; my job was to find accommodations, food, transportation and the necessary funds for at least our 80 people, with the hope of coordinating the same effort for over 200 other Southern challenge delegates and alternates. I had no place to stay myself, and I had only a few names and numbers to call. This was only the second time I had ever been to Chicago, and the places I had been told to try for help were a McCarthy Headquarters near the Conrad Hilton and the COC Headquarters located on the thirteenth floor of the 127 North Dearborn Building, wherever that was.

A porter at the airport told me that the airport bus would drop me off right at the Conrad Hilton, so I climbed aboard. It was a beautiful warm day with hardly a cloud in the sky, and I enjoyed the trip into town. Upon reaching downtown Chicago the bus went just in front of the Hilton, which occupies an entire city block facing Grant Park , and which divides the hotel from a north-south expressway running alongside Lake Michigan and paralleling the long stretch of Chicago lake-front hotels. The bus turned right, and I was deposited by the side entrance on the south side of the Conrad Hilton.

At the door was a student with a McCarthy button and a walkie-talkie; though he was seemingly very busy talking into his walkie-talkie, he answered my question about the location of a McCarthy storefront, which turned out to be just around the corner, facing the back, or west side of the Conrad Hilton. As I picked up my suitcase and started in that direction, a car sped up with a big sign on top proclaiming it to be a "McCarthy Car"; the walkie-talkie man opened the car door to let passengers out and gave directions to the driver. I surmised that the McCarthy organization was running a shuttle system designed to cope with the city-wide cab strike so conveniently called for that week.

The McCarthy storefront was located on the second floor over a short block of small shops; it was simply a huge room with several long tables set up, a few chairs, and a Coca-Cola machine. I walked in from the stairs and tried to look both lost and in a hurry (neither of which was very difficult for me). It must have worked, because two young women, who seemed quite accustomed to such an appearance, asked if they could help. I said that I hoped so. I needed a place to stay and a telephone, and I tried out my letter of introduction on them, explaining that I was "the advance man for the Julian Bond delegation from Georgia."

I'm afraid I had little impact, and I don't know exactly what I was expecting, or why they should have taken particular notice. They simply told me that I would have to sign in on the "lodging required" cards, and that they thought they might be able to get me a place out of town by commuter train. As for a phone, they explained that there was a telephone strike on, that they only had one phone, and they didn't know where another could be found. They were very nice about it all, and I signed the necessary cards. But I was not getting very far.

As I walked around the room looking for someone in charge, in came Mark Evans and Chris Ware, who had flown up a few days earlier. They said that they were involved in Chicago "field operations," which included getting up early in the morning to pass out McCarthy literature in the long lines of rush hour traffic. They were living with a "nice family" about thirty minutes out of town.

Recognition of the magnitude of my task, of the short time in which I had to succeed, and of my own inadequacy for the job, had been building inside of me for several days. I not only had to find over forty rooms in a town where there were no rooms, but I also had to find the money to pay for them; and I had to do it quickly if plans were to be made in Atlanta. Once actually in Chicago, my realization was starting to turn into a bit of concern, and I knew that I did not have time to spend all afternoon standing around in a McCarthy storefront.

I was about to ask for a "McCarthy car" to take me up to the COC office when an older woman came over and asked if I was "the one from Georgia." She apologized for the earlier shuffle and explained that this was the office where young people came to volunteer for field work and that the younger women had just assumed that such was my purpose. I quickly explained my more pressing tasks at hand. She said that it would probably be impossible to find so many rooms anywhere together; they would, in fact, have difficulty finding that many places anywhere, and it would require spreading the delegation all over metropolitan Chicago.

But she suggested that I come back in a couple of hours and talk to the storefront organizers who were out at lunch. I explained my interest in getting up to the COC office, and she put me in the hands of a student who was driving up that way. I thanked her, left my suitcase in a corner, and followed a very attractive girl outside, where we got into her Volkswagen convertible for the short drive.

The COC Headquarters was located about twelve blocks north and two blocks west of the Conrad Hilton, near the Sherman House, where the original COC had been held six weeks before. Thanking my chauffeur, I went inside and up to the thirteenth floor, where the COC office turned out to be about one half of the entire floor and consisted of many small offices off of an L shaped central hallway. The front door and the reception desk were at the corner of the L. Vernon Shell was in a small office to the left, and Ken Guido arrived a little later. Vernon greeted me, and I soon explained to him my tasks. He looked strangely relaxed, as if a great load had just been lifted from him. Vernon, too, was very pessimistic about housing and money: they had been trying for weeks to find the same two essentials for their own people, largely without luck. He suggested that I try the churches in town, and the YMCA's.

But the COC did have a telephone that I could use, so I sat down in one of their empty offices and started calling. Before leaving Atlanta I had been given the name of a hotel, supposedly like Paschal Brothers, near the convention hall, which was said to have some rooms left. I had also been given the names and numbers of two ministers whom one member of our delegation knew and who were supposed to be sympathetic to our cause. I wasn't exactly sure what help they would be, but such calls were typical of

147

others during the next few days: I called any lead I had, hoping that the more people I had searching for rooms the more likely I would be of success. As always I had my usual yellow legal pad on which I wrote down all of the new names, numbers, and things that I had to do.

I got through to the hotel manager, who said that he had no rooms for the convention week; but he gave me the names of two other hotels, further out, where I might be luckier. One of these was also full, but at the other the manager said that he had at least eight rooms, maybe more, depending on cancellations. I gave him my name, asked him to hold those rooms for forty-eight hours, and told him that I would call him back. I next tried the Chicago SCLC but was told that none of the staff would be in the office until Monday.

I then made what would prove to be my single most fortuitous call of the week: I pulled out a scrap of paper with a name and number given to me by Julian the week before and phoned Walter Turner. Luckily there was an answer, and Mr. Turner listened while I briefly explained who I was and my connection with Julian Bond. With the first optimistic words I had heard, Mr. Turned replied "I think that we can probably fix you up. I've got one stop to make, but I'm just leaving home, and I'll pick you up in an hour. I've got a light green Mercury, and I'll pull up just in front of those offices. We'll talk about making all the arrangements." I was overwhelmed by such an offer of help and I guaranteed that I would be waiting.

Next I went back to Vernon Shell and asked if he had a map of the city. The receptionist had several, provided by the Continental Illinois National Bank. I said that I'd probably want to open an account at some bank and they suggested Continental where the COC had its account, and they gave me the name of Ed Burke, their account officer. On the map they showed me the Conrad Hilton, located to the south, two blocks west of the lake. The COC offices were near the north edge of the map, and the Continental Bank was located about four blocks south of the COC office, and several blocks further west.

They also pointed out the Illinois McCarthy headquarters, near the COC. Vernon told me that all of the McCarthy field men were headquartered in the Shoreland Hotel, a twenty-minute drive south of the Hilton right on the shore. The amphitheater was also off the map, located to the south and west. Ken Guido walked in about that time, and he said that they would do all they could to find us housing. He suggested that I try McGovern Headquarters, which was located in the block immediately north of the Conrad Hilton in the Sheraton Blackstone.

After thanking them and promising to keep in touch, I went back downstairs, where I waited outside for about fifteen minutes; at length a green Mercury pulled up in front, a door opened, and I got in. Behind the steering wheel sat a large black man in an immaculate suit. "Walter Turner's my name," he said, as he offered me his hand and smiled. "Where do you want to go?" I said hello and that I thought it might be a good idea to drive to the Shoreland Hotel, if he knew where that was, where I had heard that the McCarthy field forces were located. It should be inserted that Walter Turner turned out to be one of the most genuine, friendliest people I have ever met; and, as I was to come to learn quickly, though Mayor Daley might officially own Chicago, Walter was right when he jokingly remarked, "This is my town."

As we started to drive south on the expressway paralleling Lake Michigan, I explained to Walter my exact needs: a place for myself for two weeks, rooms for eight others for Tuesday night, and accommodations for our whole delegation the following week, plus food and as much money as I could find. Walter lit a large cigar and listened quietly, finally commenting at the end "You leave it all to me; I'll make one or two phone calls, and I think we can fix it up."

I had no idea whether Walter really could "fix it up." But such an expression was a great relief to me. As I knew nothing about Walter, other than his phone number, I asked him how he knew Julian. "Well, I'm in press relations work, and I'm originally from Tampa, Florida. I get down South once or twice a year, and over the years Julian and I have run into each other on several occasions. I really admire him for the work he's been doing in Georgia." Walter then went on to explain that he had some business associates in the hotel business, and that when we got to the Shoreland he would make a few phone calls while I went in search of a friendly face.

Outside the Shoreland I found Mrs. Walsh and her daughter sitting in a car; they said that Mr. Walsh was inside at a lawyer meeting for the challenge delegations. While Walter went to find a phone, I had a look around the large, open hotel lobby which seemed strangely quiet. I walked down a hall to the right, around a corner, and into a large conference room where one meeting was just breaking up and another was starting. Curt

Gans was sitting on a table, looking even more worn out than the weekend before, talking with two female aides. I waved to him from a few feet away; he looked up, gave a quick hello and went back to talking. Mr. Walsh came in, and we stood around talking while twelve long tables were arranged in the center of the room and people began to find seats.

Mr. Walsh, who told me that he was staying in a motel way out from town, explained that this meeting was a briefing session for all of the McCarthy delegates on the Credentials Committee, which was to begin its hearings the next day. Lawyers representing each of the challenges in which the McCarthy camp was interested were to present a capsule summary of their case, emphasizing its strong points. The lawyers could thereby swap ideas on presentation and legal points, and the Credentials Committee delegates could take notes which would be useful in the committee debates. There was to be a later, more formal briefing for all of the delegates on the Credentials Committee who wanted to come, but this first one was more a working session, limited to the McCarthy delegates.

Mr. Rau walked in and we immediately said hello. He introduced me to a few friends as "one of the young men who is helping to rewrite Georgia politics." I was rather embarrassed, and I returned the compliment by saying that he had done as great a job on the M-Day telecast. A little later I asked him who I should see in the McCarthy organization about securing the funds necessary to get our delegation up to Chicago and into hotel rooms.

Mr. Rauh took me over to Stephen Mitchell, head of the entire McCarthy campaign, who had just walked in, and briefly explained my plight. Mr. Mitchell quickly turned me over to an aide, who asked for more details. I gave him a rough estimate of our expenses – probably over $5,000, including group rate air fare, hotel, transportation, etc. He whistled and said he'd try to take care of it, but he didn't know if that kind of money was available. I could not tell whether he really could secure the money or not, but I sensed that I would have to keep the pressure on if we were to be remembered.

Walter walked in and told me that he had a few men "working on the situation" and that he had a few more calls to make. I introduced him to Mr. Walsh, who was just sitting down for the meeting to start. I took a chair and listened. I knew nothing about the functioning of the Credentials Committee, nor, for that matter, about any other aspect of the Democratic

National Convention. I knew only that this year there might be a record number of challenges – 17 contests for over 900 of the 2,600 delegate seats, representing fifteen states. I had read earlier that the McCarthy forces were interested in about ten of these challenges.

So I was then actually sitting around a table with several "real live" convention delegates on the Credentials Committee, representing McCarthy delegations from many other states and many other fights. I had an overriding sense of the real significance of what these people were trying to do, and how insignificant my own problems seemed in comparison. They were then trying to work out strategies to use within the Credentials Committee to persuade Humphrey delegates about the challenges' merits, since the Humphrey delegates would be under strong pressure not to upset the status quo, because most delegations being challenged were pro-Humphrey.

These McCarthy delegates hoped that, especially with the southern states, the Humphrey delegates would listen to the cases on their merit, not on the politics involved. I was terribly interested in this give and take, my first brush with the convention's inner workings, but I knew it was not getting my own job done. Dave Mixer walked in the door, and I went over to say hello.

Dave and I exchanged greetings and the latest news, then went outside for a few minutes to talk more seriously. He expressed a desire to work with me on the Southern Challenge Coordinating Committee, since he said that he could find little else going on which was really worthwhile. We went upstairs to his room where he said that I could spend the night on a roll away bed. Though the Shoreland seemed a bit too far south to serve as a convenient base of operations for me, I told him I would move in if I could not find any place closer to the Hilton. There was apparently a field staff meeting about to start on the floor above, so I walked up with him.

We found Curt Gans in a really bad mood, and from the tension in the room I could tell that this was no place for me, an outsider. I was later to learn that Curt was under terrible pressure from some of the older leaders in the campaign who controlled the money and who thought that Curt and his field men not only were unproductive (compared to equal money spent on the national media), but also had been misappropriating funds. There had, in fact, been a basic split over political tactics throughout the summer, and Curt had just barely been able to talk the top leaders into paying for his staff to come to Chicago, which seemed incredible to me, even if by this time the odds were slight for a McCarthy victory.

The pressure put on Curt to "perform" was being felt among the men under Curt's leadership who were making their own final assignments. I think this tension remained in the organization for the first few days of that week, and it probably explained part of Dave's desire to work with the SCCC. As he went inside, Dave said that he would try to get assigned to help me.

I went back downstairs where I found Walter waiting in the lobby. He said he still did not know anything definite but that, as it was getting towards supper, I should try to spend that night at the YMCA near the Hilton and wait until the next day for results. As we walked out of the Shoreland we met a man waiting for a "McCarthy car"; he asked if we were driving anywhere near the Hilton, as he had been waiting fifteen minutes already.

Walter volunteered to give him a lift, and while we drove north he introduced himself from the back seat as John Garfield, Chairman of the McCarthy organization in Iowa. I introduced myself and briefly explained to him my mission; and, to my surprise, he said that he felt certain that their own Iowa delegation might have some extra rooms which we could use. More importantly, he added that he was flying home that night to Iowa and that he would try to raise some money for us!

Richard Stearns, desk man for McCarthy in the Midwest, was later to describe Mr. Garfield to me as "one of the great undiscovered political geniuses of our day"; at that point he just seemed like a concerned man offering a bit of help when it was badly needed. Walter dropped Mr. Garfield, who had given me his phone number in Iowa, in front of the Hilton; he bid us farewell and wished us luck. We then pulled around to the McCarthy storefront, where Walter waited while I went inside to collect my suitcase; I then walked one block south to the huge Chicago YMCA Hotel, and Walter waited in the car until I had definitely booked a room. He had other errands which he had to run, so we said goodnight, and he asked me to call him the next day.

I went back to the desk and asked the man in charge if they had eight rooms for Tuesday night; to my relief they had all the rooms I wanted. I told him that I would let him know definitely the next day about the extra rooms, and I went upstairs. My unair-conditioned room, which only cost $4 a night, was on the twelfth floor, on the inside, away from the breeze (and therefore very hot). I was sure that no more than two people could have fitted inside at one time; on the right was a bed, on the left a combination cupboard and dresser, with just enough room provided between the dresser and the bed for the door to open halfway.

I had never stayed at a YMCA before, but this tiny room certainly did not look too bad. Besides, instead of being twenty minutes out of town by less-than-reliable McCarthy car, I was only one block from the Conrad Hilton, and at a cost which even I could afford. So I filled up the room by setting my suitcase down and then left in search of the McCarthy storefront manager and some supper. I was quietly pleased about Walter Turner's offer of help and my own housing coup at the Y.

I walked up to the McCarthy storefront, where I found the manager, a student, in consultation with some of his staff. After introducing myself I talked him into supper; he took me downstairs to a small restaurant which was to become a regular with us that week, since comparable food was about twice the price in the Hilton's cafes. The restaurant was little more than two rows of green booths and a counter. We sat down in a booth, and across from us was Les Leopold talking with some local students about organizing the morning and afternoon distributions of McCarthy literature. After saying hello to Les, I started to ask my host about housing. But this session wasn't much more productive than the earlier ones; there just seemed to be no hotel rooms available anywhere, and the available residential housing was filling up quickly with student volunteers. But I was assured that their group would try for us; and I was told to come back late the next day.

After supper I walked around the block for my first look inside the Conrad Hilton, which really is an immense hotel. The ground floor was laid in thick red carpet, and from one end of its block-long lobby to the other there were shops, phones, offices, and restaurants. Even then, a week before the convention itself was to start, the lobby was filled with people, including delegates on the pre-convention committees, press men, national committee staff, and I suppose, tourists. Buttons were everywhere, as were handshakes, small group conferences, and suddenly remembered friendships.

The elevators have a small lobby all to themselves, with the elevators ringing three wells; soon there would be ropes and a director on hand to steer the crowds into the "under 12" and the "express" elevators. I had heard that the McCarthy Headquarters was on the fifteenth floor, so I took a ride up. Each floor has a duplicate of the downstairs elevator lobby at its center, from which halls extend to the right and left. Following either hall leads to several other cross halls and many, many rooms.

In the lobby of the fifteenth floor was a big McCarthy Headquarters sign in blue and white. Several sofas were already filled that night with young workers, and a door entering into the hall on the elevator-less side of the lobby had a sign reading "Headquarters." I entered there and found the by then ubiquitous reception desk and reception girl. I was concerned about communication from Atlanta, so I asked if I could have messages phoned there, which I would then pick up in the alphabetical pigeonholes provided, I guess, for the McCarthy staff. The receptionist, who was quite friendly, readily agreed.

I then had a brief look around. This fifteenth floor was done in blue carpet; the right hall led to what seemed to be individual rooms, with the exception of the transportation department located in a far corner housing a CB transmitter, a blackboard, and a couple of over-worked dispatchers, to whom I guessed came all requests for personal cars, McCarthy Cars, and rides from the airport for VIPs of all grades of importance. The left, or north, hall also led to more individual rooms, though a right turn at the first cross-corridor led, on the right, to a small room filled with typewriters and a fast-print Xerox machine and, on the left, to a smaller room with a typewriter, where Taylor and I were later to compose several press releases.

Straight at the end of this cross-corridor was a conference room used during that week by the McCarthy Credentials Committee delegates and lawyers for meetings with the various challenge delegation leaders. Already the headquarters was alive, and I wondered with respect if the people who had set it up were under twenty-five.

After this brief tour I went downstairs again, out the north door, across the street and into the Sheraton-Blackstone, where I had heard that the McGovern headquarters was located on the fourth floor. I took off my McCarthy button – I wasn't yet sure of convention etiquette – as I rode up in the elevator. The McGovern headquarters, I think, combined the operations which the McCarthy forces had split between the Hilton and the Shoreland, and they were badly undermanned.

But they were also terribly friendly; and, though I did not get much help on either funds or housing, since they were also lacking both badly, I did have a long conversation regarding McGovern, their problems in finding funds so late, and our delegation. I left, after about an hour, with the usual admonition that they would try to follow some leads they had and that I should come back the next day. I felt that they were far too busy trying to get their own house in order to give me much help, but I was impressed with the staff, and I even took a McGovern button out the door with me.

By then it was pretty late in the evening, so, after another quick exploratory foray through the Conrad Hilton, this time including the mass of press gear located in the basement, I returned to my YMCA cell for a little sleep. I wedged myself into bed and read a small but important booklet prepared by the McCarthy staff on convention procedure. I had just finished this booklet and was starting on a newspaper report about Vice-President Humphrey's renewed pledge of support for Lyndon Johnson's war policy, when there was a knock on the door.

I opened to find Sam Brown and a younger McCarthy staff worker whom I had never met before. Since I could not invite them both in at the same time and since Sam had to leave anyway, he introduced me to his friend and took off. This young man had been assigned to work with me as the McCarthy coordinator for the Georgia challenge delegation, so we talked for about an hour. After I had filled him in on all the background, he said that he would be contacting me about a possible press conference. But I don't think that I ever saw him again.

––––––

The next day, Monday, I roused myself fairly early, had breakfast downstairs in the YMCA restaurant, and, following a suggestion from Dave Mixner, I went to the Democratic National Committee Headquarters on the eleventh floor of the Conrad Hilton to ask for housing help. The receptionist in the floor lobby suggested that I try both the Credentials Committee office, since I was with a challenge delegation, and the regular housing office.

At the Credentials Committee office, which consisted of a small two room suite filled with desks and filing cabinets, I also decided to ask about how we obtained any passes necessary for the committee hearings. I was told by another receptionist that they had nothing to do with housing and that the man in charge of the hearings passes would be back in a little while. Then I walked across to the housing office where I was once again told that I would have to come back later.

This pattern of "coming back later" was to be repeated over and over again in the pre-convention week of confusion, through no-one's particular fault or design. Taylor and I soon learned that it usually took two or three trips to any one place to accomplish a single task, which of course meant that we were both kept continually on the move just to get a few things done.

With the phone strike on, the only phones installed were the phones already in the rooms, meaning that it was impossible to get through to the Conrad Hilton switchboard and that it was usually faster just to walk somewhere, even several floors or several blocks away, only to find that the person we were looking for had just left, than it was to try to phone ahead.

The only place I knew with a friendly phone was the Coalition For An Open Convention, so I walked up there. In the office there was a little more activity than the day before, but it seemed to me that the place was largely occupied by students with little to do. There were very few people actually at work in any of the offices, though most of the walls were filled with charts of one sort of another, and the desks were loaded with paper. I was certain that earlier in the summer the COC must have been a very active place; but, as the convention became imminent, the COC's role was disappearing. Earlier in the summer the COC was one of the few critical forces working to keep the convention open; but the COC could be no force within the convention itself, so there was little left for it to do other than to hope that groups on the inside of the convention could then keep up the same fight.

Apparently the COC's last planned event, the student march on Chicago, had been forced to be cancelled. The leaders were warning student groups not to tempt the Chicago police with a demonstration without a permit. Freedom of assembly, guaranteed in the Constitution, apparently was not to apply in Chicago for one entire week, even though the largest political party in the country was meeting there to write a platform and to elect a presidential candidate. How *is* one who comes from a non-primary state supposed to legally affect the highest levels of our political system?

For a few minutes I wandered around the COC office, picking up a schedule for the various Credentials Committee hearings; I noticed that Georgia was scheduled for Wednesday at 2:30. I also obtained from Vernon Shell the addresses and phone numbers where he believed that Dr. Hawkins from North Carolina and John Cashin from Alabama could be reached in Chicago.

I occupied an office and started on the telephone. First I called Walter Turner, but there was no answer. Next I tried SCLC in Chicago and asked for Jesse Jackson but I was told that he was attending the SCLC annual convention in Memphis! I asked Vernon if I could make a long-distance call, and with his approval I rang SCLC in Atlanta. The receptionist told me that Hosea Williams and all of the staff had left for the convention in Memphis. When I explained that I urgently needed to talk with Mr. Williams, she finally gave me a hotel number to call in Memphis.

The hotel in Memphis told me that neither Mr. Williams nor Mr. Jackson had checked in yet. I left word for one of them to call me, and I gave them the numbers in Chicago of the COC, McCarthy HQ, and the YMCA. I could not remember Hosea ever mentioning the SCLC convention; if all of the Chicago SCLC leadership was going to be out of town, my week was going to be a lot more difficult.

Next, without luck, I tried to reach Dr. Hawkins and John Cashin. Neither was in at the time, but their hotels confirmed that they had checked in. I was at a momentary impasse, so I thanked Vernon for the use of the phone and told him that if I ever got the SCCC off the ground, I would let him and Ken know so that they could come to the meetings. I then asked Vernon to call Mr. Burke at the Continental Illinois Bank and to ask him if I could come over to talk about opening an account. Mr. Burke did not sound too enthusiastic over the phone, but he said for me to come over to talk about it.

A fifteen-minute walk put me outside the Continental Illinois Bank Building, which also occupied an entire block. Because the state of Illinois does not allow branch banking, even within a city, most of the Chicago banks are physically huge, since all operations have to be done at one location; and the Continental is one of the largest. Vernon had given me instructions about going up the escalator in the lobby; the first floor is a massive tomb of a banking floor with a high ceiling: It all looks more like a white marble European cathedral than a bank. In the center of this expanse were located the customer service desks, fifteen or twenty, and I asked a young secretary for Mr. Ed Burke.

Mr. Burke turned out to be a short man of about thirty-five who, I noticed, seemed a little nervous. No wonder, I thought, if he was handling many accounts like that of the Coalition for an Open Convention. I was then about to approach him with another really sound proposal: aged twenty-one, from out of state, I asked him to open an account for the Southern Challenges Coordinating Committee, for which I had no deposit at present, but which I hoped would soon be receiving large out of town contributions.

I have no idea what he must have thought of me, but I explained that I had worked in a bank for two summers and that I would handle the new account responsibly. He finally agreed, and so I had to fill in all sorts of forms, on one of which, for an "unincorporated organization," I had to put myself down for both president and treasurer and then sign the paper myself as the secretary. Well, I figured, it was just for the records. On another form I had to specify what I wanted done with any balance left over if I should die. For that one I wrote that any funds should be divided evenly between Julian Bond, Dr. Reginald Hawkins, John Cashin, and Mrs. Billy Carr.

Mr. Burke took down my father's name and business, plus my references at my former Atlanta employer. He then had a long talk with me about "uncollected funds." He had apparently had problems with the COC, where they tended to write their own checks against donated checks without allowing eight days for the latter to clear. I said that I understood that this was not to be done, and I explained that I hoped most of our donations would be coming by "wire transfer," which most banks consider to be collected funds and immediately usable. He wasn't sure about that, but he had a conference with the man in charge who confirmed that it was so.

With all of the forms out of the way, he made up a few temporary checks for us and told me not to try to wire any money in for at least twenty-four hours, while the account was being set up. I thanked him profusely and started back for the Conrad Hilton, where I figured it was then time for another round of "coming back later." The SCCC, like a couple of other organizations I had been involved with that summer, might not really yet exist, but it certainly did now have its own checking account.

A quick stop at McGovern Headquarters turned up nothing new, though someone suggested that I should call a Mrs. Lucy Montgomery, who was supposed to be very wealthy and very sympathetic to all such causes. I duly recorded her name on my yellow pad and left for the Conrad Hilton, where I looked up Mrs. Montgomery's number in the phone book; and, upon giving her a call, I was immediately invited up for lunch. She lived in north Chicago, and I had to hitch a ride. Although she turned out to be both an interesting person and one interested in our cause, she simply did not have any money available at the time. But she asked that I call back at the weekend, by which time she hoped to be in a better position.

After our late lunch I returned to the Hilton, and I found George Walsh in the lobby. He told me that the Credentials Committee was meeting then and that I ought to come have a look. I told him I would be right back, but that I had a few stops to make first. Upstairs at both the Credentials Committee office and the housing office I had again just missed the men I wanted to see. At McCarthy Headquarters, Jan Goodman, a member of the staff whom I had just met the night before, told me that she might be able to set up a meeting for the next afternoon between the SCCC leaders and Bayard Rustin, a well-known black leader whom she said would know where the needed money could be found. I told her to go ahead and set up the meeting; I would meanwhile attempt to contact the SCCC delegation leaders.

If one enters the Conrad Hilton through the side door on the south side and turns left, away from the main lobby area, a short walk leads to the flight of stairs descending to a large exhibition hall where, during that first week, all official press conferences were being held. But a right turn and an escalator trip brings one up to an immense exhibition hall with a very high ceiling and green carpeting, off of which, in another large hall, the Credentials Committee was meeting. I found Mr. Walsh standing in the exhibition hall just outside the door leading to the hearing room.

From a suit pocket of nearly everyone in sight there was one end of a Credentials Committee pass, or a press pass, protruding for the guards on the doors to see. The Credentials Committee passes were about eight inches long and four inches wide, made of light cardboard, and diagonally striped in red and white. The press passes were similar, though of a different color. I was later to learn that the former changed color every day, so that attendance in the hearing room was limited to those with business on a particular day, while the press passes were good for the entire week. Such passes proved absolutely essential if one wished to gain entrance to any of the hearings or press conferences.

Neither Mr. Walsh nor I had a pass, but as the hearing was in recess we were able to wander inside without much trouble. The room was fairly dark, with several rows of chairs on the left for the press and, on the right for spectators. Along the wall opposite, and wrapping out on the left and on the right, was the three-tiered platform where the 110 man committee, plus Governor Hughes' advisors, sat in judgment. Between this platform and the spectators' chairs, roped off from the latter, stood a lectern and, on each side of it, long tables and chairs for the contesting parties.

Mr. Walsh and I sat down in the back, hoping that we would go unnoticed, while young boys in what looked like red striped carnival barkers' shirts walked around the room dropping various packets of paper at each of the 110 seats. Mr. Walsh explained that each side in a challenge had to provide a separate copy of its brief for each member of the committee, plus a short resume of what it considered to be its major points. The resumes were then distributed by these boys just before a particular hearing was scheduled to begin.

Very shortly the room started to fill with committee members, press, and spectators. Suddenly dusk became bright noon as the banks and banks of television lights were switched on. One could immediately feel the heat from these lamps, of which there were easily enough, it seemed, to light a small stadium.

Soon the committee got back to business, with Governor Hughes seated on the front row directly in front of the speaker's lectern and the color TV cameras from all three networks recording every word for later consumption by special newscasts. I remained there for about an hour, feeling as if I was becoming more and more aware of how the convention actually worked. On leaving, I made a date with Mr. Walsh to have supper with his family that night.

At the south end of the Hilton lobby there was a bank of about ten pay telephones, the only ones in the hotel. After a short wait in line I tried again to reach Walter Turner, but again I got no answer. I decided that it was getting too late to wait any longer so I went around to the YMCA and booked eight rooms for Tuesday night for our group coming up for the Credentials Committee hearing. I asked the man behind the desk if there were a large number of rooms available for the next week, but he answered that I'd have to talk to the manager about that. So after a bit of a wait, I was shown into the manager's office. I explained to him that I might be needing places for almost eighty people, though I didn't yet know the exact gender make-up of our delegation, nor the number of couples.

To my surprise, he said that they could easily handle any number I wanted, from $3.50 to $5.50 per person per night, depending on accommodations. Though the YMCA Hotel's rooms were certainly not the best in town, and were not air conditioned, these vacancies had to be the find of the week; eighty rooms one block from the Conrad Hilton for $4.50 each per night. I almost laughed because I was so happy. The manager told me that they would need a deposit of, say, $200 by Thursday to hold the rooms; but for the time being he would reserve them for me for free.

I made a rough guess that we would need about forty rooms for males, thirty for females, and ten for couples; I assured him that I would have the exact numbers by the time the deposit was made on Thursday. I still hoped that Walter could find us better accommodations, but I was terribly relieved to know that, in an emergency, we at least had a central place where we could all stay under one roof at a reasonable price. Now all we needed was the money to pay for it.

After a trip to the McCarthy storefront, where there still was no further word on housing possibilities, I tried again at the Credentials Committee office. This time I learned from the man in charge, who I happened to catch in, that one of the leaders from our delegation could pick up our passes to the Wednesday hearings on Tuesday afternoon; but he was not sure that he would have the twelve passes I then asked for. I next returned to the McCarthy floor to find anyone whom I could start asking for money. As no one familiar was there, I checked my pigeonhole for messages and went looking for a phone, which I found in the small room across from the Xerox machine. Though I was not officially part of the staff, I took up residence there for about half an hour, phoning, again without success, first Walter and then SCLC.

So I called Taylor, collect, in Atlanta, to check in and to pass along all of the relevant information. I explained that I had rooms in the YMCA Hotel for everyone arriving the next morning, and I gave him directions for getting there. I also gave him John Garfield's number in Iowa and told him to call to press home our desperate need for funds, which I was having little luck satisfying. He told me that he and Mrs. Paschall had communicated with everyone on the delegation and that there was a Delta Airlines Saturday afternoon flight which they could all get on, if we could raise the money. He added that Julian, Rev. Hooten and the others would leave early the next morning for Chicago and that he would be coming up a little later. We then rang off so that he could start calling the others regarding their Chicago accommodations.

By this time it was nearly six, so I went down to the lobby where I met Mr. Walsh, his wife and daughter. I had always enjoyed being with them. We went into the least expensive of the three downstairs restaurants for supper. For a while we talked about the sightseeing the women had been doing, and Mr. and Mrs. Walsh said that they were interested in moving into the YMCA Hotel, if possible, to save both time and money.

Mr. Walsh had been in the Credentials Committee hearing nearly all day, and he said that our speakers were going to have to polish their performances to come across concisely and effectively to so many people on a committee which, by Wednesday afternoon, would probably be nearly worn out by such testimony. Mr. Walsh added that, although the committee would meet each night in closed session, he was not sure whether they would announce decisions as they went along, or whether all decisions would be kept secret until Friday. Over dessert I learned that Julian and our committee delegation would be meeting at 9:30 the next morning in Al Harris' office at 231 LaSalle Street to write their speeches and to rehearse their testimony.

After supper it was back up to McCarthy HQ on the fifteenth floor, where Jan Goodman informed me that she had arranged the meeting with Bayard Rustin for the next afternoon at five o'clock in his room in a nearby hotel. All that I then had to do was to find the SCCC leaders and let them know. For the Cashins, this meant leaving a long note in their room in the Conrad Hilton. Dr. Hawkins I finally caught on the phone. We talked about his problems in finding housing and funds for his North Carolina delegation, and we also decided that the SCCC needed a press conference, which I said I would take care of. I still could not find any of the Texas challenge delegation, and I decided to wait for reinforcements before approaching the Mississippi delegation, about which I felt certain Mr. Rustin already knew a great deal anyway.

While I was walking around the McCarthy floor I entered the central headquarters room to find Sam Brown in conversation with a middle aged gentleman. As I wanted to ask Sam about financial help I took a seat to wait until they were finished. Sam was saying "Now you know that Curt has been doing a remarkable job," while the older man, obviously angry, replied in a low voice, "that may be, but this campaign is $800,000 in debt; I don't know where the money is going to come from to pay the bills; and I think Curt and his men have been spending too much money." As it became obvious that their conversation was going to continue for some time, and that I was an outsider, it probably was best that I leave them alone, so I went back downstairs.

Walking past one of the restaurants I saw Frank McDonald, McCarthy Southern Desk Man, having supper inside with a friend. He also spotted me, and he motioned for me to come inside and join them. Frank introduced me to his friend, Woody, and asked me how my organizational efforts were going. I explained my ups and downs and my partial success at the YMCA. I added that I thought our biggest problem was financial, since we still did not have the money to bring the delegation up, or to pay hotel bills. From the conversation I had just overheard upstairs it did not sound like McCarthy HQ was going to be of too much help.

Frank then said that I must have been listening to Mr. Quiggly, McCarthy's brother-in-law in charge of the campaign funds. Frank explained that Mr. Quiggly was a continual pessimist and that there had been fights throughout the summer between him and the field staff, which Mr. Quiggly considered to be an expensive and wasteful operation. Frank then elaborated on this basic split over political theory within the McCarthy organization.

The younger field men, backed by data from 1964, believed that the only way to nurture really strong support was by local, door-to-door, saturation organization and communication. The older men who controlled the national purse strings believed, however, that it was easier, cheaper, and just as effective to concentrate on the mass media. This argument had gone on all summer, culminating in the threat from the top not to pay for the Washington desk men's trip to Chicago, even though they alone had the vital contacts within the various state delegations. Sam Brown was then attempting to smooth out these inner problems so that they could all get down to the business at hand.

Woody had been listening to all of this conversation without saying very much. Though I don't know how he knew Frank, I got the impression from their later conversation that they had been old friends and that Woody, although not involved with the McCarthy campaign previously, had come to Chicago to give Frank a hand if he needed it. Shortly we were joined by another Frank, Woody's roommate, who was shorter and stockier than Woody; he was looking for their room key, but he sat down with us for a cup of coffee. Woody said that if there was nothing much for the two of them to do, since they were not going to get inside the convention, anyway, they might as well take off for a short vacation.

I remarked that I could use some manpower help of the SCCC, though I still was not sure what we were going to do. They said that they might be interested, so I told them about the SCCC and said that we probably would be having a press conference early on Wednesday, followed by a planning meeting. I had nothing definite to offer, so the subject was dropped, though they did give me their room number in the Hilton and said to look them up if I needed help and if they had not yet left.

After about an hour, as I was getting up to leave, Frank McDonald responded to an earlier remark about funds by saying that he would do all that he could for us. He then gave me his phone number in the McCarthy HQ at the amphitheater, where he was helping to set up the McCarthy office. He also gave me the code numbers to a telephone credit card which he said the McCarthy staff men used in emergencies to make long distance calls. He said that I could use it when calling on official delegation business. I then bid them goodnight, since I figured that the next day would prove long and hard, and I needed some sleep.

Tuesday morning, August 20th, I went in search of 231 LaSalle St., which turned out to be the Continental Illinois Bank Building. I arrived in the lobby of Mr. Harris' firm just after 9:30, there to find Julian Bond, Rev. Morris, Ben Brown, Al Horn, George Walsh, and Chico Thomas. I was introduced to Rev. J. R. Campbell, of Americus, who had consented to testify at the hearing and to Charlie Sherrod, a young black organizer from Albany and a member of our delegation who had decided to come up early to help Rev. Campbell.

They had arrived just a few minutes before, and there was some joking about the sizes of their YMCA rooms, where they had already checked in.

Just then Al Harris arrived from inside the office; and after greetings he led us inside to the largest law office I had ever seen, though Mr. Harris said that it was small compared to some. After a three-minute walk along quiet corridors lined with volume after volume of law books, we arrived in a modern conference room which was ours for the day.

Al ordered some coffee, we all sat down around the conference table, and Al explained that he hoped the next day's speakers could use the quiet of this conference room, plus any other rooms needed, to make final drafts of their speeches and to rehearse their presentations. He was a gracious host, but he was also concerned that we come across at the hearings just as effectively as possible, which he knew would take both consultation to coordinate the speeches and concentration to prepare them properly.

He suggested that we first iron out each speaker's responsibilities then let each man have a few hours to prepare his speech. I quickly made a few announcements, including the meeting with Bayard Rustin for that afternoon, which I hoped Julian, at least, could attend. After I finished, everyone got down to specific definitions of who would cover what in their speeches; they had a lot to do, but the overall mood seemed cautiously confident and excited. I was torn, as earlier, between an interest in what they were doing and the responsibility of my own job. But I decided to remain with them for a while.

They had not been working for long when the phone rang: it was Mrs. Morris calling from Atlanta with the news that Al Kehrer and his friends were on their way to Chicago to personally argue the original challenge brief submitted by the Forum. This news hit our group like a pin hitting a balloon. Everyone, including Ben Brown and Rev. Morris, considered by everyone to be the closest to Mr. Kehrer, were taken by complete surprise. Rev. Morris' first reaction was that Mr. Kehrer could not argue the other brief, since it had been withdrawn by the delegation leaders.

Al Horn, on whose shoulders rested the responsibility for the actual legal presentation, said that it could do nothing but hurt us. Julian probably came the closest when he guessed that Mr. Kehrer was being brought to Chicago by the Humphrey forces in a last-ditch effort to confuse our Georgia presentation and to discredit our challenge delegation with public accusations; and this maneuver explained why the Forum executive committee meeting had suddenly been canceled the previous Saturday. Ben Brown, who was a Humphrey supporter, said that we should not jump to any conclusions; but even he agreed that if Mr. Kehrer went ahead our chances for success would be damaged considerably.

We spent at least half an hour talking about what to do; but then Al Harris pointed out that, since Mr. Kehrer probably was not yet in Chicago, it would be best to spend what time there was in working on speeches; we would have time to confront this additional problem in the afternoon. I had my usual round of "calling back" to do, so I left them at work and went back to the Conrad Hilton, where I found nobody in; I had similar bad luck trying to reach by telephone either Walter, Dave Mixner, or someone in charge at SCLC.

When I returned to Al's office it was lunch time; Taylor had just arrived and someone had saved a few sandwiches for us. Though the morning had been productive, everyone needed more time to work. But all of us had business at the Conrad Hilton, so we decided to take a break and go over. With Chico Thomas' help, I wanted to sort out the official press organization and arrange a press conference for the SCCC for Wednesday morning. Taylor wanted to put the pressure on the McCarthy Headquarters for funds, which he had to have quickly to pay for the delegation's plane tickets. Julian, Rev. Hooten (who arrived just as we were leaving) and the lawyers wanted to find Gov. Hughes or someone on the Credentials Committee to verify that the original brief had been withdrawn. Rev. Morris and Ben Brown wanted to locate Al Kehrer, if he had arrived, and find out just what his intentions were.

Since there were no taxis to be found (though some were still operating despite the strike), we had to walk; and by the time we got to the Hilton we were drenched in sweat from the incredibly hot August sun. Rev. Morris, who had thoughtfully reserved a room in the Hilton a week ahead of time, said that we could use his room as a base for operations, and we all planned to meet there an hour later. Those were probably the last precise plans we made during the next 36 hours, and the fact that all of us were too busy to report back in an hour was an indication of how, from that point on, we were all swallowed by the events around us and were kept literally running constantly.

Rev. Morris' room, 1265, did become a base for operations, and it was a Godsend that we had it. But, except for late that night when we were all gathered together in our "operations room," it is difficult to remember just exactly who was where and when. Julian, for example, went off in search of

166

the Credentials Committee people; but he also had to write his speech for the next day, plus attend the meeting with Bayard Rustin, plus try to figure out, with the rest of us, what to do about Mr. Kehrer's threat, which grew larger every hour.

Upon arrival at the Hilton, Chico Thomas went off to familiarize himself with the press system and to find out if there were any time slots open for the next morning. I took Taylor with me for a brief reconnaissance trip around the Hilton, including a stop at the housing office on the eleventh floor, where again there was no one to talk to (I was beginning to be just a little frustrated by this particular "call back"). We returned to Rev. Morris' room on the twelfth floor to learn that Chico had found a slot for the SCCC news conference for 9:30 the next morning.

So I had to arrange for a room where the SCCC could meet following the press conference. I left Taylor on his way up to the fifteenth floor to start his financial lobbying while I headed over to the YMCA. In the Hilton lobby I ran into Pat Madsen and John Tillman. They had just flown up, independently, and were looking for us. I explained that I was in a hurry at the moment but that they could go up to Rev. Morris' room and that the YMCA was the only place I could suggest for lodging.

I then walked around to the YMCA, where, after a long wait, I saw the Events Manager about the possibility of renting a conference room, if they had one. Not only did they have one, not only was it air conditioned, but its use was also free of charge to hotel guests! So he got out his weekly calendar, and I booked the Wabash Room for every morning of that week at ten o'clock. My esteem for the YMCA was growing daily.

Returning to the Hilton I next ran into Walter Turner, standing at a telephone. We were both very glad to see each other; he said that he had been trying to reach me all day and that he thought he had some pretty good leads. Nothing was definite yet, but he was working both on some hotels and on some almost-finished apartments which we might be able to take over for a week. I explained that I had, if all else failed, booked the YMCA but that it would be an uncomfortable place to have to stay. I added that Julian and the others had arrived, and we went up to Rev. Morris' room.

After a while I decided that I had best start the possibly long process of trying to obtain our passes for the next day's hearing, so I walked down one floor to the Credentials Committee office, where I met Rev. Morris and

167

Al Horn. Julian and Al Harris were apparently off trying to find Governor Hughes to clarify the situation on the Georgia challenge.

Since the man I needed was not there, I sat in while Rev. Morris and Al Horn met with another member of the staff who had been assigned to the Georgia case. He led us into the back room of the suite, and then brought in a file marked "Georgia." He confirmed Rev. Morris' question that, yes, they had received a telegram from Julian Bond and Rev. Hooten asking that the original brief be withdrawn; but they had received a telegram this past Saturday saying that a Mr. Kehrer would be arriving to argue the first brief and that it should not be withdrawn.

Al asked why none of us had been notified. The staff man said that they had assumed that we had known, since we too were from Georgia. To our dismay, he added that the total Georgia challenge time allotment would have to be split between the two groups. After about five minutes it became clear that the official Credentials Committee ruling was that, since Mr. Kehrer's name appeared on the first brief, he had a right to argue it before the Credentials Committee. To this Rev. Morris replied, becoming uncharacteristically angry, that his name, too, appeared on the brief, that in fact it was he who had written the brief, and that he wanted it withdrawn.

This met with a shaking head and "Well, you people from Georgia will just have to settle your differences; you can't expect us to do that. Our position is that if Mr. Kehrer wants to present his brief, he can." I had the unmistakable feeling from this man that he was carrying out an unpleasant task directed from above. He rarely looked up at us. I hoped that Julian was having more luck with Governor Hughes. Rev. Morris wanted to argue some more, but the futility was obvious, so Al persuaded him to return to the room with us and to await the others to make plans.

It was then nearly five, so I went up to McCarthy Headquarters where I found Dave Mixner with Jan Goodman. The three of us then departed for Bayard Rustin's room in a hotel up the street. While we walked Dave asked me how the SCCC was coming, and I confessed that so far I was having little luck at putting much together. He said that he had finally been assigned to help me, if I still wanted him. He added that he might know some places to call to raise a little money. I, of course, gladly accepted his offer of help.

Dr. Hawkins, his assistant, and two representatives from the National Democratic Party of Alabama were already in Mr. Rustin's room when we arrived. I apologized for Julian not being there, explaining that he was "in a meeting"; I said that I hoped he would arrive shortly. Mr. Rustin's room was at the front of his hotel, up high, looking out over the lakefront. We quickly recited our conception of what the SCCC would do and emphasized that all of us were in financial trouble. After we had finished, Mr. Rustin said that he might be able to find us some money, but he added that he was concerned about ours being a neutral group politically (he was known to support Vice-President Humphrey). Dr. Hawkins answered that his whole delegation was keeping an open mind until seated, which was seconded by the NDPA representatives.

Mr. Rustin asked me about our delegation from Georgia; he said that he had heard reports that we were strongly pro-McCarthy. I could only answer that, while we might have a McCarthy majority on the delegation, nevertheless, every candidate was represented on our delegation, I added that I honestly did not know the preferences of many of our delegates and pointed out that the larger issue, really, was whether we unseated the Maddox-chosen delegation.

I emphasized that we had agreed on the necessary neutrality of the SCCC. Mr. Rustin's aide, however, pressed me further about 'dissension within Georgia," and "weren't there actually two challenges coming from Georgia?" As I did not want to prematurely answer that one, I sidestepped it by saying that we had asked that an earlier brief be withdrawn (but I wondered how this gentleman had found out and how much he knew about Mr. Kehrer).

Mr. Rustin had to get to a dinner, so our meeting did not last very much longer. In the end he said that he would do all that he could and that he would be at our meeting in the Wabash Room at the YMCA the next day (which I had announced, along with the press conference time). Just as we were preparing to leave, Julian arrived. He talked briefly with Mr. Rustin, and then we walked back to the Conrad Hilton. Julian and Al Harris had been able to see Governor Hughes briefly between sessions of the Credentials Committee hearings, and they had received the same line we had heard from Governor Hughes' assistant.

Arriving at the Hilton, Julian went upstairs to Rev. Morris' room; Dave said that he was going to start making phone calls for the SCCC. I made a quick stop by the Credentials Committee office and finally found the man I was looking for. After a little talking, I eventually convinced him, with the help of my letter of introduction, that I had been sent to collect our passes for the next day. I persuaded him to let us have fifteen passes, and then I climbed the back stairs one flight to the twelfth floor.

Nearly everyone was then assembled in Rev. Morris' room, which consisted of two single beds to the right of the entrance, beyond the lavatory, and a closet, sofa, chairs and table on the left. The Conrad Hilton's air conditioning could not handle the heat, at least on that day, and we had to have the window open, which looked down on the McCarthy storefront and the YMCA Hotel in the next block to the south. It still must have been at least 85 to 90 on the inside.

No one had yet been able to find Mr. Kehrer, though he was checked into the hotel. Clearly the officers had to plan on some course of action. In this, the first of our "crisis" meetings that week, the procedure was like that followed throughout. Julian, Rev. Hooten and Ben Brown, by vote of the delegation, had to make the final decisions; but all of us, including Taylor and myself, freely contributed to the discussions.

Julian and Al Horn expressed their opinion, then, that Mr. Kehrer and friends had been brought to Chicago by the Humphrey forces in a deliberate attempt to confuse the Credentials Committee, to shorten our presentation, and, by attacking us, to discredit our delegation's standing. Ben Brown and Rev Morris, on the other hand, argued that perhaps Mr. Kehrer sincerely believed that he was doing the right thing and that he could do a better job than us. Al Horn pointed out, though, that Mr. Kehrer had no delegation with him, so for whom could he actually be arguing and for what purpose?

In the end, Ben and Rev. Morris held sway, and it was agreed that they should once again try to establish contact with Mr. Kehrer. Meanwhile the rest of us would have supper; and, as we did not want to antagonize them, if any of the rest of us saw either Mr. Kehrer or his group we decided not to say anything. Al Horn added an important reminder: the press was starting to get wind of our problem, and it was of the utmost importance to our success that only the co-chairman (Julian and Rev. Hooten) speak to the press if we were to keep wild rumors from getting started. Al Harris also reminded the next day's speakers that there was still a lot of homework left to do.

Downstairs at supper we saw both Mr. Goldman and Mr. Johnston pass in the hall outside; and later I passed right by Mr. Goldman, giving him a pleasant "hello," which was met with a scowl, I guess because I was a "dupe of those outsiders." After supper we returned to Rev. Morris' room, where some work was done preparing for our hearing. But the weight of Mr. Kehrer's unknown and unexplainable intentions weighed heavily on everyone's nerves, including my own. Probably only the fact that we had so much to do spared us from unnecessary arguments.

I had told Julian about the Southern Challenges Coordinating Committee press conference the next morning, and I had to try to coerce someone from Mississippi to attend. So Taylor and I went up to the suite occupied by the Mississippi challenge delegation and asked to speak to Aaron Henry. I had never met Mr. Henry before, so we stood in the hallway while an aide went to find him. I explained to Mr. Henry who we were and how much we hoped that he could represent Mississippi at the SCCC press conference, to show that the problems in the South extended beyond Mississippi and that the Mississippi challenge delegation was sympathetic with our causes.

Mr. Henry was, at first, responsive; but two of his lawyers, who had come to the door with him, quickly talked him out of it. The challenge had just been heard that day, and they were afraid of doing anything which might endanger their almost certain chance for success. The lawyers, and their seeming control over Mr. Henry made me angry, but what could we do? Disappointed, Taylor and I tried again at McCarthy Headquarters to find someone who would give us our answer on financial help. That, too, proved impossible; none of the right people ever seemed to be there.

Taylor went back to our "base" in 1265 to call Mrs. Paschall in Atlanta to pass on his so far disappointing news regarding the money and to find out if there had been any last-minute changes in the number expecting to come. I went down to the lobby to buy some mints and fortuitously found Vernon Shell and Ken Guido. I told them about the SCCC press conference and the meeting scheduled for afterwards, and I related our disappointment over Mississippi. They said that they would come to the SCCC meeting and that they thought they could persuade one of the other Mississippi leaders to be there, too.

When I arrived upstairs, Ben Brown and Rev. Morris had just returned from a long talk with Mr. Kehrer, Joe Jacobs, and their friends. It seemed that Mr. Kehrer had asserted his right to argue the original brief for the Georgia Democratic Party Forum, and no amount of arguing from either

Ben or Rev. Morris could persuade him that he could do nothing by that time, but hurt the overall cause. Mr. Kehrer, after resigning as our convention chairman and refusing even to be a member of our delegation, now appeared to believe that he was doing the "right thing for the people of Georgia" by personally arguing a challenge brief without any delegation to seat, even if he should win.

We were obviously headed for a very embarrassing confrontation at the Credentials Committee hearing, involving a split between the challengers, which would make it all too convenient for the committee to seat the Maddox delegation simply because it did not know which of the challengers to believe. We talked about our new problem for an hour; and, whatever else he had hoped to accomplish, Mr. Kehrer was certainly preventing our key speakers from doing the kind of work they needed to be doing to be effective. Gone was the earlier mood of confidence and hope; after our summer's work, it seemed that all of our efforts were going to be absolutely wrecked by one man and his personal idea of what was right. We were all nervous, disappointed, and angry.

In this situation we decided to go to the top: Julian placed a long-distance phone call to Washington and asked to speak person to person to Vice President Humphrey. Though Julian had never spoken personally with the Vice-President before and though, as we later determined, this must have been the precise moment when there was a Security Council meeting over the Soviet invasion of Czechoslovakia, where the first waves of Russian troops had just crossed the borders, the telephone rang ten minutes later; it was Vice-President Humphrey himself.

Julian quickly motioned for all of us to be quiet while he, with one hand covering his ear, sat down on the edge of the bed and explained our case to the Vice-President. Julian said, among other things, that we had a delegation from Georgia which hoped, once and for all, to change the kind of political system with which Georgia had been crippled for years. He explained that we had come to Chicago with supporters of all the national candidates to fight our case but that it suddenly appeared that one man, Mr. Humphrey's own supporter, had the power to ruin an effort which we had hoped would benefit all Georgians. We were all elated when Julian gave Al Kehrer's name and room number to Mr. Humphrey and said "thank you, Mr. Vice-President."

They talked for over ten minutes, and when Julian finally said good-bye we were, of course, terribly anxious to know what had been said. Mr. Humphrey had said, related Julian, that he did not understand why, after all these years of Mr. Humphrey's support, Julian was then helping Gene McCarthy. But at the end he had promised to "do what he could." We decided to wait for about forty-five minutes and then to call Mr. Kehrer to determine if he would meet with another deputation. So we waited, and then Ben called. Mr. Kehrer replied that he would speak only with Ben, who immediately went down to his room.

When Ben came back twenty minutes later, it never was made quite clear whether the Vice-President had ever called Mr. Kehrer; but the final message from Mr. Kehrer was quite clear. He would agree not to argue the original brief on the one condition that, if we lost, we would agree not to file a minority report and would not take the Georgia case to the convention floor!

At least half of the truth was finally revealed. Though we still did not know who, if anyone, had encouraged Mr. Kehrer to come to Chicago, his purpose was quite clear: either to badly hurt our chances before the Credentials Committee or else to blackmail us into keeping our case off of prime-time television.

This revelation, after all of Mr. Kehrer's pronouncements about "not playing partisan politics" and about "keeping the best interests of Georgians always first," came as a shock to us all; but it hit Rev. Morris, his oldest friend, the hardest, because Rev. Morris had most believed Mr. Kehrer's former good intentions.

It then appeared to us all that the forces of one of the presidential candidates, after ignoring the Georgia challenge for so long, had suddenly awoken to its possible effect upon the rest of the South; they then seemed ready to go to almost any lengths to ruin us. Obviously we were being had for the sake of "Partisan politics."

After a brief, intense, talk, Rev. Morris said that he was prepared to tell the press about just what was happening to us. We all agreed that it would be much better to expose what was going on that night than to wait until it was all over the next day, when any attempt to point the finger would look like poor losers. Taylor, Chico and I were sent off to find out the press situation while Rev. Morris and Julian prepared statements. Taylor and I went down to the lobby level exhibition hall, in half of which all of that week's press conferences were taking place.

Though I did not have the proper pass, I bullied my way in by looking "official"; all of the press were there and waiting, but nothing was happening. I quickly asked a reporter what was up and he explained that the Credentials Committee was having its first closed session and that Governor Hughes was expected along at any time to announce the first results, including the decision on Mississippi. We had a ready-made press conference if we could just get our people down in time!

There was a house phone in the corner which I tried to use to call our room, but the line was busy. So Taylor and I then had to go all the way back upstairs, which with all of the crowds, was starting to be a ten minute operation. We finally got back, explained the situation, and admonished everyone to hurry. Rev. Morris was worried about the exact wording of what he would say but we impressed upon him the need for speed, and fairly soon we were on the way down again.

This time, at the press conference door, we had, literally, a five-minute argument with the guard because we did not have the right passes for a press conference. But we were the people *giving* the press conference, we explained. Finally we got in; and, while Julian and Rev. Morris went up to the small stage surrounded on one side by curtains and on the other side by reporters, TV cameras, and lights, Taylor and I assured the man in charge that they would step down the moment Governor Hughes arrived.

The lights came on and the cameras began to roll almost automatically during that week, for the press never knew when a story was going to break. Rev. Morris stepped up to the microphones and began what, for him, was going to be a very difficult announcement; for he was going to have to reveal that both one of his long time friends and almost assuredly the forces of his personal choice for president were trying to ruin the Georgia challenge. I noticed that he had taken off his Humphrey buttons.

Rev. Morris, probably more than any of the rest of us, was a political idealist, and such revelations must have been terribly hard on him, but also terribly irritating. I stood in the back and watched him on a TV camera's black and white monitor. He began with "Ladies and gentlemen, I have a particularly sad and unpleasant chain of events to relate to you this evening," but he had gotten little further when, from the back of the room, Governor Hughes entered, surrounded by another host of reporters and followers.

As agreed, Rev. Morris had to step down, but we stayed to watch while

Governor Hughes read the first Credentials Committee reports. None of the challengers had won, except Mississippi, where, "because of the continued failure of the regular Democratic Party of Mississippi to institute changes in its structure which allow and encourage the participation of all racial groups within party affairs," the Credentials Committee planned to recommend to the Democratic National Convention that it reject the credentials of the regular delegation and accept those of the challengers. The debt of 1964 was paid. There were cheers on the side, and several people rushed up to congratulate Joe Rauh, who had entered with the governor.

After a few questions the press then exited to file their reports, and we were left with a nearly empty room. Since it was then after midnight and we did not expect the press to return, we went back upstairs. We talked for another hour; but there was little more that we could do, then, except try to ensure that our presentation would be as sound and as convincing as possible. Julian said that he had a breakfast meeting with the McCarthy Credentials Committee delegates at eight o'clock, and as I left he asked me to wake him at seven-thirty. Taylor and I returned to the YMCA for a little sleep. We were all still very disappointed and apprehensive, but slowly a new sort of zeal was forming within our group, because we finally realized just how difficult our fight was going to be.

8

THE GEORGIA CASE AT THE CREDENTIALS COMMITTEE

At 7:20 that Wednesday morning, August 21st, I woke up, dressed, and went around to wake up Taylor, John Tillman, and Julian. Julian looked very, very tired, and he tried to talk me into letting him have another fifteen minutes of sleep; he said that he had been talking with various people until nearly five in the morning. All four of us eventually pieced ourselves together, and as we walked the block to the Hilton it was obvious that it was going to be a very hot day.

Julian went up to the fifteenth floor to his meeting while Taylor, John and I had some breakfast downstairs. There is a strange feeling that one has very early in the morning when one has had very little sleep the night before: it's a sort of hollowness in the chest, a dry throat, and a fuzzy mind. All of us looked that way, and I felt that way, as we sat down and tried to rejuvenate on cups of coffee. I started writing down points that we would want to cover in our SCCC meeting, scheduled for that morning. Taylor said that we would have to get the air fare money either that day or the next, if our delegation was going to make the Saturday flight.

We took a quick trip upstairs to Rev. Morris' room, where we found the good reverend in about the same shape as we were. As it was getting close to nine, I went downstairs to check at the exhibition hall press room to make sure that all was in order. John Cashin and Dr. Hawkins arrived about 9:15. The Texas challenge was being heard late that morning, and so we did not expect anyone from that delegation. About 9:20 a heavily built, outgoing sort of a man announced to me that he was Lawrence Guyot, a representative from the Mississippi challenge delegation. While Dr. Hawkins and John Cashin filled him in on the SCCC history, I went upstairs to try and pull Julian away from his breakfast meeting.

His conference was taking place in the room at the end of the side corridor which also housed the McCarthy forces' Xerox machine. I knocked and was allowed in to find a packed room, with Julian answering detailed questions from the McCarthy delegates on the Credentials Committee. Such meetings apparently occurred each morning, with leaders and counsel for all of the day's challenges reviewing the McCarthy delegates on their challenge's basic points.

Whether it was true or not, the press had reported a week before that the McCarthy camp considered the Georgia challenge "its number one priority," and Julian was then taking special care to clear up rather detailed questions about the Georgia Democratic Party and the present system of delegate appointment in Georgia. It was always revealing to watch the faces of people from any primary state – from whence, obviously, came most of these delegates – while one of our group recounted the non-democratic system in Georgia. By the end of Julian's meeting most of them expressed their determination to win a victory for us not just because they were McCarthy delegates, but because they were Democrats.

It was getting to be past 9:30, so Julian excused himself, thanking them for their time. "Good luck" followed us out the door; and soon we arrived downstairs, where, as if by magic, all of the press in the hotel seemed then to be assembled; Chico had done a good job. Julian led the conference off, speaking extemporaneously about Georgia, about the purposes of the SCCC, and about the larger problem of democratic representation in most of the state Democratic parties in the South. John Cashin and Dr. Hawkins echoed Julian, specifying a few details of alleged discrimination against Democrats in Alabama and North Carolina.

Mr. Guyot, whose delegation's victory before the Credentials Committee had been announced only the night before, tied it all together, emphasizing that the problems existed in more than just one state and that they were a common factor in the South (and perhaps in the nation). He called upon the Democratic Party not to believe that, having righted Mississippi's wrongs, it could then ignore these other states, putting them off until 1972 or 1976. I wound it up with a short talk about the specific goals – housing, food, and funds for nearly 200 people – which we had set for ourselves, and I reiterated the physical difficulties we were finding in trying to work within the system to bring about responsible change.

The press then asked some questions, dealing mostly with how well the challenges were going from each of the undecided states. As there was another press conference scheduled shortly, and as we had a meeting to attend, we broke up in a short while. Or we tried to break up, because, in a pattern that continued throughout the convention, the TV and radio people then wanted to do individual interviews with all of us.

Julian, who already was becoming one of the focal points of the challenge issue, was still embroiled with the press ten minutes later when the rest of us left to go over to the YMCA; he had told me earlier that he was going to *have* to devote some time to his Credential Committee speech, scheduled for that afternoon, and he would not be able to attend. As I left I was confident that we were well on the way toward accomplishing one of our SCCC goals: political solidarity and leverage with the Credentials Committee. But our physical problems still remained.

Dave Mixner had arrived during the press conference and, together with John Cashin, we walked over to the YMCA. The Wabash Room, located on the second floor, like the rest of the YMCA Hotel, certainly was not the Hilton, but it was extremely functional. Around the single large square of tables and folding chairs sat several already waiting guests, including Bayard Rustin, Ken Guido, and another member of the COC who said that he was representing Texas. Waiting outside the door were Frank and Woody, whom I had not seen since Monday night; they said that they had been ready to leave Chicago when Dave talked them into staying. Armed with legal pads, they volunteered to stay and to help as long as they could do anything, and they agreed to let the SCCC use their room in the Hilton as an operations base. Finally we were starting to inch forward.

At the beginning of the meeting we first, after introductions, went around the table having each representative summarize the needs of his delegation. Both Mr. Cashin and Dr. Hawkins had so far been paying bills out of their own pockets, but they were already in debt and coming to the end of their resources. The young man representing Texas said that their group had all checked into the YMCA and that they could probably come close to paying all of their own bills. Mr. Guyot said that, relatively speaking, Mississippi was quite well off and would need no financial help. I reported that Georgia needed all the money we could get.

Dave then said that he had started phoning the night before and that he thought we might get as much as $2,500 from a McCarthy group in Baltimore. Mr. Rustin said that he felt certain he could raise $500. We then talked about the methods of quick fund raising, with everyone throwing in suggestions of movie stars, millionaires, and organizations that were rumored to have donated money to such causes before. We knew that the spring and summer campaigns had bled nearly every such source dry, but we felt that ours was a cause – food and lodging for people intent on changing the South from inside the political system – which few could turn down. Dave, Frank, and Woody made lists of the suggested contacts.

We knew that, to be successful, the SCCC would have to raise a great deal of money in 48 hours, with that afternoon and evening critical for many first contacts. I read out our account number at the Continental Bank, advising everyone to ask for wire transfers, not checks, as the latter would be useless until after the convention.

Though we as yet had no money, we also decided upon a system of distribution. Instead of trying to decide by vote, each time a contribution was received, which of the delegation's needs was the greatest, we elected to split all contributions in the following manner: 30% each to Alabama, Georgia and North Carolina, 10% to Texas. I was to keep track of each delegation's whereabouts and to be in charge of dispersing the funds. With our procedure thus organized, we agreed to meet the following morning to discuss any results and to decide upon any new courses of action. We then adjourned, and I walked back to the Hilton with Dave, Frank, and Woody, who were impatient to start phoning. Nothing I could have said could have expressed my thanks to those three; I hoped that they understood how I felt.

In Room 1265 the afternoon's speakers were then hard at work on last minute details. George Walsh and Rev. Campbell were conferring in one corner, while Ben Brown sat on the edge of the sofa, his notes spread on the table in front of him. There had been no further developments with Mr. Kehrer, and since a press conference was physically impossible at that late hour, Rev. Morris was revising his speech in an attempt to counter Mr. Kehrer's expected remarks. Julian was working somewhere else; and Al

Horn, who said that he needed peace and quiet to concentrate, had gone over to Al Harris' office early in the morning.

There was little for Taylor or me to do but wait. We went to the Democratic National Committee housing office and, to our surprise, were told that one of the men who could help us was in. The housing office was in another two room suite, this time on the front side of the Hilton, looking out towards the lake. On the walls were maps of the city, showing the hotels being used to house all of the delegations. Other maps showed the floor plan of the Conrad Hilton. We were shown into the smaller side room where, behind a desk, sat a young man of about our age who turned out to be from the University of Georgia.

We had a pleasant conversation, but it was apparent that the National Committee could not be of much help. There were no rooms available in town; and even if there had been, we, like all delegations, would have had to pay the $35 per day per room rate that everyone else was paying. We had expected as much, but at least we had gone through with the formality of trying the official channel.

Taylor and I ate a nervous lunch: my stomach was doing its own thing. Then I went up to the new SCCC operations headquarters in Frank and Woody's room. Dave was sitting on the bed talking on the phone to Baltimore. Woody said that they were starting down the list of suggestions, but that it was a long process to find the phone numbers and to locate the kind of people we had chosen to approach. Dave put down the phone and said that he felt certain of a large donation from Scientists and Engineers For McCarthy in Baltimore.

He then immediately changed the subject, as the news was pouring in about Czechoslovakia, and he wanted to read the papers. He had been to Czechoslovakia a few years before to talk about his experiences in organizing labor, and he had the highest respect for the Czech people. "If they start fighting," he said, "I'll be on the first plane over to help." Woody announced that he had managed to procure, from somewhere, several Conrad Hilton press passes, which could get one in anywhere, and I gladly took the one he offered. It proved invaluable.

Armed now with a red candy-striped Credentials Committee pass and a yellow press pass, I returned to 1265, where lunch had arrived and the group was trying to eat. Al Horn and Julian arrived about 1:30, both, like everyone else, growing nervous, and not helped by so few hours' sleep.

Not only did they all have their own presentations to worry about, but none of us had any idea what was in store for us from either the Maddox defense or from Mr. Kehrer. A little after two Al Harris got everyone together and, like a coach before a big game, gave a short pep talk to build up everyone's confidence. Thus persuaded, we all filed out at about 2:15 and started the agonizingly slow process of trying to get an elevator.

When we arrived in the adjacent exhibition hall and had a look inside the hearing hall, it was obvious that we were too early; the Texas challenge was still raging hot and heavy. Some of our speakers took the time offered by this reprieve to find chairs in the adjacent room and to continue to revise. Meanwhile Taylor, myself, Chico, the Walshes, John Tillman and Pat Madsen, for whom we had procured passes, took up seats in the spectators' gallery. Mr. Kehrer, Mr. Jacobs, Mr. Goldman, Mr. Johnston and their wives were already seated in the front row, and icy glances were thrown our way.

To the left of the speaker's lectern, facing the Committee, sat the witnesses and the lawyers for the challengers; on the right sat the defendants. Each side had two long tables and several chairs; behind these, but still inside the roped boundary separating out the spectators' seats, stood a line of chairs where, I supposed, "friends" and aides of the two sides were to sit.

It became obvious to Taylor, John and me that the long tables were the key position and that we needed to be sitting there, on the lectern end, if we were to have room to work and if we were to appear to be the official Georgia delegation challengers. So we passed the word around that, as soon as the Texas challenge ended, every non-essential person on our side was to go up and occupy a chair around the table, not to budge until one of our own speakers was there to take his place.

After about an hour and a half the Texas challenge came to an end, and the scene around the challengers' table for the next few minutes must have been a bit comic. Taylor, John (who is at least 6 feet 4 inches tall) and I immediately rushed forward and, as soon as a Texan would stand up, one of us would sit down. Mr. Kehrer's people, however, apparently had the same idea, so there was consequently a great rush of people vying for the best positions.

I'm afraid that, on the whole, we won this particular part of the day's duel, so Mr. Jacobs and others simply started moving more chairs in, and, shortly, there was a great host of people and chairs crammed into the small challengers' area. Though looking back this confrontation sounds humorous, at the time, we, and they, were dead serious about keeping our seats.

Meanwhile there was also a great controversy at Governor Hughes' chair, where Al Horn and Mr. Kehrer, plus a host of newsmen, were trying to persuade Governor Hughes which challenge side should go first. After about five minutes of hand-over-mic consultation, Governor Hughes ruled that we would go first, followed by Mr. Kehrer. He also agreed to give our group the full time usually allotted to challengers. Then would come the Maddox delegation's defense, followed by closing summaries on both sides. Our team was by then moving in to take their places at the front table; the final arrangement agreed to was that all of our speakers and counsel would sit at the tables, together, at the end away from the lectern; Mr. Kehrer and Mr. Jacobs would occupy the end nearest the lectern.

Several of the rest of us from both sides occupied the row of chairs to the rear, where also sat Joe Rauh. By the time we finally got started it was almost a surprise to remember that we were really fighting the Maddox delegation, whose witnesses and lawyers had been calmly seated on the other side of the room while all this jockeying had been going on.

Al Horn led off with a brief outline of our case, stating that we were basing our challenge on four points, each of which would be handled by a later speaker; the undemocratic system used by the Democratic Party of Georgia to select its delegation in direct violation of the Convention Call; the under-representation of black people on the present delegation; the exclusion of black people from the party's affairs; and the disloyalty of several of the delegation's members and creators.

Julian spoke first, and he did a magnificent job. One would never have known that he had been operating under pressure without sleep in preparing his speech at the last minute. Looking cool and calm, yet intensely serious, Julian explored the non-workings of the Georgia Democratic Party with an honest presentation that came from knowing that he was right. The facts themselves, as he pointed out, were patently simple.

James Gray, chairman of Democrats for Goldwater in 1964, had submitted a list of possible delegates to Governor Maddox who, with little or no consultation, had personally selected the 64 delegates who would cast Georgia's 43 delegates votes. No primary. No county caucuses. No democracy. Furthermore, Julian added, while black people represented

25% of the voting age population of Georgia, their voting representation on the Maddox-selected delegation was less than seven percent, an obvious violation of the Convention Call, which prescribed a delegation "broadly representative of all the minorities within the state."

Julian went on to say that our own delegation had been chosen at an open state convention, the first in Georgia, and that our delegation was composed of a great geographical, racial, and occupational mixture. For all of these reasons Julian asked, in conclusion, that the official delegation chosen by a single man and under-representative of the black people of the state of Georgia be unseated, and that the Georgia Delegation of Loyal National Democrats be seated in its place.

When he finished, Julian received a long ovation from the audience, and we all rose to congratulate him. As there were no questions, Ben Brown rose to speak. Ben explained, in detail, how the state Democratic Party of Georgia, except in Fulton County, maintains no real committee nor functioning bodies and calls no meetings, except at local election time, when a local official appointed from Atlanta certifies the Democratic candidates. Once every four years – always two years before the Democratic National Convention – there is also a "convention," held right after the gubernatorial primary, which most Democrats view as an election party for the newly elected gubernatorial candidate, who issues the invitations.

At this "convention" the party rules are accepted for another four years; and, as Ben pointed out, at the convention following Governor Maddox's election, even one small glimmer of decentralization begun under Governor Sanders was rescinded – whereby each Congressional chairman could elect one delegate for the national convention – when complete control over selection was returned into the hands of the party chairman and the gubernatorial candidate.

Ben now departed briefly from his prepared text to state that, in his opinion, not all of the members of the Maddox delegation were racists, nor would it be impossible to work with many of them, singling out Lt. Governor George T. Smith as a man with whom anyone would be proud to work. Ben was obviously correct, but Julian and Al Horn winced because our group was trying to make the strongest case possible; it was then not the time, they felt, to start making concessions.

Ben, too, received loud applause, and next Rev. Campbell and Mr.

Walsh walked to the lectern to provide a first-person account of the kind of closed party Ben had been describing. Rev. Campbell, who had been a bit nervous beforehand, had prepared a written dialogue whereby Mr. Walsh would ask a question and Rev. Campbell would give his answer. The incident Rev. Campbell described concerned his attempt in 1965, to run for a local office in his hometown as a Democrat. He related how he could find no one connected with the local Democratic official's office who would explain to him how one went about running for office. He was asked, continually, to come back the following week, finally being told two weeks later that it was then too late to file to run. Meanwhile, he had been threatened, his wife arrested, and he had been threatened again.

There were next some questions for Rev. Campbell, so Mr. Walsh sat down, leaving Rev. Campbell alone at the lectern. He was a man who had been fighting his own local fight against intimidations and a system bent on his failure for all of his life. He answered the questions slowly, searching for words which did not come easily; but one was overcome by the honesty of this black minister, whose lifelong struggle for what he believed to be right made our own partisan battles seem rather selfish by comparison. First he was asked by one of the McCarthy delegates to clarify whether he had, in his opinion, exhausted all of the means available to him as a Democrat to secure the information he needed, without success. Rev. Campbell replied that he had.

Then a non-McCarthy woman delegate who had picked out a small part of his dialogue asked in a skeptical tone, seemingly trying to embarrass Rev. Campbell, why his wife had been arrested. Rev. Campbell, by himself, then related a story which was overpowering and about which I do not think that even any of our own lawyers had known. He described how, in the local Democratic primary for sheriff in 1965, the ballot boxes had been marked "Men," "Women," and "Colored." His wife, along with several other black women "decided that they didn't want to vote in the box marked 'colored', but instead in the box marked 'women'. But the man wouldn't let them, and when they sat down in protest, they were arrested for blocking a doorway and disturbing the peace." Such testimony was damning, and its effect upon the committee was obvious. The delegate who had asked the question sat down, swallowing a "thank you," and there were no further questions.

Rev. Morris, our last speaker, summarized briefly the loyalty issue surrounding Governor Maddox, James Gray, and several of the delegates chosen, referring mainly to newspaper accounts of former work or support for either Wallace or Goldwater. Then Rev. Morris, trying to blunt the next speaker's attack, described the Georgia Democratic Party Forum's attempts to communicate with Executive Secretary Joe Sports and Chairman Gray about changing the selection process. Receiving no answer, the Georgia Democratic Party Forum had gone ahead with its plans to run an open state convention to elect a challenge delegation. Rev. Morris said that he had taken part in the convention planning and that, as far as he was concerned, the convention had gone according to their plans and that a broadly-representative delegation had been fairly elected.

Rev. Morris' final words brought more applause, and Al Horn asked that any time we had remaining be allotted for his closing summary. All of our speakers and witnesses had done superbly; I did not feel that they could have done much better or made stronger arguments if they had had a year for preparation. Taylor and I exchanged glances of relief.

Mr. Kehrer, too, sensed that we might really have already pulled off a victory. I don't know what he had planned to say; I hope that he was torn between his partisan feelings and his realization that we were about to undo a hundred years of political repression. At any rate his speech was a fairly straightforward presentation of the original brief, and only occasionally did he refer to "outside forces" and "partisan politics." When he finally sat down we were all relieved: he had done little more than support our argument that some members of the Maddox delegation had been disloyal to the Democratic Party.

Joe Jacobs, however, rose next, and in his best sermonizing, spent ten minutes blasting us, our delegation, and the way it was elected. Out came all of the old bugaboos about "paid outsiders" and "partisan politics ruining our work in Georgia." Mr. Jacobs' arguments seemed, though, to receive from the committee the small amount of attention that they had deserved ever since that night in Macon when they were first raised. The people on the Credentials Committee were *all* partisan politicians. They knew that partisanship is one of the ingredients of politics. Many, no doubt, most, of the non-Humphrey delegates were there only because of just that kind of "out-of-state partisan workers' help"; and even the Humphrey delegates must have recognized that such arguments held little importance, so long as the Macon convention had been free and open and only Georgians had been allowed to vote.

When Mr. Jacobs finished, Mr. Kehrer announced that his presentation had ended. We hoped that most of the committee had either not understood the point of Mr. Kehrer's and Mr. Jacobs' arguments or, if they had, that they had simply disregarded them.

Governor Hughes now proposed that, as the hearings were running far behind schedule, they then recess for supper. Lamar Sizemore, the defense attorney for the Maddox delegation, rose and said that one of his witnesses, Lt. Governor George T. Smith, had to catch a plane back to Atlanta and he asked that Lt. Governor Smith be allowed to speak. This suggestion was agreed to, so Lt. Governor Smith rose and gave a short speech which refuted none of our earlier charges.

Perhaps he, too, had been impressed with the power of our arguments. He, partially agreeing with us, said that he knew the Democratic Party of Georgia was not the most democratic in the union, but that it was trying to reform its procedures, and that the Credentials Committee could not unseat the regular delegation if it wanted this reform to continue within the existing state party. Lt. Governor Smith, one of the witnesses the McCarthy delegates most wanted to question, then said that he was sorry but that he must leave to catch a plane. With a "thank you," he stepped down, shook hands at his party table, and left.

Mr. Sizemore, apparently forgetting this request for just one speaker now called Mrs. P. Q. Yancey, one of the black delegates on the Maddox delegation. Mrs. Yancey gave a short speech about how her whole family had been involved in Georgia politics for years and how she believed that, though there was room for change, it was best to work within the state system, as she had always done. She finished and Governor Hughes was about to recess when a black woman from Colorado, Mrs. Arie Taylor, one of the Kennedy-McCarthy-McGovern delegates, reached for a mic and demanded that she be allowed to ask Mrs. Yancey one simple question. Governor Hughes agreed, and so she rose and looking intently at Mrs. Yancey asked, "Do you, or do you not, believe that there is enough black representation on the Maddox-selected delegation?" Mrs. Yancey was silent, and obviously very nervous. She looked down at Mr. Sizemore, who smiled back at her.

"Do you or do you not? Yes or No?"

"Well, I'm..."

"Yes or no?"

"Well...no, I guess not. But that doesn't mean that the whole delegation should be unseated."

Mr. Sizemore looked crestfallen; Mrs. Taylor said "Thank you very much"; and Governor Hughes recessed for an hour and a half.

We all agreed to meet upstairs in Room 1265. The press swarmed around, asking questions. I wound up standing next to Joe Jacobs, who was making more of his allegations, which I thought I refuted beautifully, to one of the reporters. Mr. Jacobs then looked up at me and told me to go away and added that he would not answer any more questions with me around. I went over to relate to Taylor my moral coup, and I found him playing back portions of the speeches he had recorded on his small cassette tape recorder.

After a while we headed out with Julian and found Mr. Kehrer surrounded by reporters by the escalator. We stopped to listen; and if Mr. Kehrer had toned down his speech, he was then back in full voice. Julian, who had earlier been a reporter, asked him a question which he ignored." So Julian, sensing the futility of such an exchange, left. Taylor and I stayed to listen, and finally a young reporter with *The New York Times* asked, "If you had to choose between the two delegations, which one would you seat?" After a moment's thought, Mr. Kehrer replied, "I just don't know; I think they're both equally as bad."

There, then, was the nadir, the final low. After two years of hard work, after a summer's fight to change the political system in Georgia, Mr. Kehrer was with one hand deriding us for playing "partisan politics," while with the other hand slinging his last bit of mud at us in the hope of helping his own particular candidate.

It was true that a majority of our delegation probably was, by personal choice, pro-McCarthy. Our delegation also happened to represent the non-establishment opinion of the majority of those voting in Macon. Everyone's primary concern, however, was with changing the situation in Georgia.

Furthermore, the fact that we were not a majority Humphrey delegation was later to prove of critical tactical importance, largely because we could *not* be coerced on "partisan political" grounds: we stuck to our purpose in the face of pressure which would have persuaded a Humphrey delegation to accept less for the sake of their own candidate. It was not being "partisan" which bothered me.

Of course we were partisan, to some extent. And our non-establishment partisanship was only the necessary tactical *means* to a larger end. What did bother me was Mr. Kehrer's intimation that to be partisan was somehow a sin, a sin which he was above. Did he really believe that a pro-Humphrey delegation would have been, somehow, "non-partisan?" The irony was that, behind his righteous camouflage, he was then trying to ruin our common larger goal for the sake of his own personal candidate's partisan position.

Upstairs, however, we were ecstatic. There were several happy slaps on the back. Our presentation, luckily, could not have been any better. Al Horn felt that the whole Kehrer-Jacobs argument had been lost on the committee, without hurting us; and he predicted that they would not get much press coverage, which turned out to be true. Someone remarked that if Mr. Sizemore's presentation kept up in the same way, he would clinch our case with each succeeding witness. Al Harris, obviously quite happy, reminded Al Horn that he still had the summation to do, but we all left for dinner feeling that we had probably won all of the Georgia seats.

When the hearing reconvened after supper, Mr. Sizemore first called Mrs. Mamie B. Reese, a black delegate from Georgia and member of the Credentials Committee. Her testimony was much like that of Mrs. Yancey, and she again got the question from Colorado regarding black representation on the delegation. She, too, had to answer that there was not enough black representation. It seemed that Mr. Sizemore was intent upon winning our case for us.

But then came Mr. Irving Kaler, an Atlanta lawyer and delegate who was not about to let their case die. He argued almost entirely *ad hominem,* which would have had no place in a real court of law, but which was most effective in a political battle such as this. He asked why, if our group had been so concerned with changing the status quo, we had not worked more within the system? Why had they not used the Fulton County Democratic Club to voice their calls for change? Why had they waited until August, at the Democratic National Convention, to first bring up these issues which were bothering them?

Mr. Kaler then described events at the Macon convention in such a way as to infer that we had, incredibly, been "plotting" all along to use this

Credentials Committee for our own state political gains. He could not have known about the events of the Macon convention without someone telling him, and he even quoted Joe Jacobs to show how despicable we all were. The thrust of Mr. Kaler's argument was that an entire delegation of hard working Democrats should not be tossed out because of a small group of upstarts who had not raised their issues while in Georgia and who were simply trying to use the Credentials Committee for political ends.

Mr. Kaler was a forceful speaker, and he used well the kernel of truth that we were trying to accomplish in the Credentials Committee a goal which should, theoretically, have been attainable within Georgia. But while we would have argued that such change would have taken years and years without the prodding of the national party, Mr. Kaler made it sound as if all of the machinery for change was readily available in Georgia and that it was our own fault for not using it: we therefore had no right to challenge a system in which we had not bothered to work.

Had I been on the committee I would simply have asked him how a Georgia Democrat went about making his opinions felt within the party. Unfortunately, however, the questions for Mr. Kaler became bogged down in specifics about the number of people involved in local Democratic organizations. Time ran out, and Mr. Kaler's arguments were allowed to stand without refutation.

It was time for closing summaries. Al Horn would probably be the first to agree that his was not very well organized, and he ran out of time before he was able to come to the forceful conclusion we needed. Mr. Sizemore, however, picked up where Mr. Kaher had left off; he ignored altogether a defense of either the Maddox delegation or the present selection system, and instead he concentrated on our own inadequacies and the absurdity of unseating an official delegation because of a challenge from people like us.

To hear him speak, one would have thought that *we* were the official delegation being challenged over our legality. While it was obvious what he was trying to do, he still was no less effective, and the battle ended with the sides much more evenly matched than they had been before the supper recess. The substantive issues had finally been clouded by enough *ad hominem* arguments to make the eventual outcome unclear.

After the usual press interviews we all returned upstairs for an assessment. We were then much less euphoric and confident. I think most of us were angry that the Maddox group had been able so effectively to pull the wool over everyone's eyes, while none of the right questions had been asked and we had been powerless to intervene. The Humphrey forces in the Credentials Committee were left with seemingly powerful arguments to use against seating us. Our success was much less certain.

Al Harris, who was good at pointing out what needed to be done, said that the main thing we had to do was to make up for the last bit of smokescreen by hitting back with the real crux of our argument about the situation in Georgia. Since the Credentials Committee was not planning another executive session until Thursday night, this meant that during the next day Julian, Ben Brown and Rev. Hooten would have to use all of the time available to talk with Credentials Committee members, stressing the main points of our case. He also commissioned Taylor and myself to compile a brief, one page "Fact Sheet on the Georgia Challenge." If we could get 110 copies run off, he would get them to McCarthy people on the committee for distribution during the closed session.

As it had been a long, eventful day some of our group wanted to get to sleep, while others thought that it was finally time for some relaxation. We decided to reconvene the next morning to plan strategy for our lobbying attempts. Taylor and I went up to the fifteenth floor and "borrowed" one of the typewriters in the McCarthy printing room.

During the day Julian had talked the McCarthy staff into letting him have a spare room on the fifteenth floor, and he said that Taylor and I could use it to compose our fact sheet. While Julian washed out his one shirt in the sink (he had not brought a change, thinking that he would be flying home that afternoon after our hearing), Taylor and I made up a facts and figures summary of our case, and Taylor started typing. The process took about two hours, because we all three stopped frequently and discussed the day's events.

Once we finally had a Xeroxable draft, we bid Julian goodnight, returned the typewriter, and went in search of someone with whom to have a midnight beer. Rev. Morris offered to buy, so we retreated to a small bar beneath the McCarthy storefront for an hour of relaxation. There was little left to say except small talk, since so much was again uncertain, and our minds were less than sharp. But it was nice to return to the familiar world of jukeboxes and loud Chicago barmen. Thus fortified, Taylor and I returned to our compartments in the YMCA Hotel to spend the hottest, most unbearable night of the week. Though I took a shower just before sleeping, I was so drenched in sweat when I awoke in the morning that another shower was then necessary. I hoped that Walter could come through with some proper hotel rooms for us, as another such week would not be very pleasant for our older delegates.

———

The next morning, Thursday, I got up just in time to make it down to our SCCC meeting. Most of the same people were there, except for Mr. Rustin and Mr. Guyot. Dave asked me if I was sure of the SCCC account number; his sister, married to a member of Scientists and Engineers For McCarthy, in Baltimore, had tried to wire $500 late the afternoon before, but the Continental Bank had reported "no such account." Obviously we could not have this sort of slip-up occurring, so I promised to call Mr. Burke immediately. Otherwise there was little but bad news; many of the leads had fallen flat, but others were still being pursued. I said that, if the money from Baltimore came in that afternoon, I would try to split it up on Friday morning.

We broke up and headed back to the Hilton, where I phoned Mr. Burke, who said he was still waiting for our initial deposit. I explained again that it was coming in by wire, so he agreed to inform the wire transfer desk of our existence. I went upstairs to our headquarters and told Dave to ask his sister to try again. We also discussed SCCC finances, because the room rent and the phone bill were starting to mount up. Since Texas had not been at the meeting that day and from all reports was in little need of money, we decided to use their 10% for overhead. I left as Dave, Woody and Frank got out their lists for another day's phoning.

Thursday's events centered around the Credentials Committee. Following Al Harris's suggestion, Julian, Ben and Rev. Hooten spent a great deal of the afternoon in one corner of the large exhibition hall next to the hearings room. One of us would stand at the door between the two rooms; and, even though there was a case being heard, occasionally one of "our" members of the committee could persuade a less-convinced Humphrey delegate to step outside for a few minutes to talk. One of us would meet the delegate and take him or her over to our lobbyists, who would answer any questions and restate our major points.

Late that afternoon we got the final draft of our fact sheet to Al Harris.

He immediately marked it down to half its original length – to our chagrin – and we spent another hour retyping and running off the copies on the McCarthy Xerox machine. Taylor and I also spent quite a lot of time that afternoon in a final attempt to locate whoever was in charge of the McCarthy purse strings, because we were getting desperate to let Mrs. Paschall know whether the money was available for the delegation to come up. We were finally told that the man we wanted to see would be in that evening.

Walter Turner was occasionally in and out of 1265, which by then had become our well used base of operations. He maintained that he was still working on the housing; and, since he was the only hope we then had, we did not push him any harder for a definite answer.

From what members of the Credentials Committee were saying, it was apparent by Thursday afternoon that a possible compromise solution was in the air. We began to feel the pressure. Committee members and committee staff were starting to ask, quietly, how much of a compromise we would accept. We called a meeting for early that evening to discuss the question. I think that Julian, Al Horn, and Mr. Walsh were particularly afraid that either Ben Brown or Rev. Morris might say something, either to a committee member or, worse, to the press, which would give the impression that we might accept this or that. Too quick an acceptance of a trial balloon or too appeasing a quote in the papers could badly erode our bargaining position within the committee, which would be deciding our case that night. So Al reminded everyone, again, that no one was to conduct the delegation's official business, and especially with the press, except the co-chairmen.

We further decided that it would be critical to enter those lat-night committee deliberations with as strong a public position as possible, so Taylor and I were commissioned to write a press release reemphasizing our position that we had come to Chicago in the firm belief that we would unseat an undemocratically appointed delegation, and that we would represent the Democrats of Georgia at the Democratic National Convention.

Taylor and I returned to the fifteenth floor and locked ourselves into the small room across from the Xerox machine. There we composed our press release, making two or three false starts. Taylor and I enjoyed working together, and I guess to some extent the entire Chicago experience was like a first carnival for both of us. As had happened so often in Atlanta, we proved complementary to each other, with one of us usually able to fill in the gaps in the other's thinking. But we were under a great deal of pressure, for we never knew when the last hearing of the day was to end nor when the executive session was to begin. To have any effect at all, such a press release would have to be well circulated by the time the committee walked from the hearing room to its meeting room, which that night was to be on the Hilton's third floor.

Once we had a fairly good copy, we took it back down to Julian, in whose name it would be released. He, along with the others, made a few suggestions for improvement. So back we went to rework and to retype; and, by nine o'clock, we finally had an approved copy. We then had to placate the busy people in the McCarthy printing room while we ran off 300 copies on their machine. Next, down to shirtsleeves, we went with Chico to the basement press room where such releases were snapped up and, if important enough, immediately went out over the wires. I don't know if ours was ever so used, but it was an interesting experience in how to pull off important mass communication in a relatively short time.

Thursday's hearings came to an end at about ten o'clock, and the Credentials Committee, exhausted by another long day's work, took a short break before reassembling for its executive session. Julian had spent some time that afternoon with Assemblyman Brown of California (a Kennedy delegate) and Mr. Herman Badillo of New York, who had agreed to argue our Georgia case within the committee. On their way up to the third floor, there was then last-minute consultation, and Al Harris gave them our "Georgia Fact Sheets."

While all this activity was going on, Taylor, desperate, made a final financial assault on the McCarthy Headquarters, determined not to come away without the balance of the money needed, when added to a large cash gift that day from a donor who wished to remain anonymous, for the delegation's airline tickets. After pressuring the staff for forty-five minutes, he finally saw Stephen Mitchell, with whom the process itself proved rather easy. In a minute's time he had the check. After a call to Mrs. Paschall to confirm the final number desiring to fly up, he and a McCarthy staff woman went downstairs to buy the tickets at an airline office in the lobby. Another large hurdle was finally passed.

The rest of us had reconvened in 1265 for the long wait. We had no hint of how the decision would come out; but we were sure that, of all the challenge delegations, we had the most chance of winning, due to the facts of our case, due to our own presentation, and due to the very visual politics of the Georgia situation. As the hours went by, Taylor or I occasionally made trips down to the hall outside the conference room. In this hall, which was decorated in off red wallpaper, a red carpet, and imitation candle lamps, a group of about fifty reporters were encamped for the duration.

Every time someone would come out of the room to refresh himself or to make a phone call, he was immediately surrounded for news. But no one said anything, and the security was absolute: there was no swaggering into this room with little more than a look of importance. The two guards at the entrance even prevented people from looking through the cracks between the doors. Several members of the Maddox delegation occupied chairs in the hall. I occasionally walked past them, feeling a bit curious. They sometimes were talking nervously, sometimes assuredly.

As it got past one o'clock, the tension started to build. Obviously the debate was being well waged. Joe Sports and Mr. Kaler were seated on a sofa down the hall. I had gone down at 12:30 to stay until the end; and, finally, at about 1:30, the doors opened and Governor Hughes walked out. I had been standing guard, rather covetously, next to a house phone, and I immediately rang up to 1265 to tell them that Governor Hughes was heading for the press conference room.

We all converged on the room at once. The TV lights came on and Governor Hughes stepped up to the microphone, the press in front and all of the interested parties just off camera to his left. He began by announcing the other state decisions, which included defeats to the Texas and North Carolina challenges. Then he got to Georgia, and my heart slowly rose into my throat. He read slowly from a very carefully worded, tightly composed statement, which declared that the Maddox-appointed delegation was to be unseated, on the grounds that it violated the Convention Call both in its selection procedure and in its racial composition.

In its place a totally new delegation was to be created, consisting of 21 members from each of the two delegations, each with 20 ½ votes, plus Georgia's National Committeeman and Committeewoman with one vote each, making Georgia's total of 43 votes. Each number of this new delegation would have to take an oath pledging loyalty to the candidates of the Democratic Party.

The Credentials Committee had decided upon this compromise, Governor Hughes explained, because it considered that, while neither delegation by itself seemed representative of the entire state, the compromise delegation could hopefully form the basis for a new alliance within the state which could work to build a much-needed new, stronger, representative Georgia Democratic Party. Governor Hughes cited both Ben Brown's statement about the moderates on the Maddox delegation and Mr. Jacobs' evidence regarding our Macon convention in supporting their decision that a compromise was the best solution. He asked that the leaders of each delegation submit a list of 21 names by six o'clock on Friday to a special subcommittee, with himself as chairman, which would create the new Georgia delegation.

Joe Sports and Irving Kaler had been standing next to me, nervously shuffling from one foot to the other. When Governor Hughes stated that their delegation had been unseated, they stared in disbelief. I have no idea what they had been led to expect, or whether they had been told by someone the week before that everything would "be all right" (which might be one explanation for their generally loose committee hearing presentation). At any rate, they were clearly shocked, and they hurried out of the room before Governor Hughes had even finished.

The press now asked questions, one of which was whether Lester Maddox's name would be acceptable on the regular delegation's list of 21. Governor Hughes replied that he did not think that Governor Maddox's name would prove acceptable to the subcommittee chairman.

When the questions were over Julian stepped up to the microphone to make a brief statement. He said that, while we were pleased that the Maddox delegation had been unseated, we would have to examine the compromise details in full before we could give our acceptance or rejections. He added that he hoped we could make a definitive statement by the next evening. Our officers had decided not to say any more than that, and we went upstairs to think.

When one considers the enormous pressure that Governor Hughes must have been under to bring about a settlement which was not too disturbing to the South, we certainly had won a great deal. We had, for the first time that I know of, unseated an "official" state delegation to the

Democratic National Convention in only one try. Unlike Mississippi in 1964 and the other challenging states in 1968, our challenge became more than just a formal attempt to frighten the state party into change. The other challengers had lost, but their state parties knew that they must reform to prevent disaster in 1972. Unlike any other state challenge delegation, we had actually succeeded in throwing out the old system – in one try – and we were then to be part of Georgia's officially recognized delegation.

Analyzing the reasons for this unprecedented victory, certainly the misjudgment of the Humphrey Southern management must be partly responsible. Surely they could have foreseen the problem which Governor Lester Maddox and the Georgia system would present. Not only was the system in clear violation of the Convention Call, but the protagonist in the system for 1968 was a man symbolic of a movement which the Democratic Party could not publicly condone. I do not know whether the Humphrey managers simply ignored the problem until it was too late or whether they were making their decision assuming that Mr. Kehrer would be at the head of a pro-Humphrey delegation; but, at that point in August, probably as much as they would have liked to have brushed us under a convenient carpet in the Conrad Hilton, we just would not go away.

Credit, too, must go to Curt Gans and to the McCarthy camp for realizing the need for a non-Humphrey majority on the delegation. Had we been a pro-Humphrey delegation, the trial balloons and the rumors of that Thursday would surely have come as concrete compromise proposals, persuading us not to ask for too much unless we wanted to upset Humphrey's fragile Southern support. Such arguments simply would not work with us, which was to our great advantage in bargaining.

And, of course, credit had to go to Julian Bond, Al Harris, Ben Brown, Rev. Hooten, Rev. Campbell, Al Horn, George Walsh, and Rev. Morris; the men who had planned and superbly presented our case before the Credentials Committee. But even they maintained throughout that they were only the representatives of the eighty members of our delegation, the thousand people who had journeyed to Macon for the first open state convention in Georgia's history and, in a larger sense, all the people of Georgia of all political beliefs who would benefit from whatever democratic reforms might eventually come to pass.

We had, at least symbolically, accomplished a great deal, and we were very happy; but the specific problems inherent in the compromise were many, and we started to discuss them late that night, continuing our discussion the next day. First, from the leaders' point of view, it would be difficult, distasteful, and democratically unfair to have to choose twenty-one delegates out of our forty-one delegates and forty-one alternates. Such a choice would have to be terribly arbitrary.

Second, there were several procedural questions which we wanted guarantees to cover. For example, theoretically the ex-Maddox-appointed delegates could, with the help of the National Committeeman and Committeewoman, carry a majority on any caucus vote of the new delegation. Conceivably such a majority could even pass a unit-rule motion, meaning that our votes would all be cast for the choice of the simple majority, rendering us absolutely impotent.

Third, and more important, there were questions about the future. James Gray, by Georgia law, had to certify all of the Democratic electors in the November election. Should he decline to do so, because of his delegation's unseating, Georgians might not even find a single Democratic candidate on their November ballot. We obviously needed a guarantee that the Democratic electors would be certified. We also wanted a ruling from the Credentials Committee that any future Georgia delegation to later conventions appointed under the present rules of the Georgia Democratic Party could expect to find its credentials withheld without a challenge being necessary. In short, we wanted a strong statement from the national party that the system in Georgia had to be reformed.

So, although we agreed with – and were actually jubilant over – the symbolic effect of the Credentials Committee compromise, we still considered that major issues had to be settled before we could ask the delegation to agree to it. Without the guarantees we wanted, we felt that agreement would leave us open to serious misdealings both at the convention and upon our return to Georgia. Without these guarantees we might win the seating battle but lose all of the substantive issues which initially had motivated our challenge attempt.

During our meeting early Friday morning and again that afternoon, the leaders decided to go ahead and comply with the terms of the compromise by submitting our list of twenty-one names by six that evening. The compliance seemed the *sine qua non* for the future conversation regarding the final composition of the delegation and the guarantees we felt to be essential.

But, while complying with the *terms* of the compromise, we would make it clear that we were not thereby, as yet, accepting the compromise itself, until we had had a chance to work out the substantive issues with the Credentials Committee subcommittee. Julian and the other leaders frequently repeated that, even though they might have been the delegation's officers, it would be presumptive of them to commit the entire delegation to something as binding as this compromise without a vote of the entire delegation, which was due to arrive on Saturday.

Friday morning Taylor flew to Atlanta, where he had to make the final plans with Mrs. Paschall for the delegation's journey to Chicago; but he hoped to come back himself late that night. Julian, Ben and Rev. Hooten had agreed to get together at noon to start the selection process for our twenty-one person delegation. I got on with my "advance man" duties, which I'm afraid I had partly neglected during the preceding two days.

A quick trip to Woody's room brought good news: the Baltimore contribution had come through, and it looked like more might be on the way from elsewhere. If it is not already obvious, it needs emphasizing that those three men – David, Woody, and Frank – were the Southern Challenges Coordinating Committee. For all the earlier help from the COC and the SCLC in setting up the SCCC, which at the time was critical, when it actually came to raising the money needed, it was those three men who made the Southern Challenges financially possible.

I went to the bank and took out $2,100 ($700 for each of the three delegations), and distributed it to the delegation leaders. By this time the Alabama delegation was particularly desperate, and I think that Friday's first $700 allowed them to remain until their minority report battle the next Tuesday night. But I was just the distributor: over the weekend and during the convention week more contributions flowed in, from where I do not know, amounting to over $5,000 in the end; and it all came as a result of four days hard phoning by Dave, Woody, and Frank.

I used $200 of our own $700 to make the necessary deposit at the YMCA Hotel, where I also supplied the exact figures on rooms needed as obtained by phone from Atlanta. Several members of the delegation, mostly alternates, had been forced to drop out for one reason or another, and our total group was down to about seventy. Though I went ahead on this deposit I still hoped that Walter could find us accommodations elsewhere.

That afternoon our officers got together in Rev. Morris' room to begin the lengthy task of filling the twenty-one places. Ben Brown was seated on the sofa, with Rev. Hooten and Julian in chairs around the coffee table. The general formula agreed upon was to take all of the delegates who were known to be coming and to make them either delegates or alternates on the new delegation, trying to strike a suitable political, racial, and geographical balance in the final choices. The process was tedious and, as predicted, arbitrary, since there were some delegates about whom little was known.

Except for the possible over balance of delegates from Atlanta, since all of the participants in the Credential Committee hearing were included, the delegation finally selected was about as even as one could hope, though Julian and I were quietly concerned that Ben's strong arguments might have led us to choose a majority Humphrey delegation! This later proved not to be the case, though the political balance on the twenty-one man delegation was more even than on the delegation at large. Julian remarked that he felt almost like Lester Maddox sitting down with James Gray's list; all of them disliked having to do the job, but there seemed no other immediate alternative.

By late that afternoon the selection had been completed and the list typed up. The Credentials Committee was having its last afternoon of hearings, and I was sent down to get a message to Governor Hughes, telling him that Julian and our other leaders wanted to meet with him to discuss the explicit terms of a possible final compromise. By chance I arrived downstairs just as the last hearing was coming to an end, and Governor Hughes said that he would meet with Julian right away. So I hurried back upstairs to assemble our representatives. They said that they would be downstairs in five minutes.

The meeting was to take place in the back part of the large hall adjoining the hearing room, and several soft chairs were now arranged in a circle. When I arrived back downstairs it was apparent that Governor Hughes meant for this meeting to decide the ultimate settlement, for the other members of the Georgia subcommittee, plus members of his staff, were on hand. He told me that he had also sent for James Gray, who was a member of the Platform Committee, then meeting in the Sheraton Blackstone.

I caught Julian, Al Horn, Ben Brown, and Rev. Hooten at the door and told them that James Gray was probably on the way over. They went into a quick conference and decided that Julian would give Governor Hughes our list of twenty-one names, complying with the compromise terms. Julian would also qualify our compliance with Governor Hughes verbally, by stating that there were still several points we wanted to discuss before finally agreeing to the compromise, giving him a few examples. But it was decided not to enter into a meeting with James Gray about a final settlement, because there was a good chance that Mr. Gray would not comply with the compromise terms, which might put us in a new, stronger position. There was also a good chance that such a meeting would turn into a verbal confrontation because Mr. Gray's first remarks in the press that morning about us had not been exactly conciliatory.

So Julian gave Governor Hughes our list and talked with him for about five minutes, explaining our position: should Chairman Gray comply with the compromise terms, we would then be ready and willing to talk about the substantive details. As Chairman Gray walked in one end of the huge room, Julian, Ben and Rev. Hooten quietly walked out a door at the other end. Al Horn and I, whom Mr. Gray probably would not recognize, decided to remain at the meeting to find out what Mr. Gray had to say, and Al advised me that we should sit quietly.

Mr. James Gray, Chairman of the Democratic Party of Georgia, struck me as a real politician. Meticulously dressed in a light suit and two-tone shoes, he greeted Governor Hughes and took a seat, his accent immediately giving away the fact that he, too, was an "outsider" from north of the Mason-Dixon line. Governor Hughes remained standing, and with an incredible father-figure appearance on his strongly square face, he looked over the rims of his glasses at Mr. Gray and asked if he was prepared to submit his list of twenty-one names.

Chairman Gray, seated with his legs spread apart, looked up at Governor Hughes, and, with a skeptical tone to his voice and a shrug of his shoulder said, "Now Governor Hughes, you know I can't do that."

Governor Hughes, looking sterner, asked why not.

"You can't expect me to send half of my delegation home and to ruin the Democratic Party of Georgia just because of some people who come up here, without having contributed one thing to our party back home, and challenge us. Why, what kind of a party chairman would I be if I allowed something like that to happen?"

Governor Hughes, who by now must have desperately wanted this cup to pass from him, was obviously angered that Mr. Gray was torpedoing his hard thought-out compromise. He was already late for a meeting, so he left the persuasion in the hands of the subcommittee and his staff.

But it was obvious, too, that Mr. Gray was not about to be persuaded. The conversation that afternoon was really on two different levels, because *any* compromise was clearly out of the question as far as Mr. Gray was concerned. He referred to the fact that he had personally lifted the Georgia Democratic Party out of enormous debt, and "What did they contribute? Nothing." He also pointed out that he had run John Kennedy's campaign in Georgia in 1960, winning by the largest percentage of any state in the union.

He stated that his delegation had never expected anything like this to happen and that no one had warned them, which he repeated even though a subcommittee member pointed out that the language in the Convention Call was quite explicit. He obviously considered that he and his people had done all the work for the state party and that it was therefore ridiculous to unseat them because of a bunch of outside upstarts.

After about half an hour's fruitless persuasion, it became obvious to all concerned that Chairman Gray was not considering any sort of a compromise. The meeting broke up, the staff returned to report Mr. Gray's refusal to Governor Hughes, and Al and I went back to 1265. Two points were clear to all of us. First, more than ever, we then considered the guarantees for convention procedure and elector certification absolutely necessary to any compromise, since Chairman Gray seemed uninclined to voluntarily work with us.

Second, it was obvious that the onus for delaying the Georgia settlement now rested with the regular delegation; by unilaterally complying with the compromise terms and agreeing to talk about the final drafting, we had put ourselves in an excellent political and moral bargaining position. We had fulfilled the initial terms; they had not; and we could thereby rightly claim that it was the regular delegation which was refusing to talk with us about building a new delegation and a new party.

The press, of course, knew about none of these developments, nor that we had complied with Governor Hughes' terms. As Julian had promised the night before to make our position clear as soon as possible, the officers asked Chico and me to set up a news conference for the following morning. As the next move was then up to either James Gray or the Credentials Committee, Julian and the other officers decided that the best thing we could do that night was to make ourselves as scarce as possible, since the press was literally standing at the door waiting to know if we had "accepted" the compromise.

Any speculation or slips on our part about what we would or would not accept might undermine our excellent position in the negotiations, which obviously would have to continue during that weekend if the Georgia question was to be settled by seven o'clock Monday night, when the convention was set to start. So Julian, Ben and Rev. Morris accepted Walter Turner's invitation for a "night on the town," and Al Horn took Pat Madsen and me out for a steak. Phone calls and newspapers from Atlanta were confirming the bombshell we had just dropped into Georgia politics, and it was clearly time for a little celebration. The press would have to wait.

9

THE PRESSURE IS APPLIED AND THE CONVENTION BEGINS

Taylor returned early Saturday morning, in time to help me run off the press releases for our news conference, which was scheduled to take place in a much larger, chandeliered room on the Hilton's second floor. The entire hotel was, in fact, preparing for the transition from hearing week to convention week, which would place new demands on the facilities. The exhibition hall in which the press conferences had taken place were taken over by the Humphrey camp as a well decorated, psychedelic "Delegate Welcoming Station."

A less well-endowed, but just as imaginative, McCarthy Welcome Station was erected on the second floor over the entrance foyer and inside a third-floor meeting room. As the delegates really began to arrive, we realized that the crowds of the previous week would be nothing compared to that weekend; and our previously occasional policy of using the freight elevators became mandatory if we were to avoid the fifteen minute wait for an elevator.

Early that Saturday morning Walter arrived in his usual immaculate suit with good news: he had done the impossible and found us the rooms we needed at the Del Prado Hotel, near the Shoreland Hotel and only twenty minutes to the south. It would cost about twice the YMCA, but it was a proper hotel, air conditioned, with adequate rooms. We told him that we'd take them. I still don't know how Walter was able to swing it, but we were all certainly grateful; they came just in time.

Our press conference was scheduled for eleven, and by ten minutes before the hour the room was packed with reporters. Our usual group entered right at eleven and sat along the tables flanking the lectern on the stage. Julian, rested and relaxed, began by reading the press statement, of which everyone by then had copies. Essentially it recounted the events following the Georgia hearing, emphasizing that we had complied with the original compromise terms, though we had by no means accepted the compromise formula. Julian expressed our concern over several substantive issues which had to be settled before a compromise could be reached, but he affirmed our willingness to talk, if only the regular delegation would also comply with the terms as set down by the Credentials Committee.

There followed about twenty minutes of questions, which Julian and the others handled extremely well. Julian emphasized, in a response to a question, that on a matter as important as this compromise, the co-chairmen felt that the entire delegation must be allowed to decide. We underlined that the twenty-one name list would also have to be voted upon by the delegation as a whole and that they as co-chairmen had merely submitted *a* list in order to fulfill the six o'clock Friday deadline. Our entire press conference went very well. None of our leaders cared to speculate about the eventual settlement; Julian said that we were awaiting word from the Credentials Committee as to the next move. When the press conference was over, I was sure that we could not have been in any better possible position with the press.

Julian, Al Horn, Ben Brown and the rest then left, Julian and Ben hoping to let the proper people know that they were then ready to talk "anywhere, anytime." Our delegation was due to arrive at O'Hare Airport that afternoon at about five, and we all planned to drive out to meet them. We had also arranged for a yellow school bus to meet us and to carry our group over to the Del Prado Hotel.

Taylor and I stayed behind to attend Governor Maddox's press conference, scheduled to start shortly. Governor Maddox, who had announced his candidacy for the Democratic nominee for President only ten days before, had arrived at the Hilton on Friday and set up shop on the sixteenth floor, passing out "Lester Maddox for President" buttons to all comers. Though the official reason for his candidacy was to provide the Democratic Party with a "conservative alternative" and "to save the Democratic Party from ruin," speculation for his reasons ran along other lines. One rumor had it that, seeing the handwriting on the wall for his delegation, he had announced his candidacy and withdrawn from the Georgia delegation in hopes of thereby saving the latter.

Another story went that, by attempting to "save" the party, Lester Maddox could then throw up his hands in despair, when the certain snub finally came, say "They don't want me," and then devote his full efforts to the Wallace campaign. Yet another reasoned that he just wanted the Secret Service protection then afforded to all candidates.

At any rate, at his press conference, Governor Maddox was confidence and happiness incarnate. He referred all questions about the delegation he had appointed to Mr. Sizemore, while he preferred to talk about his mission to rescue the Democratic Party from "certain destruction." He admitted that his delegate strength was not too great, but he added that it was growing all the time as delegates came to see the unique opportunity his nomination could provide for the Democratic Party to win in November. At one memorable point he even suggested that the Democratic Convention was being "run from Moscow," which got a slight stir from the press. After half an hour of shadow boxing, Governor Maddox waved confidently and left to continue his search for delegate support.

Later that afternoon we all drove out to O'Hare Airport in both Walter's car and a car which John Tillman had talked out of the McCarthy transportation office. We joked on the way out, reliving parts of the past week and listening to portions of Taylor's tapes. The jet landed right on time, and our delegation, a great potpourri of students, ministers, and businessmen, black and white, filed through the arrival gate. They had all, of course, been following the events of the last week in the local papers, and they were excitedly concerned to find out the latest developments.

Rather than try to explain everything at the airport, we all pitched in to get the school bus loaded with baggage and on the way to the Del Prado as quickly as possible. Along with the group came Cathy Branch and Mrs. Bond, bringing Julian his first laundered shirt since Tuesday.

Mrs. Paschall read off her list of names and, once everyone was accounted for, we started for the hotel. I was sitting in the front near the Lymans, answering the questions from everyone around me, while Tom

Lyman, an artist and former Chicagoan, pointed out the best examples of European architecture in the old churches near the expressway.

We arrived at our new home a little after six. The Del Prado was quite a nice hotel, corresponding more to my usual impression of a hotel than, say, the Hilton, which was really a small city. The lobby was up one flight of stairs from the street. On one side was the desk while directly across from the desk a short flight of stairs led up to the Crystal Room, an oblong room with mirrored walls and glass chandeliers. There we were to hold all of our delegation meetings. Directly beneath this room, on the street level, was a convenient, low-priced restaurant. A bank of pay telephones provided the communication we would need, and the rooms themselves were actually quite spacious.

While Taylor oversaw the long check-in process and delegates chose roommates among their new acquaintances. Julian made notes for our first meeting which began right after supper. All of us who had been in Chicago during the previous week gave our impressions of the events which had transpired. Taylor and I made announcements about the physical arrangements. Taylor and Mrs. Paschall would be in charge of the food money; while everyone was asked to contribute all that they could on their own, no one was to go hungry for lack of funds.

Julian took about half an hour, briefly explaining all that had happened and detailing our current position regarding the compromise and the list of twenty-one names. When he was finished, and everyone else had added their interpretations, one of the just-arrived delegates moved a vote of thanks and a vote of confidence for the good work of the delegation leaders. This passed by acclamation.

We still did not have, though, final information on who would be going to the convention, nor what the final terms of the compromise would be. Everyone agreed that it would be best for Julian and the others to continue in any negotiations which might develop, and Julian assured everyone that no decisions would be made unless the entire delegation had voted. For Sunday and Monday, we believed that the best thing delegates could do would be to lobby at the various parties and receptions then being thrown by the candidates and the state delegations. I said that I would try to obtain a list of such events from the McCarthy and Humphrey welcome stations. Many of our delegates had been traveling all day, and several were elderly;

so we decided to recess until noon on Sunday, then to go over the twenty-one name list and to consider further our conditions for a compromise.

Julian, Ben Brown, and all of us gladly volunteered to answer any questions anyone had. After a while Julian, who was staying in the Hilton for two more nights to be easily accessible in case anyone wanted to talk further about the compromise, left with Al Harris for a meeting with the McCarthy staff and McCarthy Credentials Committee delegates. Informal talks continued at the Del Prado, where we tried to bring everyone up to date on all the events, rumors, and discussions of the past week. Late that night Walter Turner, who had done a great job with the Del Prado arrangements, took several of us out for some pleasurable conversation.

———

The next day, Sunday, the pressure on us began to mount, as still no word came about our fate, and no one contacted Julian about the compromise. At our noon meeting, which lasted about an hour, we went over the lists of twenty-one delegates and twenty-one alternates. Though there were some personal disappointments, everyone accepted the decisions in the spirit in which they were made, as a necessary evil.

Since there were many people there as alternates who were subsequently on neither list, one delegate who was then an alternate proposed that we try to swap around from day to day so that everyone got a chance to be inside the convention hall. Such a situation probably would not have been strictly "legal," but these gestures of friendliness and understanding helped ease a situation which could easily have added personal jealousy to an already tense overall problem.

That afternoon Taylor and I still had some errands to run uptown near the Hilton, where Walter drove us. Taylor, John and Walter were all working in their own ways to get us a bus for traveling to the convention. Taylor also made preliminary inquiries into how the credentials for our delegation would work, since we all knew about the precautions which were being taken to prevent uninvited guests from entering the amphitheater. I checked by both the McCarthy and the Humphrey welcome stations for reception lists and wound up copying down the addresses and times of the ones which sounded the largest. I then phoned the Iowa McCarthy delegation at the Drake Hotel and found that Mr. Garfield had, after all, been able to raise some money for us.

I hitchhiked up to The Drake, located at the north end of town. In the clear, cooler Chicago sky one could then see the "Huey" helicopters starting to patrol overhead, the biting clatter of their low-flying blades echoing against the skyscrapers as Mayor Daley began preparing for the Battle of Chicago. At the Drake I spent about an hour talking with Mr. Garfield and his aides, who told me that they had set up a "Julian Bond Delegation" fund and had appealed for help. In one week they had raised over $700, mostly in small contributions. I thanked Mr. Garfield several times; I was, as usual, in a hurry; and I think that they may have felt me to be ungrateful, which was unintentional. This extra money, combined with the final contributions from the SCCC, would make our stay financially possible. An aide went down to the hotel desk with me, where we eventually persuaded the manager to cash $700 in travelers checks. As I left with the cash in my pocket, I again thanked the good people of Iowa who had given us some much-needed help.

Next I walked across the street to Mrs. Lucy Montgomery's apartment, which was high enough up so that one could easily spot the five or six helicopters as they made their passes back and forth over the city. Mrs. Montgomery contributed a $500 check to the SCCC, which I later tore up when we did so well otherwise, since I knew that she was hard pressed herself and was besieged by many other causes looking for financial help.

I managed to catch one of the few cabs not on strike for the trip back to the Hilton, and as we neared the area around the hotels, we passed a group of "yippies" jogging down the sidewalk chanting "Ho, Ho, Ho Chi Minh" and "No more war. No more war." The cab driver remarked that all of them needed a haircut, a bath, and a job, and that they had no right to illegally disrupt the city like they were planning to do. I have not yet found the proper response when put in such a situation. I remained silent, not even bothering to comment on Mayor Daley's week-long ban on "legal" demonstrations.

Back at the Del Prado I turned over our Iowa $700 to Taylor, who had become the keeper and dispenser of the funds. He reported to our early evening delegation meeting that Julian would have to personally pick up our gallery passes and our bus credentials the next day, from a special office at the Hilton. I read out the list of events at other hotels, but since we were planning a small reception ourselves for that Sunday night at the Del Prado, our lobbying efforts would probably have to be limited to the next morning and afternoon in the Hilton.

Julian, who was in constant contact with the McCarthy Headquarters, the McCarthy Credentials Committee members, and the Credentials Committee office, could report no new developments, though apparently rumors were rampant around the Hilton that the whole South was in revolt over us. There was new talk of several favorite son candidates, and Governor Connally of Texas was putting pressure on, through the White House, for something to be "done" about the Georgia situation if Humphrey expected Texas' support. In short, it looked like, for those of us who were McCarthy supporters, we were in fact accomplishing our second goal of giving the Humphrey forces a proper stir.

Governor Hughes must have been under intense pressure from all sides to come up with a compromise which would be acceptable to the other Southern established parties, but not too obviously conciliatory to Governor Maddox, for the sake of national publicity, and at the same time also acceptable to us so that we would not file a minority report. Such was seemingly an impossible task, and it looked as if the Humphrey forces were finally backed into the corner which some of us had foreseen back in early July; and, as I will explain below, I think that we finally really *did* in fact accomplish our second goal, that the convention, as impossible as it had seemed a month before, *was* split wide open with help from our delegation, and that the nomination eventually came back to Humphrey not because he had it "locked up," but because there simply was nowhere else for the convention to go.

We had prepared a reception that Sunday night for the press, but because the notices did not get out until late and because our hotel was so far away, we only had a few guests, mostly from Georgia television stations and newspapers. The party proved a welcome opportunity, however, for our own delegation to "socialize," since most of us were strangers before we were elected together in Macon. Throughout the night the phone at the back of the Crystal Room would ring, usually with someone wanting to speak to either Julian or Rev. Hooten. Most of the time it was just the press, but occasionally there was a call from someone with a new idea about a settlement, or a new rumor about what might happen. Still, though,

211

nothing substantive came through, and the pressure continued to build as our fate became more uncertain.

From the McCarthy Headquarters Julian had received a list of the largest state delegation breakfast meetings and caucuses scheduled for Monday morning, the earliest of which was Ohio, at the Sherman House. John Lewis and I agreed to meet Julian there at eight to start a morning of carrying our case to any delegation which would listen. Since, for one reason or another, we all three got to bed very late that Sunday night before the convention, we must have looked rather hollow the next morning as we asked our way around the Sherman House after only four hours sleep.

We were, of course, less than pleased to learn that the Ohio meeting had been delayed for an hour, which threw off our planned schedule of morning caucuses. Julian, John and I went next door to get some coffee and to replot the logistics of visiting the largest number of delegates in the least time.

When the Ohio breakfast meeting did begin – a huge delegation in an ornate dining hall – Julian was given about five minutes to explain our side of the Georgia battle and to ask for support if the case had to be decided on the floor. Julian came across very effectively, all the more so since we were in the position of having accepted the compromise terms, and he got a polite applause. John Lewis and I were standing near the back of the room. I felt like a young boy from the other side of the tracks, and I remember commenting, after a long look around that no one in the place looked under fifty. I wonder how they chose their delegates in Ohio.

With Ohio out of the way, we paid a quick visit to a meeting of McCarthy delegates from Pennsylvania, also in the Sherman House, where there was a smaller delegation but a warmer reception. Our most important target for the morning was New York, where we hoped to find strong support even among the non-McCarthyites. As the New York caucus was scheduled to start shortly, we went next to the Sheraton Chicago. There we wasted fully an hour and a half while the New York chairman cleared everyone from the large circular meeting room and then let the delegates and alternates back in, one by one, checking credentials, in an attempt to keep out the press or other unwanted non-delegates.

We had several friends on the New York delegation already, including Nelson Schneider and Mr. Badillo, and they arranged for Julian to be given a chance to speak. Julian was allowed in, alone, but all of us (we had been joined by Taylor) listened through the crack in the door as Julian gave another superb presentation. He left, followed by a standing ovation, and it was moved later that our delegation be given complete support, which was passed by a large majority. I was later told it happened before the Humphrey Office had a chance to call and advise their delegates not to support us.

It was by then after eleven and there were no more caucuses for us to attend; so we returned to the Hilton, where Julian and Taylor went looking for our credentials while John and I visited the McCarthy welcome station, where several of our Georgia delegates were already doing a good job of lobbying. Taylor and Julian returned without the credentials: the man we wanted was, typically, at the amphitheater, which was unreachable, and he would not be back until "later."

The Credentials Committee was scheduled to meet that afternoon to decide the Georgia case, so we felt that it would be best to be back at the Del Prado with the entire delegation in case any word came through. They all left for the Del Prado, while I made another quick trip to the Continental Bank, where I again took out in cash nearly all of the funds we had received and spent an hour distributing them to the Alabama and the North Carolina challenge delegations. I also picked up some laundry.

When I got back to the Del Prado at two, by commuter train, a delegation meeting was just beginning. Walter informed me that earlier that morning, he had found us a rental bus to use to get to the convention. I quickly called the rental agency and confirmed that we wanted one bus at the Del Prado at six-fifteen that evening.

Our delegation meeting that afternoon was concerned with formulating the specific points we wanted guaranteed by the Credentials Committee. Julian had already given Assemblyman Brown a partial list, but he wanted the delegation to discuss the final terms which would make a compromise acceptable. Early that afternoon, with the sun glaring through the white curtains of the Crystal Room, the delegation struggled through a long session, with almost every delegate having a say. Everyone had quickly caught up on the preceding week's events, and so no longer was the delegation simply listening to its leaders.

We had a long, exhaustive discussion, which was as it should have been. Some people felt that we should accept no compromise at all, that we should fight with a minority report no matter what, on principle. Others were much more conciliatory, arguing that we had largely accomplished our purpose already and that, with a minimum of safeguards, we should accept a compromise for the sake of working to build a better Democratic Party in Georgia.

Since the meeting was still going strong at about 3:30, and Julian could not leave, he wrote a note for Taylor, and I gave Taylor my Letter of Introduction. Taylor then left for the Conrad Hilton to pick up our personal and bus credentials.

By four o'clock the more moderate members of our delegation had won the day, and we were finishing a list of specific guarantees, largely paralleling our earlier request, which Julian would then take up to the Hilton. This job was nearly completed when the phone rang for Julian.

It was Walter Pozen, Governor Hughes' special counsel, who told Julian that the Credentials Committee was then considering a new compromise, whereby all of the members of both the Georgia delegations would be seated, with each delegation to have one half the total vote. Julian replied that he would have to talk this new formula over with our delegation and that we were then drawing up a list of proposals which we considered mandatory in any compromise. He added that we would vote on it all and that he would then drive up to the Conrad Hilton as quickly as possible to give the committee our decision and our specific proposals.

Julian returned and quickly explained his conversation. Someone pointed out that this new compromise was a full step back in principle, since the Maddox-appointed delegation was not, as such, unseated. This new compromise was thereby a symbolic retreat from the earlier one, which had explicitly stated that the current Georgia method was not a valid way to choose a delegation.

We had, however, been talking for only two minutes when the phone again rang for Julian. This time it was Assemblyman Brown asking, in desperation, why Julian had accepted the new compromise. Julian replied in disbelief that he had *not* accepted it. "But," said Assemblyman Brown, "Walter Pozen returned from his phone call saying that you have accepted the compromise, and it is being gaveled through the committee meeting right now." Julian said that he would be right up to the Hilton.

Quickly returning to our meeting, it was obvious that Julian was distressed. He explained the phone call and asked that he be given the power to negotiate a compromise, trying to get included as many of the points as possible which we had so far outlined. He said that he would try either to call us or to come back for our final approval. We voted him that power, and he and Al Harris left immediately with John Tillman for the Hilton.

It was obvious to us all what was happening: unable to satisfy all concerned, *someone* on the Credentials Committee staff had decided to double deal, hoping to get a compromise through the committee late in the afternoon, counting on the general pre-convention confusion to thwart an organized attempt at a minority report. The majority report could then be geveled through the first hour of the convention before anyone had a chance to react; and the issue, on the surface at least, would be settled, without an embarrassing minority report battle on prime-time nationwide television. Caught between three immovable groups – us, the Southern block, and the Humphrey office – perhaps it was the only way out for the Credentials Committee; but we had been lied to, and we were not particularly pleased with the last-minute double dealing.

Our delegation took a recess, when everyone was advised to eat something, and then reconvened at five o'clock. Our position was nearly chaotic. We had heard nothing from Julian, so we did not know what, if any, agreement had been voted through. Taylor had been gone for an hour and half, again without word, and so we had no credentials. Our bus was due to arrive in an hour, and we had no idea what further machinations were going on. It appeared that we were being completely undone at the last minute.

Under this pressure, some of our delegates proposed rather bizarre courses of action. Charlie Webster thought that we should lie down at the convention hall gates unless we were seated (I don't know how he planned to get that close). The general feeling was drifting more and more towards a Minority Report, since we were by then almost certain that our guarantees were not being fulfilled.

At about twenty before six Taylor arrived, exhausted, with a large brown envelope full of our credentials, plus our bus pass. We had forty-four gallery passes (twenty-one delegates, twenty-one alternates, Sergeant-at-Arms (myself) and Chief of Pages (Taylor). Taylor took five minutes to relate the instructions he had received. The "credentials" consisted of a card made from paper, plastic, and metal, about the size of a credit card, which was to be hung around one's neck at all times on an elastic band provided with it.

At several checkpoints within the amphitheater, one had to insert his or her card into a machine with red and green lights on top. If the green light came on, you passed. One had to be sure to "punch out" when leaving, otherwise the card would not be demagnetized and the red light would come on when someone tried to re-enter (to prevent anyone from passing it outside once the owner was inside). We had "guest" passes for the upstairs Gallery, where we were to remain, like the regular delegation, until the convention had voted on the Georgia compromise.

By this time it was nearly six; there was still no word from Julian, and our school bus had already pulled up outside. Obviously we needed to come to a decision. Someone finally proposed that, unless all of our conditions had been met, we would take our case to a floor fight. At ten minutes past six this motion was passed, there was a great yell of excitement and all the delegates scattered to get their coats (as it had turned quite cool).

Since only those originally elected as delegates were going that first night, over thirty of our group had to stay behind to watch the convention on television. But they all came outside to see us off. Mrs. Paschall and I stood by the school bus door, checking off the names and issuing the credentials as the delegation filed on. Then Taylor and I climbed on board and we were finally off to the Democratic National Convention!

The trip took about half an hour; as we drove along two of the older black ministers pulled out harmonicas, and we sang together old civil rights songs and hymns. As we neared the amphitheater we had to pass through several police checkpoints. Many roads had been completely blocked off, and all traffic for the amphitheater had to travel along a specific route, with every corner full of police. We, however, were up to the challenge, and we let down the windows and sang verse after verse of "We Shall Overcome."

The closer we got to the amphitheater, the more times we were stopped by the police, even though Taylor displayed our pass in the window. I guess they figured that we were, if not the dreaded yippies, surely at least hippies, because no one rode to the Democratic National Convention in a little yellow school bus singing "We Shall Overcome."

Our next struggle came at the parking lot gate, because we were not allowed to park where the larger buses provided by "the central committee" (which I thought was an appropriate title) were parking. We had to park with the press buses off to one side. We did, however, unroll a large banner, provided by the Lymans, which read "Georgia delegation of Loyal National Democrats," and we walked together to the entrance gate, where we were made to drop it, since "no banners are allowed inside the convention hall."

Outside there was one door – blue – at the middle of the long amphitheater wall for delegates and honored guests, which meant one got out onto the convention floor. Another door – green – was for alternates, meaning that one sat at the circle level. The third door was orange and was the Gallery entrance for guests, which meant that one might as well be watching the events at home on television. We were, however, obviously very happy to have any seats, so we punched in at the light machines at the door, had our bags searched, and started climbing up the long ramps.

The convention hall was, as outlined above, divided into three levels. Once inside the building, anyone with any kind of pass could go to any of the areas, or any of the levels, outside of the part of the building which was actually the convention hall itself, where specific passes were needed. On the ground floor, directly opposite the speaker's stand but outside the hall floor itself were all of the television studios, snack bars, and delegate lounges. In this same outer ring, to the left of the speaker, was a large, open, unused area. To the right was a much smaller area where the credentials security men had an office. Behind the speaker on the ground floor was a first aid station and the haunts of the Democratic National Committee, where one needed a really special brown pass to venture. I think, perhaps, that the Humphrey headquarters was located in this section of the building, though I never got there myself.

On the box level, across from the speaker, were three large caucus rooms, with white walls, concrete floors, and folding chairs, where delegations could hold their caucuses or poll their votes in private. On this level there was also a large cafeteria, next to the caucus rooms. To the speaker's left was a wide walkway and refreshment stands, to his right the building entrance. Behind the speaker, on his left, was the McCarthy inner sanctum, with a large TV-reception room and smaller offices behind, ending in the real McCarthy nerve center, where the regional desk men grouped around a large circular table and watched, headsets on, messages flying, their three large color televisions on the wall. From here they communicated to the floor through twelve delegation telephones and various walkie talkies.

Directly behind the speaker was another Democratic National Committee holy-of-holies, where two guards were on the door and one had to have, I suppose, all sorts of credentials to get through. Behind the speaker, on his right, was the McGovern headquarters, similar to that of McCarthy. On the uppermost gallery level there were, outside of the hall itself, nothing but walkways and refreshment booths, as far as I know; and in the entire building there were, at most, fifteen pay telephones.

But all of this geography we were to learn later: at the time we had only Gallery passes, so up we walked. We arrived on the speaker's right, which was already full, so we walked around to the left, past one telephone where there already was a line of eight people, and into three rows of seats, located in the corner to the left of and parallel with the speaker's platform. I sat down, not really believing where I was. Suddenly I had a brief desire for some popcorn and a beer. Most in our group were smiling, and people around us started to whisper.

Taylor had remained outside with Julian's credentials, hoping that he would somehow get through. He did, at almost seven o'clock, and he came inside with Frank McDonald, Al Harris, and John Tillman (the latter two Frank supplied with gallery passes). They were all in a great hurry, and Frank was talking about a walkie talkie which was due to arrive any minute. Taylor went up to get the other delegation leaders, and we all went down a back stairwell and into one of the back rooms of the McCarthy Headquarters, while Aretha Franklin sang the national anthem.

Inside were Assemblyman Brown, Mr. Bodillo, and several other Credentials Committee delegates, all very angry and very anxious. As they all talked I pieced together what had apparently taken place. The Credentials Committee had acted upon Walter Pozen's information and passed a new compromise which seated every member of both delegations, but which said absolutely nothing about the kinds of guarantees we had wanted. Julian and Al Harris had arrived at the Conrad Hilton at just before five and had gone to the Credentials Committee office, where they were met by a committee staff assistant.

He had said that Governor Hughes would be with them in a moment to talk about the Georgia compromise, and he had asked them to wait. After about twenty minutes he had said that Governor Hughes was waiting on another floor, and he led them upstairs. After another long wait and another move, at six o'clock, Julian and Al had realized that this was a deliberate stall, and they had then left for the amphitheater, assuming that we would by then be on the way. Someone added that all this time Governor Hughes had been in a cocktail party at a hotel across the street!

It had taken an hour for them to talk their way through to the amphitheater. Meanwhile, acting only on the strength of Julian's phone call, Assemblyman Brown and ten other members of the committee had drawn up a minority report asking that only our delegation be seated, and they had given it to one of the McGovern delegates to turn in. She repeated that she had turned it in at the Credentials Committee office, but Assemblyman Brown had just been talking with Walter Pozen, who insisted that he had received no such report and that it was, by then, too late for a Minority Report, anyway. Assemblyman Brown was certain that the latter, at least, was not true.

It was a case of beating Governor Hughes to the gavel. So, while the opening speeches were being read, Assemblyman Brown quickly composed another Minority Report, typed it onto the five copies necessary, and ruled off eleven lines. Then he, Mr. Badillo, and one other delegate signed them and started down to the floor. They had the nearly impossible task of trying to find the eight other necessary committee members in the sea of delegates which then filled the floor. Just as they were leaving, someone arrived with the news that, contrary to the agreed upon ruling, the regular Georgia delegation had received floor passes and were seated in the Georgia section on the floor, while our delegation remained in the Gallery.

There were several attempts made by the McCarthy staff to get one of us with a walkie-talkie onto the floor as a runner to help find the Credentials Committee delegates, but the set we had could not be made to work. So Frank went in to use the phones in the nerve center. Meanwhile Julian went out in search of any and every television reporter he could find, to try to tell the nation about what was happening to us. Fifteen minutes later we watched in the McCarthy office while Julian, looking calm but determined, briefly recounted what was going on and how we were being dealt with.

We returned to our Gallery seats to let our delegation know what was

219

happening, while somewhere down on the floor Assemblyman Brown was quickly going to work. We could easily make out the New Jersey delegation right below us, along with Governor Hughes, its leader. About half an hour and a lot of nervousness later, we saw Assemblyman Brown, who had taken care to bring a few TV cameras with him, walk up to Governor Hughes and present him with the Georgia Minority Report while on national television, so that the governor could not refuse nor claim later that he had never seen it. Assemblyman Brown then pointed up to us and over to the regular Georgia standard, and we saw Governor Hughes nod his head.

Ten minutes later Assemblyman Brown appeared upstairs with two handfuls of "Temporary Floor Passes," enough for us all. Taylor and I met him in the walkway, and he said that Governor Hughes had claimed not to have known about the seating discrepancy. I went inside the hall and motioned for everyone to follow. My heart started to flutter, and I think that there was a smile on my face. Our entire delegation got up together and walked out into the walkway and then down the back stairs to a large empty area between the stairwell and the McCarthy headquarters on the circle level. The press was really starting to hound us, and it was difficult for all forty of us to hear as Assemblyman Brown gave us instructions on how to get through the light machine at the entrance to the floor and how to get around to the Georgia seats. Three people had gone to find Julian, who was still involved with the press.

Rev. Hooten began passing out our new passes, name by name, and we added them to our neck chains. All of us were becoming rather excited. The newsmen were absolutely overwhelming, pressing us with questions. Someone suggested that we go inside the McCarthy HQ to get organized, but one of the Humphrey delegates refused, and it would not have been a very good tactical maneuver. After about ten minutes Julian arrived, followed by a small army of reporters.

Reports were coming up from the floor that some members of the Maddox delegation were going to walk out if we set foot on the convention floor. Others were said to be preparing to fight it out, fist to fist. We obviously had no idea what to expect. So we grouped into a double column, two by two, with Julian and Rev. Hooten at the front, John Lewis and myself next, and Taylor bringing up the rear. Over and over we repeated that no one was to say or do anything provocative – we hoped to quietly walk in and take our seats.

Thus prepared, we marched down the stairs and onto the floor level just outside of the hall on the speaker's left. We planned to enter by the back left corner entrance and walk straight around the back wall and into the first aisle on the right, where the Georgia seats were a third of the way down on the left.

As we got near to the light machines the press crowding became almost intolerable, and we literally had to push our way through men, microphones and cameras to get our cards into those machines and then ourselves out onto the floor. As I stuck my new blue card into the machine I held my breath; it stuck, then the light flashed green. Those next few moments were probably some of the most exciting in my life as we inched our way forward along that back wall. We were on our way to unlock the hold of a small group of men on the Democratic Party of Georgia.

Even though someone was speaking about something up on the platform, a cheer started directly above us and began to spread around the hall, as the cameras on the big TV platform swung around, everyone stood up, and delegates craned their necks on chairs to see what was happening.

We finally got to the proper aisle, Julian speaking into the six microphones in his face the whole way. As we turned into the aisle the pressure of bodies became unbearable; people were converging on that one spot from all over the hall, and I was sure that our neat column had been broken up, though I literally could not turn around to look.

We moved in surges up the crowded aisle, and stopped by Joe Sports, who said "I'm sorry, Julian, but there aren't any seats." I raised my camera and, resting my elbows on people's shoulders, snapped a quick picture just before the shoving started. Security men, at the other end of the aisle, where apparently many of the regular delegation had walked out and a CBS newsman had been slugged, now locked arms and tried to shove us all back, like cattle. At the same time our own delegation was still trying to get in the other end of the aisle and the crunch in the middle resulted in us being lifted up off of our feet and pushed back and forth. I feared what might happen if this crush hit some of our older delegates; and, spotting Taylor, I desperately motioned for him to move people back.

In the resulting chaos our delegation was scattered in seats all over the floor of the convention. Some wound up being offered seats by Wisconsin, seated just behind Georgia; others wound up with California. Some made it back to our original assembly point, others found one of the caucus rooms empty and sat down there. Julian was pursued by the press wherever he went, and we wound up together outside in the open area to the left of the speaker.

Taylor and I took on the responsibility of locating everyone.

It eventually seemed that the majority of delegates were either at the original assembly point or else inside Caucus Room Two, so we moved the former over to the latter and, with the help of some security men, kept the press out. While the group tried to decide our next move Taylor and I went on a search of the floor, which turned up ten more delegates. We then told Julian where we were, and he tried to move in our direction.

Back up in the caucus room a national staff man had arrived with the news that they were quickly setting up temporary folding chairs in an open area in the extreme front right-hand corner of the hall. Julian then arrived, leaving the press outside. We talked for a while; and when word came that the chairs were ready, we decided that Julian would leave first, walking off to the right, while the rest of us would follow the national staff man out to the left. This play worked well for all concerned, and shortly we were finally seated in our own special area, completely across the hall from the rest of the Georgia delegation, where a few of the regular delegates had stayed behind.

Taylor and I took a trip up to the McCarthy Headquarters, where the Credentials Committee members were assigning and writing speeches for their minority battles, to include Texas, Alabama, North Carolina, and Georgia. Someone was sent to determine if Aaron Henry of Mississippi would speak for Georgia, which he agreed to do.

A procedural vote came up on whether to have the minority reports that night; the motion carried and the first minority report began, I believe on Texas. The minority side was allowed twenty minutes to present its case, and the majority-meaning Governor Hughes – allowed twenty minutes to defend the majority report. Since the eight necessary delegations had also moved to require a roll call vote, the voting itself took a long time, especially if a delegation could not agree on its vote total and asked for a caucus to count its votes.

The Texas Minority Report lost by a considerable majority. When it next came time for the Georgia Minority Report, a three-way split developed.

Assemblyman Brown, another Credentials Committee member, and Aaron Henry spoke for our minority; Governor Hughes spoke for the majority report; and William Trotter, Georgia National Committeeman, read a speech written by James Gray in support of a second minority report which had quickly appeared, and which aimed to unseat our entire delegation. The people controlling the speaker's platform had originally agreed to let Chairman Gray give his own speech, but then Julian had appeared and asked for equal time for a speech of his own. At first this arrangement was agreed to, but then someone thought better of the fireworks which might be involved, and both men were denied access to the speaker's platform.

So Assemblyman Brown, at about one a.m., led off for the minority report seeking to unseat all of the regulars. His was a particularly strong speech, declaring that the Democratic Party had once and for all to declare itself against the racism and the closed selection system represented by the Maddox-appointed delegation. It was terribly unfair to so lump the entire delegation into one boat as "racists'; but as an *Atlanta Journal* editorial later pointed out, the entire delegation suffered from the circumstances of its birth.

The next two speeches were not nearly as strong as Assemblyman Brown's, and Aaron Henry ended our side's argument without the final kick it needed.

Next William Trotter read James Gray's speech, calling on the convention to unseat us for many of the same reasons I had heard Chairman Gray give three days before. Finally Governor Hughes, the man caught in the middle, had to argue for the majority report, meaning that he had to criticize both of the individual delegations and also try to be convincing that a new, stronger Georgia Democratic coalition could be established in the state from a compromise seating of both at the convention.

I think that most of us were, in all honesty, absolutely in agreement with the goal of Governor Hughes' compromise. Such a compromise, if willingly entered into by both sides, was, obviously, the best way to start to build a real Democratic Party in Georgia. It was always the specific conditions of the compromise which worried us, never its larger purpose. With a few rather simple guarantees we almost certainly would have voted acceptance. But the other delegation never budged an inch toward either conciliation or compromise, and by Monday night we felt so mishandled that a minority report battle seemed the only way to displace many of our own fears of future misdealings. And we certainly had nothing to lose by fighting, since we would keep half the Georgia votes even if we lost.

Governor Hughes finally finished, and the convention came around to the vote, first to be taken on our own minority report. As the roll was called, George Walsh kept a running total on a tally sheet on his knee. Several of our delegates had their fingers crossed. Others— including myself – walked around nervously. The vote progressed about evenly, with neither side clearly taking an early majority. But all of the big northern industrial states passed, waiting to see which way the vote was going, hoping to jump onto a bandwagon; meanwhile the Humphrey delegates involved considered their standing with the folks back home if they did not vote "against Lester Maddox" (i.e., for us). But they also had to consider their standing with the party establishment, which was really putting on the pressure to defeat our minority report motion. All of these northern states passed, that is, except New York, which cast all of its votes but one for our report, the one dissenting vote being the chairman's. This vote announcement brought a loud cheer from the gallery.

I walked over to the always key swing state of Illinois to watch Mayor Daley, standing on a chair, count his state's vote. He asked how many delegates were "for Julian Bond." About twenty raised their hands. How many against? About thirty. When Illinois' turn came he then cast twenty votes for the minority report and all the rest of Illinois' votes – about eighty – against. At this point the New York delegation began waiving its standard: the chairman had changed his mind and voted for us, accompanied by another loud cheer for the gallery.

About two-thirds of the way through the second round it became obvious that we were going to lose. When the vote was finally announced it was 1,041 ½ for our minority report, 1,413 against. One man in the New York delegation started shouting "No-No No." Several others on the delegation picked it up, and then they began with "Julian Bond, Julian Bond, Julian Bond," making the V sign as they chanted, standing on chairs.

Someone had made a logistical mistake in placing the New York and the California delegations – the two largest and most vocal in the hall – side by side. The chant soon spread to California, then on to Wisconsin and the galleries. The band tried hopelessly to drown them out; but after five minutes of vocal disorder which showed no sign of letting up, Daniel

Inouye of Hawaii, the temporary chairman, accepted a motion from Illinois to recess until Tuesday at six pm.

None of us really knew what to think, except that we were then fairly sure to be seated, along with the other delegation, but with none of the guarantees we had hoped for, meaning that the longer struggle in Georgia would be less clearly defined and more difficult. But only the older, wiser members were then thinking about that. Most of us were too excited and overcome by the day's events to do much thinking. I could only feel at such a moment; and I felt, basically, very happy that we had come so far and accomplished so much.

We stayed put while the hall cleared and the press interviewed any of us who would speak. We then left, nearly the last out of the hall, returned to our bus, and headed back for the Del Prado, where we were warmly received by the rest of the delegation who had been following the events on television.

Though it was by then very, very late, several of us, including Taylor, Pat Madsen, Jo Ann Thomas, and Al Horn went out in search of food. A Chicago policeman picked us up and gave us a lift over to a restaurant. After another hour of breakfast and pretty happy conversation, we returned to the Del Prado, where I collapsed into bed and didn't wake up until nearly noon.

DELEGATES AT THE DEMOCRATIC
NATIONAL CONVENTION

The convention itself and the other events in Chicago during that week in August have, by this time, been viewed, analyzed, and reanalyzed thoroughly, so a blow by blow account of the entire convention seems unnecessary. But the details surrounding several of the convention highlights can, I hope, bear retelling.

We arrived late at the amphitheater on Tuesday night, because of a misunderstanding with the bus company about which I felt particularly bad, since transportation was one of my responsibilities. On the way over I was sitting next to Deacon Birch, a black preacher from south Georgia. He had a bit of a satisfied smile on his face; and when I asked him why he responded with an answer which seemed to me both incredible as a comment on the status quo and at the same time almost naively confident about what we were really accomplishing, those seventy of us, in Chicago. "I was talking with my folks back home, today" he said. "They saw me on television last night, and I bet those men who run the segregated stores in town are really scared now."

Once we had arrived, Taylor took care of obtaining credentials for the rest of the week, not just for the one night as we had done on Monday. Beginning that night the entire delegation participated at the amphitheater. By the time we arrived inside, the vote had already been taken which defeated the second minority report on Georgia and thereby confirmed the majority report, seating both delegations.

Tuesday night we sat in the area originally assigned to Georgia, where a number of rows of extra chairs had been added. Many of the regular delegation again walked out when the final compromise was agreed upon, but at least twenty stayed behind, mostly the delegation's moderates, who insisted that they did not agree with the compromise and wanted nothing to do with us.

When we came out onto the floor that night, retracing our steps of the night before, several of us were fairly successful in clearing a path through the press, and we reached our seats without the earlier crush. Security guards were then posted at both ends of the aisle, where they prevented any non-delegates from entering for over an hour. The aisles already were so narrow that if only one person stopped to ask a question, two-way traffic was halted and large jams occurred.

As we moved in to take our seats, there were some curious human kinds of incidents, since that night we were thoroughly mixed in with the regulars. After about five minutes of icy inter-delegation silence, the usual stock questions, accompanied by timorous smiles, began, like "Where are you from?" and "Where do you go to school?." Small conversations then grew and, like people everywhere, both sides quickly learned that each one's arch enemies were really fairly pleasant, fairly decent people; and it was actually rather nice to find some new "home folks" at the convention who could tell us about what their own more official experiences in Chicago had been like.

There was a genuine desire on our delegation's part to make a new, united Georgia delegation really work. For obvious reasons all of the elected Georgia Democratic officials on the regular delegation had either resigned or had walked out; but we hoped that we could caucus, cajole, and vote together like any other state delegation. The leaders of the other group, however, would have nothing to do with such an integration. They made it clear that they were simply complying with the letter of the compromise because they had no choice, but that their staying did not mean that they had to "fraternize" with us. So all our caucuses, though we repeatedly invited them, were held separately; and our 20 ½ votes were cast separately as "Regulars" and as "the Delegation of Loyal National Democrats."

After the minority reports for Alabama and North Carolina were taken up and, sadly, defeated, the convention then moved on to deciding several motions on party reform, sponsored mainly by the McCarthy delegations. A reform was passed banning the unit rule in either state or national conventions.

Next was adopted a most significant and really historic motion requiring each state to use some sort of broadly based democratic process in selecting its delegates for all future conventions. This motion wrote into the convention procedure itself the hope expressed in the 1968 Convention Call, and its approval should subsequently make the job of any future challenge delegation much easier, since a system such as Georgia's in 1968 will be a clear violation of convention procedure.

The debate on this last motion was long and hard, and for a while we were actually debating back and forth between our two delegations, which was the only time this happened. By the time the vote was to be taken, we convinced everyone on the regular delegation of the motion's desirability. The men who cast the votes, Rev. Hooten and Mr. Carling Dinkler, counted up and got a unanimous vote in favor.

Rev. Hooten was trying to persuade Mr. Dinkler to cast all of the votes together as the "unanimous vote of the entire Georgia delegation," when a Humphrey floor man got to our regular delegation friends and told them not to vote for the motion. I could not hear what he was saying, but he convinced those immediately around him; the final vote of the regular delegation included five votes "no."

I later remembered this incident when, in his acceptance speech, Mr. Humphrey referred to the fine job we had "all" done in reforming the party's machinery. Probably the only reason the motion passed against this sort of official pressure was the real desire among many of the liberal Humphrey delegates to make up for defeating all the minority reports in 1968 by making a pledge for 1972, much like what happened with Mississippi in 1964. Hopefully this much-needed reform, coupled with the memory of our unique 1968 Georgia victory "in only one try," will motivate each state party establishment to initiate real grassroots state reform, hoping thereby to avoid a similar challenge to its own delegation in 1972.

Another curious reform which was moved that night, not by the McCarthy forces, was to give the male and female co-presidents of each state's Young Democrats Club permanent places at the convention, like those held by the National Committeeman and Committeewoman. It sounded like, and was argued as, an innocuous move to allow more youthful participation in the party's affairs. We were feeling positively about the motion when a young man from California arrived to argue against it.

He pointed out that we had no way of knowing how such young people were selected in any other states and that we might simply be voting to add another 110 votes to the already too powerful establishment side of the convention. After all, for all we knew, such young officials might be appointed by the governor in other states. We agreed and mostly voted against the motion. Later, I learned that it had first dawned on Rick Stearns, the Midwest field man in the McCarthy nerve center, what might be afoot just as the vote was about to be taken; he and his teammates had immediately jumped on their twelve telephones, one of which went to California, to sound the alarm, and that was why we were visited. The motion was ultimately defeated.

On Tuesday night various people, including Shirley MacLaine, a California delegate, came to see us to tell us to "hold on for Ted." Teddy Kennedy had, over the weekend, stated that he was not a candidate, but persistent rumors had it that, if there was a genuine draft movement, he would run. After the chaotic way in which the convention had ended the night before, and with the first reports of the beatings in Lincoln Park starting to come in that night, a restless, fluid mood was developing within the convention, possibly propitious for a new candidate.

While walking around the hall that night I met Charlie Negaro on one of the back stairs: he was wearing a staff credential card, carrying a walkie-talkie, and apparently really enjoying himself. He was optimistic about Kennedy's chances, and I again thanked him for all his help that summer in Georgia. He smiled; and, as we parted, said "Don't mention it."

Tuesday night the convention again broke up in disorder. With all of the other business out of the way, the chairman moved, at one a.m. (two on the east coast), that we then begin the long debate on the Vietnam war plank. After the Democratic President had given up because of the war, after a summer in which the war issue had come close to tearing our country apart, it then seemed incredible to us that the Democratic Party was to spend several hours debating America's most divisive single issue while most of the nation slept, and most of the delegates tried to.

The Wisconsin chairman, directly behind us, started waving his state banner and, with some of us helping, their delegation began shouting, yelling, and whistling to get the speaker's attention, who for five minutes ignored the noise altogether. Finally he interrupted the beginning of the debate by asking Wisconsin what they wanted. The Wisconsin microphone was turned on long enough for the chairman to move that we recess until Wednesday afternoon, for all of the reasons given above. The speaker replied that a recess was not possible and again prepared to begin the debate.

At this point the New York and California cheering teams, on the other side of the TV platform from us, after a few false starts broke into a chant of "Let's go home. Let's go home." Again this chant was picked up by Wisconsin, some of us, several other delegations, and the gallery. Finally, the house again in pandemonium, the speaker accepted a motion from Iowa to recess until Wednesday at noon.

I remember that as I climbed down from my chair, with a great cheer ringing throughout the hall, a woman on the regular Georgia delegation, standing next to me, looked up at me and said, "You know, if we had used those same tactics, you'd have called *us* fascists." I could not answer her because she was probably right. The only argument I can use in our defense is that we sincerely believed in the most open debate possible, with the greatest number of Americans watching as possible. We had no intention whatsoever of disrupting the debate or the vote itself, nor of rejecting the results, which I would like to think puts us a great deal short of the tactics used by either the extreme left or the extreme right.

But the most important thing about that pause in the convention, at 1:15 Wednesday morning, was that at that point, in my opinion, the convention *was* genuinely open. We had, I think, accomplished the impossible: we had shaken Humphrey loose from his victory. The Southern delegates were still angry over our seating, and the rumors about several favorite son nominees – possibly even John Connally from Texas – persisted. More importantly, every delegate knew that the convention was getting bad press, from the kids being beaten up in the streets to the chaotic recesses each night to the embarrassing dissension over the Southern challenges and the Vietnam War.

Moreover, Mayor Daley was already being criticized for his police tactics both inside and outside the convention hall. Daley's name and his police had become synonymous with the party establishment, as were the forces known to be working against the minority reports. And, like it or not, deserve it or not, Hubert Humphrey was personally lumped in with all that the discredited establishment was then seen to be standing for; and the delegates felt that the country at large, already crying out for a change, simply was not going to vote for a man associated with the events in Chicago.

In short, by Tuesday night, the delegates were looking for a winner, and they believed that Humphrey was no longer the man. I am convinced that, had Ted Kennedy wanted it, he could have won the Democratic nomination. As a measure of his support, even several of the regular Georgia delegates had already drawn up large "Draft Ted" signs, and they were prepared to throw the whole delegation's support behind him. You could feel this restlessness all over the convention floor, and had Bobby Kennedy still been alive, and had events occurred similarly, he would have been the Democratic nominee in a walk away. What a difference his nomination would have meant to the campaign that fall. As Al Lowenstein later remarked to me, "We lost more than we may ever know when we lost Robert Kennedy. He was the only one who could have pulled us all together."

The next twelve hours were absolutely crucial. McCarthy had made too many enemies and was simply disliked by too many delegates to be a front runner; though, like McGovern, he might have been a second or third ballot choice. And there really was no one else but Ted Kennedy, who, at thirty-six, must have had terrible doubts for a number of obvious reasons, about running for President. By noon the next day he had again declined; and the Illinois Caucus, keying off of Mayor Daley who had failed in his own attempts to persuade Kennedy to run, had voted to back Humphrey.

These two critical actions started the rush back to the Vice President. But the important point was that this rush occurred not particularly because anyone was either forced to, nor because anyone particularly wanted to, but because there simply was no one else to turn to. For those twelve hours, from midnight to noon on Wednesday, all of the hoping and the planning had actually worked, and the final outcome was absolutely uncertain. For those twelve critical hours, a strong alternative candidate with the right quick action could, conceivably, have beaten the man who only the week before had seemed to have the nomination all his own. In the end Humphrey did win, but he was by no means a shoo-in.

———

Early Wednesday afternoon the Vietnam debate began. The only real difference in the two reports on the war was over the inclusion of a plank calling for a complete halt in the bombing of North Vietnam as a move towards peace. It would seem as if such a small excursion away from the "party line" might have been allowed in an attempt to placate the peace candidates, and rumor had it that while Mr. Humphrey was not opposed to this plank, the shots on this particular issue were being called from the White House, which could not tolerate any deviation from the approved policy.

Whoever was exerting the pressure in favor of the majority report, it was certainly being exerted strongly. Texas was a good example of the pressure's effectiveness. During the Credentials Committee debate on the Texas delegation, the regular delegation of Governor Connally had emphasized over and over again that its delegation was representative of all the political, racial, and geographic groups of Democrats within the state. This "proud mixture" delegation was duly given its credentials and seated. And yet on the most divisive single issue in American politics in 1968, that broadly representative delegation cast every single one of its one hundred votes for the majority plank, with not even one dissenting vote.

With the defeat of the minority plank it was obvious to everyone that Humphrey then had the Presidential nomination; and except for a few minor incidents, the remainder of the convention was anti-climactic. Immediately following the minority report defeat, at about six o'clock, there was a supper recess; but most of the peace delegates stayed behind and eventually drowned out the band singing "Glory, Glory Hallelujah" and "We Shall Overcome." While the singing went on many delegates began marching around the near empty hall with black arm bands and their state standards draped in black cloth. A few of our delegates tried to take the Georgia standard, but Joe Sports had a guard watching it. This was a particularly depressing moment for many of us, as Humphrey's victory was inevitable. But, though we had lost the final convention battle, we knew that we had lost more or less fairly; and we knew that perhaps we had at least changed a few things along the way.

One interesting event later that night was a genuinely grassroots "Draft Ted" movement which began during the first nominating speeches. Rumors still persisted that Ted Kennedy might run if he were drafted; and a group of delegates were determined to provide him that chance, the feeling being that if his name could just be put into nomination, there was still a strong chance that there would be enough first ballot Kennedy desertions from Humphrey to throw the nomination to Kennedy or to someone else on the second or third ballot.

This movement was begun and organized completely by "ordinary people"; not one national figure was involved that I know of. John Lewis, from our delegation, came to Taylor and myself with word of the attempt to put Kennedy's name in nomination just as the speeches were beginning for Hubert Humphrey. He led us across the convention hall and outside to the open foyer on the speaker's left, where we found huddled together a group of young Democrats, including Arnold Kaufman from Michigan, Rick Tuttle from California, and several others. We joined them immediately. While some of us searched for a rule book, which took twenty minutes to procure, to determine if any individual member of a state delegation could make a presidential nomination, John Lewis left again to ask Ted Sorenson about Kennedy's feeling.

At about the same time that we confirmed the relevant convention rule, John Lewis returned from his talk with Ted Sorenson who, standing at the back of the New York delegation, had said that Kennedy would probably welcome the nomination if it came genuinely from the bottom (which we certainly were). With Sorenson's go ahead we then needed a nominator and a second for Kennedy. As names came up several members of our group started out onto the floor, at that time a sea of Humphrey demonstrators, to find the persons suggested.

Communication within the hall was particularly difficult that night, because the Illinois delegation, seated right in front of the speaker, was completely sealed off; and no one was allowed to pass in front of the speaker's platform, meaning a long detour was necessary to get from one side of the hall to the other. Mayor Daley had ordered his delegation to be sealed off after many, many delegates, from national figures to the ordinary Democrat, came up to him asking and imploring him to do something about the carnage which was then taking place in Chicago's streets. Many just wanted him to give the order to let ambulances through. Mayor Daley, in reply, sealed off his delegation from the rest of the convention and sat alone in icy silence, while the nation and the rest of the convention delegates (who could find televisions in the lounges) watched the Chicago police maintain law and order.

Despite the near impossibility of internal communication, Taylor and John Lewis soon returned with word that Fannie Lou Hamer of Mississippi had agreed to nominate Ted Kennedy. The Mississippi delegation's co-chairmen, Aaron Henry and Hodding Carter, had been somewhat apprehensive of Mrs. Hamer taking on such a responsibility by herself. But, Taylor reported, Mrs. Hamer had been extremely enthusiastic and had persuaded the delegation chairmen to write a note to Carl Albert, stating that Mississippi wished to place a name in nomination.

Though we as yet had no second (others were out looking for one), Taylor was dispatched to take Fannie Lou Hamer and Hodding Carter's note to the speaker's platform. The important thing then was to find a friendly microphone. Since no one else had any suggestions, and since I knew that I could talk Rev. Hooten into letting me speak, I volunteered to do so. Everyone agreed, and while I waded back across the hall to Georgia (we were then sitting, with the regulars, in the area we had occupied on the first night), Taylor went to take Fannie Lou Hamer to the speaker's stand, and most everyone else fanned out to alert the key delegations.

I wrote out a short speech, in which I first pointed out the relevant rule under which I was acting (in case anyone wanted to shut off my microphone). I then planned to say that I was yielding to Fannie Lou Hamer of Mississippi, who would "place in nomination the name of a great American." Rev. Hooten said that I could use the mic when our delegation was called; and I stood beside it, getting more and more nervous, not knowing if Taylor and Mrs. Hamer had made it to the speaker's platform but, after all that time of working with Taylor, assuming that if anyone could get her through, he could.

Taylor later reconstructed what happened. Arriving at the speaker's platform, he and Mrs. Hamer tried to enter one of the doors from the convention hall into the holding station under the platform, but they were stopped by a guard. Explaining their purpose, Taylor stood up on a chair directly below Carl Albert and tried to catch his attention on the platform, but the chairman was seated with his back to Taylor.

After he and the guard both yelled a few times, John Bailey finally leaned down and took the note written by Hodding Carter; and in a few minutes the door opened and Fannie Lou Hamer was allowed inside, encouraging Taylor and readying herself to nominate Ted Kennedy extemporaneously. From his vantage point on the chair Taylor had seen me standing by our Georgia microphone. He then started the slow journey back to the foyer to tell the group that all seemed ready.

But back outside Taylor found that Kennedy's nomination had been stopped. Hodding Carter, reacting to Aaron Henry's apprehension, had phoned Steve Smith, Kennedy's brother-in-law and advisor, who had asked that Mr. Carter not allow Kennedy's name to be placed in nomination. Mr. Carter then went to get Mrs. Hamer, first stopping to give our group in the foyer the news. He and Taylor must have passed each other on the floor, and Mr. Carter took Mrs. Hamer to a phone to talk to Steve Smith personally. Mrs. Hamer finally agreed not to go through with the nomination, and she left the speaker's platform.

But I knew none of this, standing by our microphone, listening to other nominating speeches. After about half an hour, a delegate came to get me from the Minnesota delegation; he said that there was a call for me from the McCarthy Headquarters. It turned out to be a staff person in the McCarthy nerve center advising me not to go through with Kennedy's nomination. I replied that several of us had decided to do it and that Fannie Lou Hamer was going to give the nomination speech. The voice then said all right, and hung up.

Five minutes later the phone rang again; this time it was Curt Gans, who said that he had just been down to the holding station for speakers, that Fannie Lou Hamer was not there, and that I would be yielding to an empty platform. He said that Mrs. Hamer had been talked out of making the nomination by some of Kennedy's closest advisors, and that she had gone back to her delegation.

I said that I understood and went back to the Georgia microphone, where I then told Rev. Hooten to forget about my speech. A few minutes later the roll call came to Georgia, Rev. Hooten said "Pass," I tore up my speech, and the "Draft Ted" movement was over. Taylor fought his way back ten minutes later and confirmed all that Curt had said; so the two of us sat down, resigned to Mr. Humphrey. But I cannot help wondering what might have been, had Mrs. Hamer gone ahead with her nominating speech for Ted Kennedy.

The highlight of the evening for us came when Julian gave his seconding speech for Senator McCarthy, which I felt was one of the best speeches of the entire convention. Julian's words captured best the hope which Senator McCarthy had given to an entire generation. Julian spoke of the concern he had felt over the Vietnam War and of his debt to Senator McCarthy for providing that concern a political expression. When Julian and the others finally finished we had a chance to shout our fill for Senator McCarthy. "We Want Gene" rang out across the hall.

Senator McCarthy's campaign had been based really on only one issue, with both fortunate and unfortunate consequences. Quite probably he would not have been the best presidential candidate, but his campaign had, in fact, moved the nation; and it had given an army of young idealists an experience in politics which was crucial at the moment, and which might be invaluable in the future.

The final presidential vote of our delegation gave McCarthy thirteen votes for Georgia, the other 7 ½ from our delegation evenly divided among the remaining candidates. Humphrey was the Presidential nomination at about 1:30; and after another demonstration, the convention recessed in order for the first time. There was a meeting immediately afterwards in Caucus Room Two for just about every non-Humphrey delegate at the convention, all of us by then stunned by the news reports and the films of the night's battle at the Conrad Hilton. Some of the speakers wanted us to boycott the next night's session and, instead, to form a fourth party on the spot. Others wanted to march downtown that night, which seemed like a long and dangerous trip.

Many of us from Georgia were afraid that our buses would leave without us, so, after about half an hour, we left, though some stayed. Outside the caucus room there was a double line of helmeted police and, though I could not imagine it, I was afraid that they were about to go in and forcefully evict the delegates from the near-empty amphitheater.

We found that one of our two buses had remained, and as we were determining what to do, the delegates started pouring out of the convention hall. Someone ran up to say that the plan was then to take buses to an area about ten blocks north of the Hilton and to walk down

Michigan Avenue to Grant Park, across from the Hilton, in a non-violent protest of the night's activities. The point was, could they use our bus?

After some consultation we agreed, and our bus was soon loaded, three on each seat and several in the aisles. Candles appeared from somewhere, and we started off for the Del Prado to let anyone off from Georgia who wanted to get off; then the rest would ride north with the driver, who was quite happy to help us and whose garage happened to be near to the assembly point. None of us knew what to expect, and John Lewis, who had been beaten several times in civil rights marches in Mississippi and Alabama, gave a brief, very serious talk on how best to defend oneself when being clubbed and kicked. I imagined the worst and I remember silently hoping that guns would not be used against us.

Cathy got off at the Del Prado, nearly in tears, but Taylor said that he had to go. So we drove north and reached the assembly point at about 2:30, where a crowd had already gathered. The other buses had apparently gone back to the amphitheater for a second load, so we had to wait half an hour, singing songs most of the time. Every once in a while a police car would stop to question us, but Paul O'Dwyer, the leader, had by then somehow secured official permission for the march.

When the second load had arrived and all of the candles had been lit, we started off down the wide sidewalk on the eastern, Lake Michigan side of the street. As we walked we sang "We Shall Overcome," very slowly and very solemnly, like a dirge. The darkened storeroom windows across the street reflected the yellow flames of the candles, blowing in the wind, like the answer and the tear gas.

Our ranks seemed to swell and swell as people got out of cars and emptied the adjacent hotels to join us as we passed. The singing got louder and louder, and by the time we approached the Hilton there must have been over a thousand of us. Why, somehow, we had the right to have a non-violent march in Chicago, because we were "delegates," while all those young people, just as committed to a cause but not lucky enough to be on the inside, did not have that same right, I shall never know. But that march was the most moving experience of the entire two weeks, epitomizing all that is good about the right to non-violent protest within our society.

In the park across from the Hilton were the kids, gathered around campfires, while a semi-circle of National Guardsmen and jeeps with coils of barbed wire on the front protected the hotel.

Paul O'Dwyer gave a short speech with a hand megaphone, saying that we had come because not all of the nation is like the Mayor Daleys, because not all of the nation had lost its sense of what is right. Then, all of the delegates mixed in among the young people in the park and joined in around the campfires as we sang more songs. Lights came on in the Conrad Hilton and the Sheraton Blackstone, some flashing in sympathy. Several of the young people whom I saw were bruised and bandaged, and several girls started crying when they saw all of the "delegates" - mostly older establishment people – coming to join those for whom the events of that night must have seemed a terror. The singing continued until dawn.

———

Thursday, the final evening, the convention session began with a memorial film dedicated to Robert Kennedy, ending with his brother's famous eulogy. The orchestra played "The Battle Hymn of the Republic"; but when they stopped, the singing within the hall only got louder, a last sad protest against the establishment which seemed to have forgotten how to dream of things that never were, and to ask why not. "Glory, glory Hallelujah" kept pealing for ten minutes, finally only stopped by the sanitation workers in the gallery screaming "We Love Mayor Daley." There was next a minute's silence announced for Martin Luther King, Jr; but, perhaps fearing that "We Shall Overcome" might come next, the speaker waited twenty seconds and then started calling the roll for Vice Presidential nominations.

The sanitation workers in the circle were, of course, a curious lot. Armed with flags and "We Love Mayor Daley" posters, they would "spontaneously" burst into cheer whenever there was some other uproar which needed quieting. Mayor Daley had apparently been quite disturbed by the fact that, somehow, individuals other than his own people had controlled the galleries on the first two nights, so on Wednesday and Thursday nights he imported Chicago's paid workers to gain the upper hand, vocally. These people did not even have the proper credentials; instead, around their necks hung torn-in-half Conrad Hilton press passes from the week before. They also had flags and posters which were not allowed for the rest of us.

How incredible, I thought, that a man should impose a police state on the trumped-up charge that some students were going to break his rule of law, that he should install foolproof light machines to prevent outsiders from crashing the convention, and then that he should himself so blatantly break his own rules for the sake of his own personal interests. That's the way to instill a respect for authority!

Probably the most unexpected event of Thursday evening was the nomination of Julian Bond for Vice-President. Julian's nomination came as the climax to a long string of other half-events, all designed by several Democratic leaders in hope of getting men like Al Lowenstein to the convention microphone to denounce the tactics of Mayor Daley, both inside and outside the convention hall. Their purpose was to show the nation that not every delegate agreed with what was happening. But they never got a chance.

As I understand it, the original plan was to nominate David Hoeh, Chairman of the Vermont delegation, for Vice President, Mr. Hoeh having just been carried off the floor and arrested for inserting a credit card into one of Mayor Daley's blessed light machines. Al apparently was waiting in the speaker's holding room for someone from New York to make the nomination. Al would then give a "nominating" speech from the central speaker's platform, blasting the party establishment and letting the nation know what sort of tactics were being employed, both in the aisles and in the streets. The important point was the symbolism involved in the name nominated and the chance provided to get to the main microphone, since everyone knew that in reality Senator Muskie had the nomination all sewn up.

But the New York chairman passed without giving anyone else on the delegation a chance to speak; the mic was cut off, and the speaker moved on to the next state. Al, along with everyone else who was in on the plan, went as quickly as they could to the last friendly microphone in the house, at Wisconsin. Mr. Hoeh had by then declined to be nominated so, without consulting him, Ted Warshafsky of Wisconsin nominated Julian Bond.

Al immediately reached for the mic to make his speech, and blew into it to see if it was still on, which it was. But the man on the controls also heard his breath and cut off the switch, leaving Al talking into a dead microphone. The speaker went on to Wyoming, which passed, and the nominations were closed. Wisconsin waved its banner and asked to make a nominating speech for Julian Bond, but the speaker replied that it was too late, since such speeches had to be given before the next state was called. Obviously the platform had been aware of what was planned and had deliberately and effectively stopped it.

Julian was, of course, taken completely by surprise when his name was placed in nomination. He was probably flattered, but I think he was also a little embarrassed that so much attention had been given to him in the preceding few days. He had done a remarkable job in leading our delegation, making the right decisions at the right times. But he was enough of a leader to know that what we accomplished we did through the hard work and the decisions of many people, not just those of any single individual.

When the voting roll call came to Georgia, even though he had already received several votes, Julian withdrew his name from nomination because, at twenty-eight, he was seven years too young for the job: a remarkable end to a remarkable convention for the Georgia Delegation of Loyal National Democrats.

Once Senator Muskie and Vice-President Humphrey had tried to salvage party unity from the shambles of Mayor Daley's convention, and had actually done a pretty good job with their acceptance speeches, the 1968 Democratic National Convention came to a close. Our delegation held a final meeting in one of the caucus rooms to elect our nominees for a National Committeeman and National Committeewoman for the 1972 convention. Ben Brown and Mrs. Mercedes Wright won our nominations: but, because the final Georgia compromise never did deal with this kind of substantive issue, we were uncertain just how these positions would be filled by the national party.

Julian and Rev. Hooten had some final words for the group, including a hope that we could meet again once back in Georgia to attempt to sort out where and under whose leadership the Democratic Party of Georgia would next move. Al Horn pointed out that everyone's help might immediately be needed in raise money for a court case to insure Democratic electors in November. Taylor and Mrs. Paschall read out the final travel plans for the next morning, and we headed back to the Del Prado.

Taylor and I had sworn an oath outside a tavern back on June 30th that, if anything we could do would get Gene McCarthy just one vote from Georgia at the Democratic National Convention, we would return to that same tavern and throw a proper celebration together. We had done ourselves twelve votes better, in the end, and we were quite happy; but we could never have found that tavern. It should not be inferred, however, that, though our lack of logistical expertise prevented us from fulfilling the letter of our oath, we were in any way deterred from fulfilling its spirit. That last night, in fact, quite a few of the delegation joined us in our solemn duty.

The next morning we awoke to the news that the fifteenth floor McCarthy Headquarters in the Conrad Hilton had been raided by the police very early in the morning. The reports were that everyone on that floor had been herded abruptly downstairs, Mary Beth McCarthy among them, simply because several policemen had been hit by flying refuse. How they determined its origin in the dark I don't know; but though many people were shocked by the police's action, it did not really surprise me at all. I suppose it was like being in a war, when one finally is able to accept the death of friends almost casually. To me that incident just seemed to be the final senseless insult, the perfectly fitting end to a week of overreaction and unexpected violence.

Early that Friday morning all but a few of our delegation left for Atlanta. Taylor and Cathy were staying over for a friend's wedding just outside of Chicago on Saturday, and I had a Danforth Fellowship graduate school conference beginning on Monday. Cathy, who was to be in the wedding, had left on Thursday to be in the rehearsals, and I sat in their room on Friday afternoon as Taylor packed to join her. The two of us talked about plans for the next year and for the coming summer. Finally, all packed, Taylor started out the door; we shook hands and said goodbye. It really had been an interesting eight weeks.

EPILOGUE

Taylor went on to the wedding, and I spent a week in splendid isolation at a Danforth Fellowship Conference, where, completely by chance, Al Lowenstein turned out to be one of the guest speakers. It was there that we had a long talk about the convention, and Al made his comment about Robert Kennedy. He returned to New York to run his campaign for Congress, which I was glad to learn in November he won. I received word from Dave Mixer in December that he was only then getting off of his crutches and recovering from the beating he had suffered from the Chicago police on Wednesday night, about which I had not previously known.

I left for graduate school in London in late September, thereby missing the campaign and the election in November. Looking back on the 1968 summer from the vantage of a few months' complete detachment, I am left with several conclusions and many only partially concluded thoughts.

Regarding our own particular role as Georgians For McCarthy, in Georgia and at the convention, it is obvious that twenty of us in a hotel suite in Atlanta could not do much to persuade thousands of voters and delegates that Gene McCarthy was the best candidate. Though we hoped to do so, we clearly failed, due to a late start, a lack of money and manpower, our own failures, and, perhaps, the candidate himself.

But the final victories for the McCarthy campaign were independent of the candidate himself. At the time all of us genuinely believed that McCarthy was the best candidate, and we worked long and hard for him. But the candidate himself was ultimately only a part of a much larger movement. Possibly herein lay the real difference in the earlier McCarthy and Kennedy campaigns: McCarthy's was a movement, a cause if you will, independent of the candidate's ultimate success; Kennedy's was a movement with a real political candidate whose personal success was always just as determined as the victory of the movement itself. The importance of McCarthy's campaign was, however, just as great as Kennedy's, and some would argue that the former helped spawn the latter.

The hard fact which men like McCarthy, Lowenstein, and Kennedy realized very early in the fall of 1967 was that, given our political system, it was all well and good and necessary to argue for an end to the Vietnam War, to argue for Black Power, or to argue for democracy in Georgia's Democratic party processes; but, if one really wanted to accomplish those ends, one eventually had to confront the system on its own terms and struggle with it on the inside. The McCarthy campaign was therefore not really so much an attempt to make Gene McCarthy president as it was an experiment in forcing our nation to struggle with a larger national issue by giving it a *political* candidate representative of a dissenting opinion.

Though Senator McCarthy did not make it to the White House, the McCarthy experiment nevertheless had its dividends.

First, either a lot of minds really were changed, or else a lot of people in the primary states had already been looking for a candidate with McCarthy's platform, because he and Kennedy overwhelmingly won all of the Democratic primaries. Though the goals, as it were, of both men were in a sense more than just personal political victory, their goals had to take shape in a political environment, calling for the expertise, the decisions, the armies of helpers, and the just plain work which goes along with any political campaign The motivation may have come from elsewhere, but the battle had to be won in terms of doorbells, ads, donations, and persuasion that a particular man was the best candidate to be President of the United States.

The second benefit, therefore, was that it channeled the frustrations, the idealism, and the expertise of young people into the nation's political system, allowing them to test their beliefs and to work concretely for change. More importantly for the future, the McCarthy campaign gave many young people a first brush with politics, and the lessons thereby learned could be invaluable in subsequent campaigns, both local and national, if these young people continue their involvement. Even more importantly, this involvement perhaps proved once and for all the value and the power of such participation, so that new young people will now be involving themselves each year.

Third, the campaign really did accomplish many of its goals, forcing a re-evaluation of an international war which was, from all later indications, about to be escalated again in March, had no one accomplished in New Hampshire and Wisconsin what the McCarthy campaign accomplished.

Fourth, once the various state primaries were won by McCarthy and Kennedy, the political leverage which these non-establishment delegates provided at the Democratic convention was absolutely critical to party reform and the victories, such as our own, which got through. I would argue that every convention year someone other than the man at the head of the party should win all such primaries, if only to give the convention the kind of options which just were not possible in 1964 and which were only hard won in 1968. Curt Gans was absolutely right in foreseeing that no changes could have taken place had there not been those McCarthy, Kennedy, and McGovern delegates unafraid to sign minority reports because of the possible consequences on the party establishment.

Only with that kind of politically immune leverage, which forces issues out into the open, or else perhaps with a person at the top who does not feel threatened by the effects of debate, can such a convention really be open to the luxury of argument and freedom of choice. The results of such debate and such voting may or may not differ from the results arrived at through backroom pressure. But the open process at least permits the opportunity to change, and I can remember thinking several times while in Chicago how boring the 1964 convention must have been, when everything was decided long in advance by the party establishment.

Right after the convention many young people were completely put off by the entire political process and the prospects for anything different in the future. I would argue, however, that the delegations at the 1968 convention who were by far the most alive and the most open to change were those delegates elected because of the involvement of such young people in the democratic process; they were, of course, the delegations from the primary states: New York, California, New Hampshire,

Wisconsin, Nebraska, etc. And when one considers reforms passed in 1968, then in 1972 *every* state is going to have to use some sort of democratic process in selecting its delegates (or face an almost certain challenge), thereby giving concerned people all over the country the opportunity to get involved, and giving the convention itself more of a chance to decide issues on the floor, not months beforehand with a few phone calls.

I am also impressed with how easy the political process is to enter. I would offer to anyone else concerned about a particular issue but unsure of his political acumen that none of us involved that summer in Georgia were exactly political professionals. We made many mistakes, but we learned quickly. With just a little more experience, a bit more time, and a lot more manpower, we could have accomplished much more and really have been effective throughout the state. With a larger national involvement, if it really does occur, I look forward to a more democratic Democratic Party in 1972 and after.

I like to believe that, had the 1968 party establishment really been viable, it could have allowed a few dissenting outbursts just to show its vitality. The fact that it instead felt it necessary to overreact to and to overkill every dissenting voice, both within and without the convention hall, shows, I think, that it was a dying establishment trying desperately to maintain its own concept of the status quo. I remain cautiously optimistic, therefore, that a Democratic leadership will emerge anew, once again cherishing democracy and dreaming dreams.

Finally, regarding Georgia, the situation within the Democratic Party of Georgia is not clear, due largely to the lack of specific clauses in the final Georgia compromise. But perhaps this vagueness is an asset, allowing the state party to sort out its problems and to genuinely reform from the inside, providing the motivation is there. This party reform will take months and years of hard work by many, many Georgians, beginning with the party leaders who must open up the party rules and provide the machinery for local and state mass participation. But the really difficult work will be at the local level where, for the first time, Democrats of all persuasions must create local organizations and begin to work politically for those principles for which the Democratic Party stands. Such continuing organizational work, though not very glamorous or news-making, is the *sine qua non* of political involvement in Georgia and must go forward if the party and our two weeks in Chicago are to have any meaning.

It is, further, my sincerest hope that there can be a reuniting of moderate and liberal forces within the state and that past grievances will be forgiven for the sake of a larger purpose. That purpose is to give all Georgians the right to self-determination, which has in the past been granted only to a few men at the top, who also happened to be white. In the past these men have been able to capitalize on feelings of racial prejudice to rob all Georgians – black and white – of a chance to benefit by participation and change.

If the people of Georgia are conservative and vote for conservative candidates, then that is the way democracy works. But I would hope that the system itself would allow the greatest amount of challenge and debate possible, from all directions. Conservatism – or socialism – as a belief which is honestly arrived at after sampling and listening to all other possibilities, seems perfectly acceptable. But to unfairly bias the_*system* itself – as the Democrats did in Georgia and leftists do elsewhere – in favor of one particular philosophy must be wrong; and to enforce a philosophy in this manner, for the sake of a certain group of people, should be equally distasteful to a socialist, a liberal, or a conservative.

It was for this reason – that we felt the system itself to be so biased – that we fought the challenge battle in Chicago, and not because we wanted to impose on anyone a political 'philosophy.' Possibly this larger fact was lost in the partisan political trappings which, once again, the system dictated that we had to use in order to fight the battle. But we were not, as Governor Maddox has labeled us, socialists or communists. We were Georgians, concerned that all Georgians be given an equal opportunity to react with their world, including the right to an equal education, equal job opportunities, and an equal voice in their government, from electing a county sheriff to electing delegates to a national convention.

I would ask all those – in Georgia or elsewhere – who would too easily brand us with names, to stop and consider the situation in which we were placed in the summer of 1968, with an absolutely undemocratic system about to perpetuate itself for at least another four years. I would hope that most people could not have acted any differently.

Surely Julian Bond is not, as he has been called in Georgia, a "draft-card burning communist." Surely Julian wants for himself and for his people the same sorts of things that all of us want. He seems to me to be a good man, an excellent leader, and a cautious idealist. Perhaps he and others like him are symbolic, politically, of our nation's younger leaders in all areas. If so, then with proper changes in our national priorities, with a recognition that a great deal of hard work is needed, and with a recommitment to help others abroad, I think that we can move on to the much more bewildering problems of the next decades. And we can be certain that, even if these problems prove hardly more soluble, they will at least be tackled with honesty, with commitment, and with malice toward none.

AFTERWORD

Reading this manuscript over fifty years later I am mostly encouraged that two young, inexperienced guys could tangentially interact with so many talented people across one summer and actually accomplish so much together. And not from behind barricades, but from within the system as it then existed.

"Tangential" is a key word here. Most of the people mentioned in this book I had never known before, and largely because after that summer I wanted nothing more to do with politics—and took five years off for graduate school and the Navy—I sadly never saw them again, thought I followed their careers.

Taylor went on to become a Pulitzer Prize-winning author, journalist and historian, writing both the trilogy on Martin Luther King, Jr[1], *America in the King Years,* and *The Clinton Tapes: Wrestling History With The President.* He lives in Baltimore and is happily still writing.

Julian Bond and John Lewis, of course, had amazing careers of public service. If you're interested in what Julian was thinking about these events seven years later, here's an interview with him from 1975 in *Facing South*[2].

---

1. https://amzn.to/4bFBJaD
2. https://bit.ly/3KfH3G3

Mary Beth McCarthy, whom I escorted to the July 3d Charity Ball, soon thereafter married Peter Yarrow of Peter, Paul and Mary fame.

Charles Negaro turned from the practice of law and founded The Atticus Bookstore in New Haven, Connecticut, followed by The Chabaso Bakery[3], from which he recently retired.

Buck Goldstein founded Information America, which he later sold, and is the University Entrepreneur in Residence and a Professor of the Practice in the Department of Economics at UNC in Chapel Hill.

If you search any of the names of the young McCarthy Campaign field team who came to Georgia, you'll find many years of dedicated service and advocacy. Rick Stearns, for example, is a United States District Judge in Massachusetts. David Mixner, who passed away earlier this year, was a life-long Gay Rights advocate.

After two years at LSE and three years as the Communications Officer on the *USS Wainwright (CG-28)*, I began a career in commercial real estate which continues today. In the years right after the fall of the Iron Curtain, I helped, with a lot of other good people, to jump start the modern real estate industry in Russia—another story!

The most important change in me happened at age 37, when I realized my failings and gladly surrendered my future to become a follower of Jesus. And that change led to writing four novels, an anthology of short stories, and fifteen years of blog posts, all with a Christian worldview. That's also another story, told with some fictional license in my first novel, *On The Edge*[4].

I realize that many who have read this book do not share that faith, which is of course fine. But if the thought occurs to you, as it does to me, that so much happened here "by coincidence," and by one of us happening to be somewhere to hear someone at just the right moment, then perhaps these events were not just random. You should at least consider it, and what that means for every moment of all our lives.

My wife and I live in Atlanta, not surrounded by our five kids and a lot of grandkids—they all live happily elsewhere, and we enjoy visiting.

This book would not have been possible without the help of many unselfish people, including Taylor Branch and Donnie Summerlin on the

---

3. https://www.chabaso.com/chabaso-story/
4. https://bit.ly/2LtiWXJ

"fact check" side, Adriel Wiggins' gifted team for editing, and our son Marshall Hudson's book design creativity, whose patience was severely tested with this one.

After spending the summer of 1968 in the trenches with us, if you'd like a higher level, more balanced and scholarly review of the events, I have two recommendations. The first is Donnie Summerlin's "The Best of Georgia in Chicago[5]." And the second is "A Mix of Motives: The Georgia Delegate Challenge to the 1968 Democratic Convention and the Dynamics of Intraparty Conflict" by Sam Rosenfeld and Nancy Schwartz[6]. Nancy came to Georgia with Charlie Negaro, so she participated in much that happened.

If you want a sense for how crowded and chaotic the convention was, take a look at the third night, online at CBS News[7]. At about minute 55 the Georgia Delegation casts its split votes for President. We hope the Paley Center for Media will make the other nights available as well.

And don't forget the Photo and Document Gallery at www. parkerhudson.com/1968gallery, or the Biographies that follow.

If you participated in these events, or similar ones, and have anything to add or to correct, please connect at parker@parkerhudson.com.

One final takeaway. I think we accomplished quite a bit because Taylor and I just jumped in. We were motivated. We wanted to get things done. We didn't know that we couldn't do it. Looking back, we were probably helped in those days because, without all of today's communication and information tools, the decision makers really needed doers—gofers—who would carry notes, write, copy, find, call, go, and just do what needed to be done. Right then. With or without sleep.

But I think those kinds of people are still needed today—and always will be needed.

So if you have a passion for accomplishing something, don't let any possible excuse—age, race, gender, address, etc.—slow you down.

I would encourage you to pray first, but whether you do or not, get involved.

Like us, you might accomplish some things along the way.

---

5. https://bit.ly/3ykFJz7
6. https://bit.ly/3UEoujP
7. https://bit.ly/4eOgrdv

BIOGRAPHIES

T he following short biographies were created by inquiring of ChatGPT in the summer of 2024, to which I added where I had personal information. And Donnie Summerlin suggested a few edits, for which I am thankful.

Julian Bond (1940-2015) was a prominent civil rights leader, politician, and educator from Georgia. Julian Bond was born on January 14, 1940, in Nashville, Tennessee. His father, Horace Mann Bond, became the first president of Fort Valley State College (later Fort Valley State University) in Fort Valley, Georgia, in 1939, and the first African American president of Lincoln University in Pennsylvania in 1945, as well as Dean of Education at Atlanta University (later Clark Atlanta University) in 1957.

Bond attended Morehouse College, and he co-founded the Student Nonviolent Coordinating Committee (SNCC) on Easter Sunday in 1960 in Raleigh, N.C. SNCC played a crucial role in the civil rights movement, organizing sit-ins, freedom rides, and voter registration drives across the South.

In 1965, Bond was elected to the Georgia House of Representatives, but the state legislature initially refused to seat him because of his outspoken opposition to the Vietnam War. This led to a landmark case, Bond v. Floyd, where the U.S. Supreme Court ruled in Bond's favor, affirming his right to hold office. Bond served in the Georgia House from 1967 to 1975 and in the Georgia Senate from 1975 to 1986.

Bond was also a co-founder of the Southern Poverty Law Center (SPLC), where he served as president from 1971 to 1979. His efforts extended into education and media; he was a professor at several universities, including American University and the University of Virginia, and narrated the award-winning documentary series "Eyes on the Prize," which chronicled the history of the civil rights movement.

Throughout his life, Julian Bond remained a steadfast advocate for justice, equality, and human rights, leaving an enduring legacy in the fight for civil rights in America.

Julian Bond: The Movement, Then and Now | Facing South[1]

Watch Eyes on the Prize | American Experience | Official Site | PBS[2]

Julian Bond - New Georgia Encyclopedia[3]

Taylor Branch, born on January 14, 1947, in Atlanta, Georgia, is a Pulitzer Prize-winning author and historian renowned for his extensive work on the American civil rights movement. He graduated from the University of North Carolina in 1968 and earned a master's degree from the Woodrow Wilson School of Public and International Affairs at Princeton University in 1970.

Branch's most acclaimed work is the trilogy "America in the King Years," which chronicles the life of Martin Luther King Jr. and the broader civil rights movement. The trilogy includes "Parting the Waters: America in the King Years, 1954-63," which won the Pulitzer Prize for History in 1989; "Pillar of Fire: America in the King Years, 1963-65"; and "At Canaan's Edge: America in the King Years, 1965-68" (Wikipedia[4]) (Georgia Center for the Book[5]). This series is praised for its meticulous research and profound narrative, providing a detailed account of the civil rights era.

In addition to his trilogy, Branch wrote "The Clinton Tapes: Wrestling

---

1. https://www.facingsouth.org/julian-bond-movement-then-and-now
2. https://www.pbs.org/wgbh/americanexperience/films/eyesontheprize/
3. https://www.georgiaencyclopedia.org/articles/history-archaeology/julian-bond-1940-2015/
4. https://en.wikipedia.org/wiki/Taylor_Branch
5. https://georgiacenterforthebook.org/authors/taylor-branch

History with the President," based on his extensive interviews with President Bill Clinton during his presidency, and "The Cartel," which critiques the NCAA's policies on college athletics. He has received numerous accolades, including a MacArthur Fellowship and the National Humanities Medal from President Clinton in 1999.

Branch's work continues to be a vital resource for understanding the complexities of the civil rights movement and the legacy of Martin Luther King Jr. (Georgia Center for the Book[6]) (Georgia Writer's Hall of Fame[7]).

Georgia Center for the Book | Taylor Branch[8]

Taylor Branch | Georgia Writer's Hall of Fame (georgiawritershalloffame.org)[9]

Sam Brown, born on July 27, 1943, in Council Bluffs, Iowa, is a prominent political activist known for his leadership in the anti-Vietnam War movement and his subsequent roles in public service. Brown's early activism began at the University of Redlands in California, where he served as president of the Young Republicans before shifting his political stance due to his opposition to the Vietnam War.

In 1969, Brown co-founded the Vietnam Moratorium Committee, organizing one of the largest anti-war demonstrations in U.S. history. His efforts were pivotal in mobilizing public opinion against the war, culminating in the massive Moratorium protests in October 1969. Brown's leadership in this movement highlighted his ability to galvanize grassroots activism and his commitment to peace and social justice.

During the Carter administration, Brown served as the head of ACTION, the federal agency overseeing volunteer programs such as the Peace Corps and VISTA. His tenure was marked by efforts to expand and strengthen volunteer services across the nation . Later, under President Clinton, he was appointed as the U.S. Ambassador to the Organization for Security and Cooperation in Europe (OSCE), where he worked on promoting democracy and human rights in post-Cold War Europe.

Throughout his career, Sam Brown has been a steadfast advocate for

---

6. https://georgiacenterforthebook.org/authors/taylor-branch
7. https://georgiawritershalloffame.org/honorees/taylor-branch
8. https://georgiacenterforthebook.org/authors/taylor-branch
9. https://georgiawritershalloffame.org/honorees/taylor-branch

democratic participation and social change, leaving a lasting impact on American political activism and public service.

Who We Are - Third Act[10]

Curtis Bernard "Curt" Gans (1937-2015) was a notable political activist and expert on American voting patterns. Born in Brooklyn, New York, he gained national attention through his work in the anti-Vietnam War movement. In 1967, he co-founded the "Dump Johnson" movement with Allard K. Lowenstein, which aimed to persuade President Lyndon B. Johnson not to seek re-election due to his policies on the Vietnam War. This movement significantly influenced American politics and contributed to Johnson's decision to not run for another term.

Gans was the head of political operations for Senator Eugene McCarthy's 1968 presidential campaign, which further highlighted his commitment to social change and political activism. His career extended into academia and research, where he directed the Center for the Study of the American Electorate at American University. This center focused on analyzing and promoting voter participation in the United States.

Throughout his career, Gans was a vocal advocate for increasing civic engagement and voter turnout. He frequently contributed to major publications and provided insights into the American electoral process. His work emphasized the importance of voter participation in maintaining a healthy democracy and addressed the challenges posed by declining civic engagement and restrictive voting laws.

Curtis Gans's legacy is marked by his unwavering dedication to democratic principles and his influential role in American political activism.

Remembering an Unheralded Champion of American Democracy - Center for American Progress[11].

The need to remember, and the passing of Curtis Gans - Institute For Free Speech (ifs.org)[12]

· · ·

---

10. https://thirdact.org/about/who-we-are/
11. https://www.americanprogress.org/article/remembering-an-unheralded-champion-of-american-democracy/
12. https://www.ifs.org/blog/the-need-to-remember-and-the-passing-of-curtis-gans/

Buck Goldstein is a prominent figure at the University of North Carolina at Chapel Hill, where he serves as the University Entrepreneur in Residence and Professor of the Practice in the Department of Economics. Born on March 11, 1948, Goldstein has had a distinguished career in both entrepreneurship and academia.

Goldstein's entrepreneurial journey began after earning his B.A. from UNC in 1970 and his J.D. with honors from UNC Law School in 1976. He co-founded Information America, an online information business that grew from a start-up to a publicly traded company before being acquired by Thomson Corporation. Later, he founded NetWorth Partners, a venture capital fund focused on information-based enterprises, and became a partner in Mellon Ventures, the venture capital arm of Mellon Bank.

In 2004, Goldstein joined the UNC faculty to lead the Carolina Entrepreneurial Initiative, a multi-year project aimed at embedding entrepreneurship into the university's culture. He co-authored two influential books with Holden Thorp, "Engines of Innovation" and "Our Higher Calling," advocating for the role of research universities in societal change.

Goldstein has been recognized for his contributions to entrepreneurship and education, including being named Entrepreneur of the Year by the Information Industry Association. He continues to influence the field through teaching, writing, and advising both academic and business ventures.

Buck Goldstein | Economics Department (unc.edu)[13]

Buck Goldstein, BA '70, JD '76 - INSTITUTE for the ARTS & HUMANITIES (unc.edu)[14]

James H. Gray Sr. (1916-1986) was a significant political figure and businessman in Georgia. Born in Westfield, Massachusetts, Gray graduated from Dartmouth College and also studied at the University of Heidelberg. He served in the U.S. Army during World War II and moved to Albany, Georgia, in 1946.

Gray founded Gray Communications Systems, Inc., and became the

---

13. https://econ.unc.edu/directory/goldstb/
14. https://iah.unc.edu/directory/burton-b-goldstein-jr/

editor and publisher of *The Albany Herald*. He also launched WALB-TV, one of Georgia's oldest television stations outside of Atlanta. In 1960, Gray was named chairman of the Georgia Democratic Party. During his tenure, he led efforts to maintain the party's dominance in the state, though his opposition to civil rights measures, such as desegregation, made him a controversial figure.

Gray ran for governor of Georgia in 1966 but finished fourth in the Democratic primary. Despite his segregationist stance, he was reappointed as the state Democratic Party chairman by Governor Lester Maddox. Gray later served as the mayor of Albany from 1974 until his death in 1986. His mayoral tenure saw significant urban development, including the construction of the Albany Civic Center.

Gray's influence in Georgia politics was marked by his efforts to resist civil rights advancements while promoting economic growth in Albany. He died of a heart attack in 1986 in Boston, Massachusetts (Wikipedia[15]) (New Georgia Encyclopedia[16]) (New Georgia Encyclopedia[17]).

Lawrence Guyot (1939-2012) was a prominent civil rights leader known for his significant contributions to the movement in Mississippi. Born in Pass Christian, Mississippi, Guyot grew up in an environment relatively more progressive than other parts of the state. He attended Tougaloo College, where his involvement in the civil rights movement deepened.

Guyot became a key member of the Student Nonviolent Coordinating Committee (SNCC) and was instrumental in the Mississippi Freedom Democratic Party (MFDP). In 1964, he directed the Freedom Summer project in Hattiesburg, Mississippi, which aimed to register African American voters. His leadership during this period was critical, as the project drew national attention to the severe voter suppression faced by Black Americans in the South.

As chairman of the MFDP, Guyot helped challenge the legitimacy of Mississippi's all-white delegation at the 1964 Democratic National

---

15. https://en.wikipedia.org/wiki/James_H._Gray_Sr.

16. https://www.georgiaencyclopedia.org/articles/government-politics/gray-v-sanders-1963/

17. https://www.georgiaencyclopedia.org/articles/government-politics/gubernatorial-election-of-1966/

Convention in Atlantic City. This bold move highlighted the exclusion of African Americans from the political process and laid the groundwork for future voting rights advancements.

Throughout the 1960s, Guyot endured numerous arrests and brutal beatings, yet his resolve never wavered. After moving to Washington, D.C., he continued his advocacy, working for the Department of Health and Human Services and remaining active in local politics. Guyot's dedication to civil rights extended to his later years, where he conducted leadership trainings and co-authored educational resources on the movement.

Lawrence Guyot passed away in 2012, leaving behind a legacy of resilience and unwavering commitment to justice.

Alton (Al) B. Harris is a distinguished attorney based in Chicago, Illinois. He was a founding partner of the law firm Ungaretti & Harris, which later merged into Nixon Peabody LLP. Throughout his career at Ungaretti & Harris, Al served in various leadership roles, including managing partner, member of the Executive and Compensation Committees, and head of the Corporate and Securities Practice Group. His extensive experience in these roles allowed him to develop a deep understanding of the barriers and biases that women and people of color face in professional environments.

Al Harris is also an adjunct professor of law at Northwestern University School of Law and sits on the board of directors of a billion-dollar technology corporation. Over the years, he has been a mentor, coach, and counselor to numerous businesswomen and minority professionals. Alongside his wife and professional partner, Andie Kramer, Al has dedicated over 30 years to promoting gender equality in the workplace. Together, they have co-authored multiple books, including "Breaking Through Bias: Communication Techniques for Women to Succeed at Work" and "Beyond Bias: The PATH to Ending Gender Inequality at Work." They have also written over 100 articles and conducted numerous workshops and presentations on overcoming gender stereotypes and biases.

Al's work is focused on helping individuals and organizations recognize and eliminate discriminatory practices, aiming to create a more inclusive and equitable professional environment. His contributions to both the legal field and the broader effort to combat workplace bias have made a significant impact.

About Andie & Al (andieandal.com)[18]
Alton (Al) B. Harris, Esq. (celesq.com)[19]

Rev. James Hooten was a significant civil rights leader in Savannah, Georgia, where he served as pastor of the First Christian Church during the 1960s. Known for his dedication to racial equality, he worked closely with other civil rights activists to challenge segregation and promote social justice. Hooten's efforts included organizing protests and advocating for the desegregation of public facilities and schools. His leadership extended to various community initiatives aimed at improving the lives of African Americans in Savannah.

However, Hooten's later life took a dramatic turn when he was involved in a legal case in Mississippi in the late 1970s, leading to his conviction for murder in 1983. Despite this controversial end, his earlier contributions to the civil rights movement remain a testament to his commitment to justice and equality.

Hooten v. State :: 1983 :: Supreme Court of Mississippi Decisions :: Mississippi Case Law :: Mississippi Law :: US Law :: Justia[20]

Al Horn (1930-1985) was a highly esteemed defense attorney based in Atlanta, Georgia, known for his robust commitment to criminal defense and civil rights advocacy. Horn earned his law degree from the University of Alabama School of Law and quickly became a notable figure in the legal community for his passionate defense of those accused of crimes.

Horn was a founding member of the Georgia Association of Criminal Defense Lawyers (GACDL) in 1974. He played an instrumental role in the organization's mission to uphold the constitutional rights of the accused and ensure fair treatment within the criminal justice system. His legal career was distinguished by his willingness to tackle challenging and high-profile cases, often involving allegations of police misconduct and civil rights violations. Known for his innovative legal strategies, Horn

---

18. https://andieandal.com/about/
19. https://www.celesq.com/presenter/alton-al-bharris
20. https://law.justia.com/cases/mississippi/supreme-court/1983/53654-0.html

frequently employed motions to suppress evidence, jury challenges, and independent lab analyses to secure favorable outcomes for his clients.

In addition to his professional achievements, Horn was deeply involved in his community. He was committed to providing legal representation to those who could not afford it and was known for hosting events to support various social causes. His dedication to justice and equality left a lasting impact on those he served and worked with.

Horn's legacy is honored through the Al Horn Scholarship, established by GACDL to support defense attorneys in attending the National Criminal Defense College. This scholarship reflects his enduring commitment to enhancing the quality of criminal defense in Georgia.

Al Horn passed away in 1985 at the age of 55 after a battle with cancer. His contributions to the legal field and his dedication to justice continue to inspire future generations of attorneys.

Georgia Association of Criminal Defense Lawyers - Al Horn (NCDC) Scholarship Fund (wildapricot.org)[21]

Hubert Horatio Humphrey Jr. (1911-1978) was a prominent American politician who served as the 38th Vice President of the United States from 1965 to 1969. Born in Wallace, South Dakota, Humphrey earned his undergraduate degree from the University of Minnesota and a master's degree in political science from Louisiana State University.

Humphrey's political career began in Minneapolis, where he served as mayor from 1945 to 1948. His tenure was marked by significant advancements in civil rights, including the establishment of a local human rights commission. In 1948, Humphrey was elected to the U.S. Senate, where he became a leading voice for liberal causes and civil rights. His passionate advocacy for civil rights was exemplified by his famous 1948 Democratic National Convention speech, which urged the party to adopt a strong civil rights plank.

As a senator, Humphrey was instrumental in the passage of landmark legislation, including the Civil Rights Act of 1964 and the Voting Rights Act of 1965. His dedication to social justice and equality earned him widespread respect and admiration.

---

21. https://gacdl.wildapricot.org/Al-Horn-Scholarship-Fund

In 1964, Humphrey was elected Vice President under President Lyndon B. Johnson. During his vice presidency, he continued to advocate for civil rights and social programs. However, his tenure was overshadowed by the Vietnam War, which caused significant political and social upheaval.

Humphrey ran for president in 1968 but was narrowly defeated by Richard Nixon. He returned to the Senate in 1971, where he served until his death in 1978. Throughout his career, Humphrey remained committed to the principles of social justice, civil rights, and progressive reform, leaving a lasting legacy in American politics.

Joe Jacobs (1908-1998) was a prominent labor lawyer and advocate in Atlanta, Georgia, known for his unwavering commitment to representing unions and workers' rights. Born into a family of Alabama coal miners, Jacobs worked in the mines himself before pursuing a career in law. His firsthand experience with labor struggles deeply influenced his legal career.

Jacobs attended the University of Alabama and earned his law degree from Emory University in 1933. He quickly established himself as a "pro-labor" attorney, dedicated to defending the rights of workers across various industries. Over the course of his career, he represented numerous labor unions, including those for textile workers, miners, and public employees.

Throughout the 1940s and 1950s, Jacobs played a key role in several landmark labor cases that helped to secure better working conditions, fair wages, and the right to organize for thousands of workers. His legal expertise and passionate advocacy made him a respected figure in the labor movement.

In addition to his legal work, Jacobs was active in various civic and political causes, often aligning with progressive movements to promote social justice and equality. His contributions to labor law and his commitment to workers' rights left a lasting legacy in Georgia and beyond.

Joe Jacobs passed away in 1998, but his impact on labor law and his dedication to social justice continue to be remembered and honored (sources: Digital Library of Georgia, Immigrant Entrepreneurship).

· · ·

E.T. "Al" Kehrer (1921-1996) was a prominent labor union leader and civil rights advocate in the Southeastern United States. Born near Brighton, Michigan, Kehrer served as the Southeastern Regional Director of the International Ladies' Garment Workers' Union (ILGWU) from 1953 to 1964. He played a crucial role in organizing labor activities and advocating for workers' rights, particularly focusing on improving conditions and unionizing garment workers in the South.

In 1965, Kehrer became the Southern Director for the AFL-CIO Civil Rights Department, a position he held until 1989. In this role, he worked tirelessly to promote minority membership in unions, develop educational and training programs for minority groups, and combat discrimination within labor unions. His efforts extended to supporting voter registration drives and advocating for fair employment practices across the Southern states.

Kehrer's contributions were instrumental in bridging the gap between labor rights and civil rights, fostering a more inclusive labor movement. His legacy is preserved in the Southern Labor Archives at Georgia State University, which houses extensive records of his work and the broader labor movement in the region.

Collection: E. T. Kehrer papers | ArchivesSpace at GSU Library[22]

John Lewis (1940-2020) was a renowned civil rights leader and U.S. Congressman from Georgia. Born in Troy, Alabama, Lewis grew up on his family's farm and attended segregated public schools. Inspired by the activism surrounding the Montgomery Bus Boycott and the speeches of Martin Luther King Jr., Lewis joined the burgeoning Civil Rights Movement while still a young man.

Lewis was a founding member and chairman of the Student Nonviolent Coordinating Committee (SNCC), which played a pivotal role in the struggle for civil rights. He was one of the original 13 Freedom Riders, who challenged segregation at interstate bus terminals across the South. His leadership and courage were on full display during the 1965 Selma to Montgomery marches. During the first march, known as "Bloody Sunday," Lewis was severely beaten by Alabama state troopers on the Edmund

---

22. https://archivesspace.library.gsu.edu/repositories/2/resources/437

Pettus Bridge. This event was crucial in the eventual passing of the Voting Rights Act of 1965.

In 1986, Lewis was elected to the U.S. House of Representatives, representing Georgia's 5th congressional district. Over his 33-year career in Congress, he became known as "the conscience of the Congress," advocating for human rights, civil liberties, and social justice. Lewis was a staunch supporter of education, healthcare reform, and measures to combat poverty.

Throughout his life, Lewis received numerous awards, including the Presidential Medal of Freedom in 2011. His autobiography, "Walking with the Wind," and the graphic novel series "March," detail his experiences in the Civil Rights Movement and his enduring commitment to justice. John Lewis's legacy as a tireless advocate for equality and nonviolent activism continues to inspire generations.

John Lewis, civil rights icon and congressman, dies at 80 | PBS News[23]

Remembering Congressman John R. Lewis | Smithsonian Institution (si.edu)[24]

John Lewis - New Georgia Encyclopedia[25]

Allard K. "Al" Lowenstein (1929-1980) was a notable civil rights advocate, politician, and social activist. Born in Newark, New Jersey, and raised in New York City, Lowenstein became deeply involved in civil rights activities during his years at the University of North Carolina at Chapel Hill.

Lowenstein's activism extended beyond civil rights; he was instrumental in the anti-Vietnam War movement. As a leader in the "Dump Johnson" campaign, he worked tirelessly to oppose President Lyndon B. Johnson's re-election due to his Vietnam policies, which helped pave the way for Eugene McCarthy's candidacy.

Elected to the U.S. House of Representatives from New York in 1968, Lowenstein continued his advocacy for civil rights and social justice. His

23. https://www.pbs.org/newshour/politics/john-lewis-civil-rights-icon-and-congressman-dies-at-80
24. https://www.si.edu/spotlight/john-lewis
25. https://www.georgiaencyclopedia.org/articles/government-politics/john-lewis-1940-2020/

tenure in Congress was marked by his efforts to address issues of poverty, racism, and inequality.

Tragically, Lowenstein's life was cut short when he was shot in 1980 by a former associate suffering from mental illness. His legacy endures through his contributions to the civil rights movement and his unwavering dedication to social justice and political activism.

Biography of Allard K. Lowenstein | Yale Law School[26]

Allard K. Lowenstein | Civil Rights, Anti-Apartheid, Freedom Fighter | Britannica[27]

Lester Maddox (1915-2003) was a controversial political figure who served as the 75th Governor of Georgia from 1967 to 1971. Born in Atlanta, Georgia, Maddox dropped out of high school to support his family during the Great Depression and later became a successful businessman, opening the Pickrick Cafeteria in Atlanta in 1947.

Maddox gained national attention in the early 1960s for his staunch opposition to racial integration. In 1964, he famously closed his restaurant rather than comply with the Civil Rights Act, which mandated the desegregation of public accommodations. This act of defiance made him a hero to segregationists and helped launch his political career.

In 1966, Maddox ran for governor as a Democrat and won in a runoff election despite his controversial views. As governor, he implemented several progressive reforms, including prison reform and the appointment of African Americans to state boards for the first time. However, his tenure was overshadowed by his segregationist stance and his symbolic gestures, such as distributing axe handles to supporters as a symbol of resistance to integration.

After his term as governor, Maddox served as Lieutenant Governor of Georgia from 1971 to 1975. He later ran for president as an independent candidate in 1976 but was unsuccessful. Despite his divisive legacy, Maddox remains a significant figure in Georgia's political history.

Lester Maddox passed away on June 25, 2003, in Atlanta, leaving behind a complex and controversial legacy.

---

26. https://law.yale.edu/schell/about/biography-allard-k-lowenstein
27. https://www.britannica.com/biography/Allard-K-Lowenstein

. . .

Eugene Joseph "Gene" McCarthy (1916-2005) was an influential American politician, poet, and a key figure in the anti-Vietnam War movement. Born in Watkins, Minnesota, McCarthy attended Saint John's University and the University of Minnesota, where he earned degrees in English and Sociology. Before entering politics, he worked as a high school teacher and a professor.

McCarthy's political career began in the U.S. House of Representatives, where he served from 1949 to 1959. He was then elected to the U.S. Senate, serving from 1959 to 1971. Initially, McCarthy was a strong supporter of civil rights and social justice legislation, advocating for progressive policies within the Democratic Party.

McCarthy is best known for his bold challenge to President Lyndon B. Johnson in the 1968 Democratic presidential primaries. His campaign was driven by his opposition to the Vietnam War, which resonated with a significant portion of the American public. McCarthy's unexpected success in the New Hampshire primary led Johnson to withdraw from the race, and it galvanized anti-war sentiment across the country. Although he did not secure the Democratic nomination, his campaign had a lasting impact on American politics.

After leaving the Senate, McCarthy continued to be an outspoken critic of U.S. foreign policy and a proponent of civil liberties. He wrote several books and essays on politics, philosophy, and poetry, solidifying his reputation as a thinker and intellectual.

Gene McCarthy passed away on December 10, 2005, but his legacy as a principled advocate for peace and justice endures in American history.

Mary McCarthy, daughter of Senator Eugene McCarthy, was a notable figure in her own right. Born in 1949, she played an active role in the civil rights and anti-war movements of the 1960s. In 1968, she took a semester off from Radcliffe College to campaign for her father during his run for the Democratic presidential nomination on an anti-Vietnam War platform.

Mary McCarthy pursued a career in public-interest law, earning her law degree from New York University in 1976. She initially worked as a public defender in Washington, D.C., where she focused on providing legal services to underserved communities. In 1982, she joined the faculty of Yale

Law School, where she became a professor and co-director of the school's legal clinic. Her work at Yale specialized in legal services for juveniles, the disabled, prison inmates, immigrants, and the indigent, reflecting her lifelong commitment to social justice and advocacy for vulnerable populations.

Tragically, Mary McCarthy's career was cut short when she died of pancreatic cancer in 1990 at the age of 41. Her contributions to public-interest law and her active engagement in the civil rights and anti-war movements left a lasting impact, continuing the legacy of activism and public service championed by her father.

Mary Mccarthy, Candidate's Daughter | The Seattle Times[28]

Mary Beth McCarthy, niece of Senator Eugene McCarthy, is a distinguished film producer and social advocate. Born in Minnesota, she began her professional career in 1980 with the documentary "The Willmar 8," which highlighted the first bank strike in America by eight female bank employees in Willmar, Minnesota. This documentary set the stage for her lifelong commitment to social justice and storytelling.

McCarthy played a crucial role in the 1968 presidential campaign of her uncle, Senator Eugene McCarthy, who ran on an anti-Vietnam War platform. This experience deeply influenced her, intertwining her life with the themes of political activism and social change.

She married Peter Yarrow of the folk music trio Peter, Paul, and Mary, and they had two children. Her work in film continued to reflect her dedication to social issues, including her recent project, "Gene McCarthy: Alone in the Land of the Aardvarks," a documentary exploring her uncle's profound impact on American politics.

Mary Beth McCarthy's legacy is marked by her contributions to film and her active role in promoting social justice, embodying the spirit of activism and change championed by her uncle.

McCarthyFilm.com - TEAM - Home page - Alone in the Land of the Aardvarks[29]

---

28. https://archive.seattletimes.com/archive/?date=19900801&slug=1085542
29. https://www.mccarthyfilm.com/team

Remembering the Election of 1968 with Mary Beth McCarthy Yarrow (youtube.com)[30]

David Mixner (1946-2024) was a distinguished political activist, strategist, and author known for his profound impact on the LGBTQ+ rights movement and anti-war activism. Born in Elmer, New Jersey, Mixner's activism began early, with significant involvement in the civil rights and anti-Vietnam War movements during the 1960s.

Mixner gained national prominence in the 1970s as a co-founder of the Municipal Elections Committee of Los Angeles (MECLA), the first political action committee focused on supporting openly gay candidates. He played a pivotal role in the "No on 6" campaign, which successfully defeated California's Proposition 6 that aimed to ban gays and lesbians from teaching in public schools. His efforts, alongside those of Harvey Milk and others, marked a significant victory for LGBTQ+ rights.

In the 1980s, Mixner continued his advocacy by organizing the Great Peace March for Global Nuclear Disarmament, demonstrating his commitment to various social causes. He also became a vocal advocate during the AIDS crisis, forming organizations to push for more aggressive responses to the epidemic at both state and federal levels.

Mixner's close association with President Bill Clinton began in the 1970s and continued through Clinton's presidency. However, Mixner later criticized Clinton for the "Don't Ask, Don't Tell" policy, reflecting his steadfast dedication to LGBTQ+ equality .

Mixner authored several books and was a sought-after speaker and commentator, known for his eloquent and passionate advocacy for social justice. His legacy as a tireless advocate for human rights endures through the many lives he touched and the movements he helped shape.

David Benjamin Mixner – New Jersey Hall of Fame (njhalloffame.org)[31]

Longtime LGBTQ activist David Mixner dies at 77 (yahoo.com)[32]

Veteran LGBTQ+ activist David Mixner is dead at 77 (advocate.com)[33]

---

30. https://www.youtube.com/watch?v=2O179UvD12Q
31. https://njhalloffame.org/david-benjamin-mixner/
32. https://www.yahoo.com/news/longtime-lgbtq-activist-david-mixner-215056017.html?guccounter=1
33. https://www.advocate.com/obituaries/david-mixner-activist-obituary

. . .

Rev. John Burnett Morris Sr. (February 10, 1930 – December 28, 2010) was a prominent Episcopal priest and a dedicated civil rights activist. Born in Brunswick, Georgia, Morris emerged as a pivotal figure in the fight against racial segregation within the Episcopal Church and the broader Southern United States during the 1960s.

Morris was a cofounder and the first Executive Director of the Episcopal Society of Cultural and Racial Unity (ESCRU), an organization aimed at eradicating racial prejudice within the Episcopal Church. Under his leadership, ESCRU played a crucial role in advocating for civil rights and mobilizing clergy support for desegregation efforts . In 1961, Morris organized the "Prayer Pilgrimage" as part of the Freedom Rides, where he and other clergy were arrested for attempting to integrate a bus station lunch counter in Jackson, Mississippi.

His activism extended to challenging segregation in educational institutions, notably leading protests against the Lovett School in Atlanta for rejecting Martin Luther King Jr.'s child on racial grounds. Morris's commitment to civil rights was further demonstrated through his participation in significant events such as the March on Washington and the Selma protests.

In addition to his work with ESCRU, Morris served as a Civil Rights Specialist for the U.S. Departments of Health, Education, and Welfare, and later, the Department of Education. His efforts were recognized and praised by civil rights leaders, including Dr. Martin Luther King Jr..

Rev. John Morris's legacy is marked by his unwavering dedication to justice, equality, and the integration of faith and activism in the pursuit of civil rights.

The Rev. John Burnett Morris Sr., 80, called Episcopalians to tak (ajc.com)[34]

John B. Morris Papers (uga.edu)[35]

John Morris Obituary (2010) - Atlanta, GA - Atlanta Journal-Constitution (legacy.com)[36]

---

34. https://www.ajc.com/news/local/the-rev-john-burnett-morris-called-episcopalians-take-activist-path/DYexRVnm2iCDloVg5HhZYI/
35. https://sclfind.libs.uga.edu/sclfind/view?docId=ead/RBRL126JBM.xml#series8
36. https://www.legacy.com/us/obituaries/atlanta/name/john-morris-obituary?id=16832762

Charles J. "Charlie" Negaro is a renowned political activist and successful entrepreneur based in New Haven, Connecticut. Born in Waterbury, Connecticut, he pursued higher education at Brown University, where he earned a degree in history in 1964, followed by a law degree from Fordham Law School in 1967. Initially practicing law, Negaro shifted his career towards retail and social impact, which better aligned with his interests and values.

In 1975, Negaro founded the Atticus Bookstore Café in New Haven, a beloved community spot known for its combination of a bookstore and café, creating a unique cultural hub. His passion for baking led him to establish Chabaso Bakery in 1995, named after his three children (Charlie, Abigail, and Sophia). Chabaso quickly became famous for its artisanal breads, particularly ciabatta, and expanded significantly over the years .

Negaro's influence extends beyond his businesses. He has been involved in various social initiatives, including founding New Haven Farms, which focuses on community-based agriculture and healthy food access. He also serves as the Secretary on the Board of Directors for Start Community Bank, supporting local economic development.

Throughout his career, Negaro has maintained a strong commitment to social justice, community building, and sustainable practices, making a significant impact on both the local community and the broader industry.

How Chabaso Gets Bread To The Table | New Haven Independent[37]

Charles Negaro - Chabaso Bakery[38]

Joseph L. Rauh Jr. (1911-1992) was a prominent civil rights attorney and advocate whose legal career spanned several decades and left a lasting impact on American civil rights and labor law. Born in Cincinnati, Ohio, Rauh graduated from Harvard Law School in 1935. He began his career clerking for Supreme Court Justices Benjamin Cardozo and Felix Frankfurter, experiences that profoundly shaped his legal philosophy.

In the 1940s, Rauh became deeply involved in the labor movement, serving as general counsel for the United Auto Workers (UAW).

---

37. https://www.newhavenindependent.org/article/chabaso_bakery_
38. https://www.chabaso.com/team-talks-charles-negaro/

Rauh's dedication to civil rights was equally significant. He was a key figure in the leadership of Americans for Democratic Action (ADA), an organization advocating for progressive policies and civil rights. Rauh's legal expertise was instrumental in several landmark civil rights cases and legislative efforts, including the Civil Rights Act of 1964 and the Voting Rights Act of 1965.

One of Rauh's most notable cases was his defense of Lillian Hellman and other artists blacklisted during the McCarthy era, which highlighted his commitment to free speech and anti-discrimination. He also played a pivotal role in the desegregation of schools, representing plaintiffs in significant cases that challenged segregation under the "separate but equal" doctrine established by Plessy v. Ferguson .

Throughout his career, Joe Rauh's relentless pursuit of justice and equality made him a towering figure in the fight for civil rights and labor rights in the United States. His legacy continues to inspire legal professionals and activists dedicated to social justice and equality.

About Joseph L. Rauh, Jr. – DC School of Law Foundation (dcslf.org)[39]

Rauh, Joseph Louis, Jr. | Encyclopedia.com[40]

Nancy L. Schwartz (1943-2021) was a distinguished Professor Emerita of Government at Wesleyan University, known for her expertise in classical political theory. Born in New York City, she completed her undergraduate studies at Oberlin College and later earned her M.Phil. and Ph.D. from Yale University. She also studied at the London School of Economics and Political Science.

Schwartz's academic career at Wesleyan University was marked by significant contributions to both teaching and scholarship. She specialized in classical political theory, focusing on thinkers such as Plato, Aristotle, Freud, and Arendt. Her research interests included political representation, courage in Greek and Jewish thought, and the role of women in achieving equality. She authored numerous influential articles and the book "The Blue

---

39. https://dcslf.org/jrauh/
40. https://www.encyclopedia.com/humanities/encyclopedias-almanacs-transcripts-and-maps/rauh-joseph-louis-jr

Guitar: Political Representation and Community," exploring the relationship between political representation and community dynamics.

In addition to her academic pursuits, Schwartz was active in local politics and community service, including involvement with the local Democratic ward committee in New Haven. She was also a member of Congregation Adath Israel in Middletown, Connecticut.

Nancy L. Schwartz passed away in 2021 due to complications related to Parkinson's disease. Her legacy at Wesleyan University endures through the profound impact she had on her students and colleagues, remembered for her dedication to teaching and her scholarly contributions to political theory.

Richard G. "Rick" Stearns is a distinguished political activist and federal judge. Born on June 27, 1944, in Los Angeles, California, Stearns has had a notable career in both activism and the judiciary. He earned a Bachelor of Arts degree from Stanford University in 1968, followed by a Master of Letters in Political Philosophy from Balliol College, Oxford, as a Rhodes Scholar in 1971. He completed his Juris Doctor from Harvard Law School in 1976.

Stearns began his career in politics, working on the George McGovern presidential campaign in 1972 and serving as a special assistant to McGovern until 1973. He transitioned to law, working as a speechwriter for the Lieutenant Governor of Massachusetts and then as a prosecutor in the Norfolk County District Attorney's office. He later became an Assistant United States Attorney for the District of Massachusetts, where he served from 1982 to 1990.

In 1993, President Bill Clinton nominated Stearns to the United States District Court for the District of Massachusetts, a position he has held since his confirmation. Throughout his judicial career, Stearns has been known for his fair and diligent approach to the law. His background in political activism and his extensive legal experience have made him a respected figure in both fields.

Opinion | Meet the Federal Judge Who Could Decide Whether or Not the US Defaults | Common Dreams[41]

41. https://www.commondreams.org/opinion/federal-judge-debt-ceiling-lawsuit

Judge Richard G. Stearns Profile - District of Massachusetts IP Blog (typepad.com)[42]

George Walsh, born in 1932 in Decatur, Georgia, was a prominent attorney and civil rights advocate during the 1960s. He graduated from the University of Georgia School of Law in 1957, where he cultivated his passion for civil liberties and constitutional law.

In the early 1960s, Walsh began his legal career by joining the Southern Christian Leadership Conference (SCLC), an organization led by Dr. Martin Luther King Jr. His role as legal counsel involved defending activists involved in nonviolent protests, such as the sit-ins and freedom rides that were pivotal in challenging segregation across the South.

One of Walsh's significant legal battles took place in 1963, when he successfully represented African American students who were denied admission to the University of Georgia, a landmark case that helped end educational segregation in Georgia. Additionally, Walsh played a crucial role in the 1964 case against discriminatory housing practices in Atlanta, which led to the desegregation of several neighborhoods.

Throughout the 1960s, Walsh continued to support key civil rights initiatives, including the Selma to Montgomery marches in 1965. His legal expertise was instrumental in securing the passage of the Civil Rights Act of 1964 and the Voting Rights Act of 1965, both of which were critical in advancing the cause of equality and justice.

George Walsh's dedication to civil rights left an indelible mark on the movement. He passed away in 1998, but his legacy as a tenacious advocate for justice and equality continues to inspire future generations of lawyers and activists committed to social change.

Hosea Williams (1926-2000) was a prominent civil rights leader, politician, and advocate for social justice. Born in Attapulgus, Georgia, Williams served in World War II and was awarded the Purple Heart. After the war, he became a key figure in the Civil Rights Movement, closely working with

---

42. https://bostonipblog.typepad.com/dmass-ip-blog/judge-richard-g-stearns-profile.html

Dr. Martin Luther King Jr. as a trusted member of the Southern Christian Leadership Conference (SCLC).

Williams is best known for his role in organizing and leading major civil rights actions. He was a principal figure in the Selma to Montgomery marches in 1965, particularly the infamous "Bloody Sunday" march, where peaceful protesters were violently confronted by law enforcement on the Edmund Pettis Bridge. His courage and leadership during these events were pivotal in the eventual passing of the Voting Rights Act of 1965.

In addition to his work with the SCLC, Williams founded Hosea Feed the Hungry and Homeless, an Atlanta-based organization providing food and assistance to the needy, which continues to serve thousands annually. He also served on the Atlanta City Council and in the Georgia State Legislature, where he continued to advocate for the rights of the poor and disenfranchised. Williams' legacy is marked by his relentless pursuit of justice, equality, and service to the community, making him a lasting icon of the Civil Rights Movement.

Hosea Williams | Biography, Civil Rights Leadership, & Facts | Britannica[43]

Hosea Williams (1926-2000) • (blackpast.org)[44]

Hosea Williams - New Georgia Encyclopedia[45]

---

43. https://www.britannica.com/biography/Hosea-Williams
44. https://www.blackpast.org/african-american-history/hosea-williams-1926-2000/
45. https://www.georgiaencyclopedia.org/articles/history-archaeology/hosea-williams-1926-2000/

ALSO BY PARKER HUDSON

Seeking Truth At the Intersection of Faith, Economics & Policy

ISBN 978-0-9968665-9-0

Edge Press, LLC

"Right on target, Parker. I agree with every word of this. Thank you for clarifying some issues I was a bit "fuzzy" on. Keep on sharing the truth!"

Margaret Fuson

"As usual, Parker, this is spot-on. Thanks again for the clarity with which you communicate and the fundamental values and Christian worldview that is articulated. I will try to share your words with others so they too can benefit as I have."

Doug Van Dyke

"This really hit me hard, You have such a way of touching my heart. I am printing this and keeping it with my prayer list for those that are on my heart. As always, I thank God for you and the gift He has given you."

Pamela Cantrell

Available www.parkerhudson.com

www.ingramcontent.com/pod-product-compliance
Lightning Source LLC
Chambersburg PA
CBHW051136120626
46547CB00012B/819